KV-648-910

Modern Chinese

The Chinese language, spoken by over one billion people, has undergone drastic changes over the past century in a way unparalleled at any time previously. This book presents a comprehensive and up-to-date account of the development of Modern Chinese from the late nineteenth century up to the 1990s, concentrating on three major aspects: Modern Spoken Chinese, Modern Written Chinese, and the Modern Chinese writing system. It describes and analyses in detail, from historical and sociolinguistic perspectives, the establishment and promotion of Modern Spoken Chinese and Modern Written Chinese and the reform of the Chinese script. Through an integrated discussion of these three areas of the language it highlights the close interrelationships between them and reveals the interaction of linguistic, historical, and social factors in the development of Modern Chinese.

PING CHEN is Senior Lecturer in Chinese Language and Linguistics in the Department of Asian Languages and Studies at the University of Queensland. He has previously taught at UCLA, the University of Oregon, the Chinese Academy of Social Sciences, Beijing, and the City University of Hong Kong. He has published widely in the area of Chinese linguistics.

Modern Chinese

History and Sociolinguistics

PING CHEN

EDINBURGH UNIVERSITY LIBRARY
WITHDRAWN

CAMBRIDGE
UNIVERSITY PRESS

PUBLISHED BY THE PRESS SYNDICATE OF THE UNIVERSITY OF CAMBRIDGE
The Pitt Building, Trumpington Street, Cambridge CB2 1RP, United Kingdom

CAMBRIDGE UNIVERSITY PRESS
The Edinburgh Building, Cambridge, CB2 2RU, United Kingdom
http://www. cup.cam.ac.uk
40 West 20th Street, New York, NY 10011-4211, USA   http://www.cup.org
10 Stamford Road, Oakleigh, Melbourne 3166, Australia

© Ping Chen 1999

This book is in copyright. Subject to statutory exception and to the provisions of relevant
collective licensing agreements, no reproduction of any part may take place without
the written permission of Cambridge University Press.

First published 1999

Printed in the United Kingdom at the University Press, Cambridge

Typeset in 9/13pt Utopia, in QuarkXPress™   [GC]

A catalogue record for this book is available from the British Library

Library of Congress cataloguing in publication data

Chen, Ping, 1954–
        Modern Chinese: its history and sociolinguistics / Ping Chen.
            p.   cm.
        Includes bibliographical references.
            ISBN 0 521 64197 7 (hardback) — ISBN 0 521 64572 7 (paperback)
            1. Chinese language — Modern Chinese, 1919–   I. Title.
        PL1083.C525   1999
        495.1—dc21   98–38449   CIP

ISBN 0 521 64197 7 hardback
ISBN 0 521 64572 7 paperback

This book is dedicated to the memory of my father, Chen Yujia.

Contents

Tables

Preface

The Chinese language has undergone drastic changes over the past 150 years in a way that is unparalleled in Chinese history. In writing this book, I have hoped to present a comprehensive account of the development of Modern Chinese mainly from the late nineteenth century up to the 1990s, concentrating on three major aspects, namely Modern Spoken Chinese, Modern Written Chinese, and the Modern Chinese writing system. I have attempted to describe and analyse the establishment and promotion of Modern Chinese in its spoken and written forms, and the reform of Chinese script in a historical and social context. Treating the topics in question in an integrated way, I hope I have been in a position to reveal the close interrelationships between spoken Chinese, written Chinese, and the Chinese writing system, and to highlight the interaction of linguistic, and historical, social factors at work in the process. In this book, which has incorporated my own research results over the years and the gains of the latest research reported in the literature in Chinese and Western languages, I have aimed to provide readers with up-to-date findings in the field.

The book was written primarily for students and teachers of Chinese language and Chinese linguistics. It may be used for the relevant subjects at the upper undergraduate and postgraduate level at university, or read by those who have studied Chinese for some years. I will be very pleased if my fellow researchers in Chinese linguistics also find something useful in it. Since the linguistic phenomena are discussed in close connection with the historical and social context, and with frequent reference to similar phenomena in other languages, it will also appeal to specialists in other fields of Chinese studies, specialists in historical linguistics and sociolinguistics, and to anyone who takes an interest in Chinese language, Chinese literature, Chinese culture, and Modern China.

I am grateful to many people for making the completion of the work possible. First of all, I must acknowledge a special debt of gratitude to Lü Shuxiang, who initiated me in the study of Chinese language both in the traditional philological approach and from the perspective of modern linguistics, and was the first to arouse my interest in many of the issues under discussion in this book when I was an MA student under his supervision in the Institute of Linguistics of the Chinese Academy of Social Sciences. He has been a shining example for me to emulate in scholarly research. I am greatly indebted to Sandra A. Thompson for her interest in this book and for her advice and encouragement from the beginning of the work. She has always been a highly valued source of inspiration and support to me in this work, as well as in many of my other research projects since my years at UCLA.

I wish to acknowledge my indebtedness to One-soon Her, Thomas H. T. Lee, Perry Link, Jerry Norman, and an anonymous reviewer for the Cambridge University Press, who read draft versions of the book, and provided valuable comments, criticisms, and suggestions. At various stages of research for this book, I benefited from advice and assistance from William Bright, Hilary Chappell, Robert L. Cheng, South Coblin, Florian Coulmas, Feng Zheng, Nanette Gottlieb, Jiang Lansheng, Liu Jian, Kam Louie, Victor H. Mair, Tsu-Lin Mei, Alain Peyraube, Alan Rix, Malcolm Skewis, Chaofen Sun, Roland Sussex, R. McMillan Thompson, Benjamin K. Y. T'sou, William S. Y. Wang, Xu Liejiong, Eric Zee, Zhong Zhemin, and Zhou Youguang. To all of them I am deeply grateful. This project was in part supported by two grants from the Australian Research Council, and by the University of Queensland through its University Research Grant and Special Studies Program. I alone am responsible for all the viewpoints expressed in the book.

Finally, I wish to record my gratitude to my wife, Jean, and to our children Fay and Laura, for their unfailing love and support.

Acknowledgements

Other versions of parts of the work have appeared elsewhere:

Chapters 5–6
Chen, Ping 1993. Modern Written Chinese in development, *Language in Society* 22(4), 505–37. Reprinted with the permission of Cambridge University Press.

Chapter 7
Chen, Ping 1996. Modern Written Chinese, dialects, and regional identity, *Language Problems & Language Planning* 20(3), 223–43. Reprinted with the permission of John Benjamins Publishing Company.

Chapter 10
Chen, Ping 1996. Toward a phonological writing system of Chinese: a case study in writing reform, *International Journal of the Society of Language* 122, 1–46. Reprinted with the permission of Mouton de Gruyter. A Division of Walter de Gruyter & Co.

We gratefully acknowledge permission by the publishers to use the copyright materials.

Abbreviations

CL	classifier
DUR	durative aspect
PFV	perfective aspect
Q	question

Chinese is the native language of approximately a billion people distributed over vast geographical areas of the world. It is the official language of mainland China and Taiwan. It is one of the two official languages in Hong Kong, where ethnic Chinese constitute more than 95 per cent of the local population. It is one of the four official languages of Singapore, where about 75 per cent of population are ethnic Chinese. It is also reasonably maintained by about 30 million Chinese scattered in other parts of the world.

Genealogically, Chinese belongs to the family of Sino-Tibetan. The earliest reliable records of Chinese in the form of *jiǎgǔwén* 'oracle bone script' date back more than 3,000 years. Much controversy surrounds the periodization of the language since then, partly due to lack of sufficient documentary evidence on the chronological changes in the language, particularly in the pre-modern periods of its evolution, and partly due to the fact that periodization based on each of the three main components of the language, namely, phonology, grammar, and lexicon may not always be co-extensive (Peyraube 1988, 1996; S. Jiang 1994; Chan and Tai 1995). The periodization adopted in this book is first and foremost based upon changes in grammar, which may sometimes be co-extensive with phonological, and to a lesser extent, lexical development of the language. As elaborated in Lü (1985a, 1985b), Norman (1988), Peyraube (1988, 1996), Ohta (1991), Mei (1994), inter alia, each period is marked by some conspicuous innovations in syntax and morphology, the details of which need not concern us here. A sketch of the periodization is presented in Table 1.1.

Archaic Chinese (*Shànggǔ Hànyǔ*) is represented by the language used in classic works of the pre-Qin period and the Western Han dynasty. Writings from the Eastern Han onward, while basically following the style of Archaic Chinese, displayed an increasing number of innovations in grammar and vocabulary, which are believed to be reflective of changes in the contemporary vernacular.[1] It is referred to as Medieval Chinese (*Zhōnggǔ Hànyǔ*), which represents a transitional period. Archaic Chinese and Medieval Chinese constitute Old Chinese (*Gǔdài Hànyǔ*). The appearance of substantial texts in mainly vernacular style in the late Tang dynasty marked the beginning of Pre-Modern Chinese (*Jìndài Hànyǔ*). A growing number of emergent grammatical, lexical, and phonological features are attested in texts of this period and thereafter, which presumably

Table 1.1 Periodization of Chinese

Archaic Chinese	Shang dynasty (ca. 1700–1100 BC)
	Western Zhou dynasty (ca. 1100–771 BC)
	Spring and Autumn period (770–476 BC)
	Warring States period (475–221 BC)
	Qin dynasty (221–206 BC)
	Western Han dynasty (206 BC – AD 25)
Medieval Chinese	Eastern Han dynasty (AD 25–220)
	Wei-Jin period (220–420)
	Southern and Northern dynasties (420–589)
	Sui dynasty (581–618)
	Early and Middle Tang dynasty (618–907)
Pre-Modern Chinese	Late Tang dynasty
	Five dynasties period (907–60)
	Northern Song dynasty (960–1127)
	Southern Song dynasty (1127–1279)
	Yuan dynasty (1206–1368)
	Ming dynasty (1368–1644)
Modern Chinese	Qing dynasty (1616–1911)
	Twentieth century

reflect corresponding developments in the language shortly before and during the period. The next ten centuries or so constituted the formative years of Modern Chinese (*Xiàndài Hànyǔ*) during which period almost all the most important characteristic features gradually took shape. By the early Qing dynasty, all the major changes in grammar, phonology, and basic vocabulary that characterize Modern Chinese had been completed. Influences from Western languages and Japanese aside, present-day Chinese differs little in grammar, phonology, and basic vocabulary from the vernacular found in *Hónglóu mèng*, a novel written in the mid eighteenth century.[2]

What is known as the Chinese language comprises dozens of dialects which may be mutually unintelligible.[3] Again, opinions differ as to their grouping. This book follows the framework in Norman (1988) and B. Xu and Zhan (1988) in classifying all the dialects into seven major groups, differentiated mainly on the basis of phonological features, and, to a lesser extent, also in terms of vocabulary and grammar. The major dialect groups are Beifanghua (Mandarin),[4] Wu, Yue (Cantonese), Min, Kejia (Hakka), Xiang, and Gan, of which Mandarin is by far the largest group, with its native speakers accounting for the majority of the Chinese population.[5] The non-Mandarin groups are also called the Southern dialects. Each of the major dialect groups is in turn comprised of a large number of varieties that are related to each other in terms of a hierarchy with three main levels, sub-dialect, vernacular, and accent. For example, following the traditional classification, Mandarin is composed of four major sub-dialects, namely, Northern, Northwestern, Southwestern, and Jiang-Huai, all of which may be further divided into different groups of vernaculars and accents. The standard form of Modern Chinese is known by several names. It is called *pǔtōnghuà* 'the common language' in mainland China, *guóyǔ* 'national language' in Taiwan, and *huáyǔ* 'Chinese language' in Singapore.

This book attempts to present a historical and sociolinguistic profile of Modern Chinese. It will focus on its development and major features of structure and use from the late nineteenth century up to the 1990s, and in the context of a modernizing Chinese society. The book is composed of three parts, concentrating on the spoken form, the written form, and the writing system respectively.

Part I

Modern Spoken Chinese

Establishment and promotion of Modern Spoken Chinese

2.1 Development of Standard Spoken Chinese before the late nineteenth century

2.1.1 Base of Standard Spoken Chinese in early times

The Chinese civilization originated in the Yellow River areas. It is recorded that there were as many as 1,800 clans and tribes inhabiting areas along the Yellow River towards the end of the Shang dynasty. As commercial and military activities among these speakers of different languages increased, the need for a lingua franca naturally arose. The earliest form of such a lingua franca, it is generally believed, took shape on the basis of the language spoken in what is now known as Yinxu in the west of Henan province, which was the capital of the Shang dynasty between about 1324 and 1066 BC. The so-called *jiǎgǔwén* is the written, and highly condensed, counterpart of this lingua franca.

The subsequent Zhou dynasty marked the beginning of the feudal system, with more than 130 states established in the early period of the dynasty, covering various dialectally differentiated areas. Subsequent wars among the states resulted in the collapsing of the smaller polities into several large states. Local dialects distinctive of the major states developed, marking the beginning of the differentiation of Chinese dialects into several major groups.

As the major dialects of Chinese respectively evolved in different parts of the land, the importance of a standard spoken Chinese, both as a standard for formal purposes and as a lingua franca across dialects, increased as there were more and more administrative, diplomatic, cultural, and military exchanges between the central government and local states, and among the states themselves. There is considerable consensus among scholars that such a standard spoken Chinese is what is called *yǎyán* 'elegant speech' in the Confucian *Analects*. It is in the Western Zhou period that *yǎyán* won full recognition both in terms of its importance, and its distinctness from other local dialects.

According to historical records, *yǎyán* was the standard language taught in schools in all the states in the Zhou dynasty, and used extensively in educational, cultural, and diplomatic activities. As observed in the *Analects*, *yǎyán* was the language used in classic literary works like *Shū jīng* (*Book of history*) and *Shī jīng* (*Book of odes*) and as well as on all ceremonial functions. The authors of *Shī jīng* were scattered across different states, yet they all followed basically the same rhyming patterns, a fact which could only be explained by mastery of a standard language in addition to their local dialect. Proficiency in the standard language was an important part of the attainments of scholars. Although a native speaker of the Lu dialect from the present-day Shangdong province, Confucius himself customarily used *yǎyán* for educational and diplomatic purposes.

Yǎyán was based upon the language that evolved from the lingua franca of the Shang dynasty and was spoken in Central China around what is today's Henan province, which had been the main focus of political, commercial and cultural activities since the Xia dynasty (ca. twenty-first century – seventeenth century BC), and the Shang dynasty. Based on the geographical features of the area, the language was also known as the dialect of the He Luo 'Yellow River and Luo River' or Zhongzhou 'Central China' area. The close connection between *yǎyán* and its base language, the Zhongzhou dialect, has led quite a few scholars to interpret the terms as synonymous. Following what is general practice in the literature, I will use the more common name, the Zhongzhou dialect, to refer to the base dialect of *yǎyán*.

From the Eastern Zhou onwards, the two major cities in the area, Luoyang and Kaifeng, served as the capitals of many imperial dynasties, which further consolidated and enhanced the status of the Zhongzhou dialect as the base of the standard spoken Chinese across the whole country. This status was more or less maintained through successive dynasties over the next two thousand years or so. On several occasions during this period, China disintegrated into more than one autonomous part. More than once, to flee from the harassment or attack of the nomadic tribes to the north of China proper, dynasties founded in the north of China moved their capitals south of the Yangtze River, where the local dialects were very much different from that of Zhongzhou. The first large migration from the north to the south occurred in the Wei Jin period. Wealthy and prestigious noble families as well as people from all walks of life followed en masse when the royal court of Jin Yuandi (317–22) moved from Luoyang to what is the present-day Nanjing. This effected the spread of the Zhongzhou dialect to the south of the Yangtze River. During the same period, states were established in the North of China, mostly by non-Han ethnic groups. They were readily assimilated into the Han culture, adopting the Chinese language as their main official language. This was largely due to the fact that, for all their military feats, the Han culture as a whole was considered far more prestigious than their own. As a result, in the ensuing Southern and Northern dynasties and thereafter, the Zhongzhou dialect was the base of the standard spoken language both in the north and the south, displaying some variations as a result of close contact with either other Chinese dialects or non-Chinese languages. Since at the time competence in standard pronunciation was generally associated with respectable background and status, elevated society was sensitive to the sociolinguistic differentiation of the standard and the substandard languages. Linguistic features and uses of the standard pronunciation, and the difference between the standard and other dialects, were common topics in writings from that period. Commenting on accents of his contemporaries, for example, Yan Zhitui (ca. 531–90), a prominent man of letters, observed that the dialect of Luoyang in the north and that of Jinling (Nanjing) in the south represented the standard pronunciation in his times.

It is also beginning from his times that the standard pronunciation was codified and promulgated across the land. What is known as the institution of *kējǔ* 'imperial examination system', initiated in the Sui and the Tang dynasties, in which officials at all levels were selected from people who passed rigorous examinations administered by the imperial court, no doubt played a significant motivating role in the process. As rhyming writing constituted an important part of the official examinations, it was imperative that at least for educational and literary purposes, aspiring scholars follow a standard in pronunciation. Among the most influential rhyming dictionaries compiled to codify and promulgate the standard pronunciation was *Qièyùn* (601). First compiled in the Sui dynasty, and annotated and revised later in the Tang and the Song dynasties, it served as the most reliable source of the phonological system of the spoken standard at that time. Although there are many disagreements as to the phonological details of *Qièyùn*, scholars have reached consensus on two points. First, it represents the phonological system of a language that was officially sanctioned as the standard one, at least as far as the imperial examinations were concerned. Second, it is essentially based upon the Zhongzhou dialect, although some phonological features prevalent in other dialects, most notably the Nanjing dialect, may have been included (Shao 1982; X. K. Li 1987). Dozens of similar rhyming dictionaries were published after *Qièyùn*, recording either the phonology of the officially sanctioned standard, or that of the particular dialects in successive periods and in major geographical areas.

2.1.2 **Standard Spoken Chinese in pre-modern times**

While the Luoyang and the Nanjing dialect did not differ significantly in Yan Zhitui's times, the divergence between the north and the south widened in the course of natural evolvement. Since the beginning of Pre-Modern Chinese, two major groups of the Northern, or Mandarin, dialects could be identified, the northern group in the Yellow River region and Northeast China, and the southern group south of the Yangtze River and in Southeast China. The Standard Spoken Chinese in the pre-modern times was based on Mandarin, although it is controversial which particular Mandarin dialect served as the national standard during particular periods.

Although references to the standard pronunciation in the late Tang and the Song dynasty were scanty, and mostly anecdotal, it seems safe to assume that the spoken standard in the Northern Song was based on the Zhongzhou dialect, as in medieval times. The imperial court moved to Lin'an (Hangzhou) in the Southern Song. Immigration on a large scale from the North turned the dialect of Hangzhou into one that was very similar to the Zhongzhou dialect.

There has been much debate over when the Zhongzhou dialect started to give way to other dialects as the base of Standard Spoken Chinese. The traditional view is that it was replaced by the Beijing dialect as early as in the Yuan dynasty, which was established with Beijing, then called Dadu, as its capital (Bao 1955; R. Li 1990).[1] After a close examination of the relevant literature, however, Li Xinkui (1980) argues, quite convincingly, that the Beijing dialect's gradual assumption of the role as the base of the national standard did not begin until much later. Whereas the national standard pronunciation in the Ming dynasty and the early Qing dynasty was also called *guānhuà* 'mandarin', *zhèngyīn* 'standard pronunciation', *Hànyīn* 'Han pronunciation', *guānyīn* 'official pronunciation', *tōngyīn* 'general pronunciation' etc., the dialect of Beijing, known as *běiyīn* 'the Northern pronunciation', was treated in the literature as a local dialect in contrast to the national standard under the various names.

While Li Xinkui claims that the Zhongzhou dialect represented the standard pronunciation of *guānhuà* before its replacement by the Beijing dialect, many other scholars, most notably Lu Guoyao (1980), Zhang Weidong (1992), Paul Fumian Yang (1995), and South Coblin (1997, 1998), propose that it was the Jiang-Huai Mandarin based on the Nanjing dialect that assumed the role as the national standard from the beginning of the Ming dynasty. The latter proposal was mainly based on studies of the writings of the Jesuit missionaries who went to China in the late sixteenth century, like Michele Ruggieri (1543–1607), Matteo Ricci (1552–1610), Nicolas Trigault (1577–1628), and Francisco Varo (1627–87), who left us with detailed descriptions of the sociolinguistic situation of China as they found it, and the phonological system of the then national standard. According to their observations, Nanjing at that time surpassed European cities and other Chinese cities in beauty and grandeur. In spite of the move of the capital from Nanjing to Beijing in 1421, Nanjing was apparently still the symbolic centre of Chinese culture, and its dialect prevailed over other dialects as the basis of a national standard.

It was as late as around the mid nineteenth century that the Beijing dialect gained ascendancy over the Nanjing dialect as the base of the national standard. There seem to be several factors that contributed to the replacement of the Nanjing dialect by the Beijing dialect. First, as the capital of three successive dynasties spanning several hundreds of years, Beijing had become increasingly influential as a political and cultural centre, and this in turn enhanced the prestige of the local dialect. Second, as Giles remarked in preface of his 1892 dictionary, 'Since the T'aip'ing rebellion [i.e. 1850–64], Nanking (Nanjing) has lost much of its pretension to give a standard pronunciation, for the simple reason that its enormous population almost ceased to exist; and the moderate number of thousands who now occupy a tithe of the city area are many of them unlettered immigrants from other provinces or districts'[2] (quoted from Coblin 1997:51). The drastic change in the relative strength of the two cities further facilitated the final acceptance of the language of the imperial court by the general public as the national standard.

As will be discussed in detail shortly, the status of the Beijing dialect as the base of the standard spoken Chinese was not formally recognized until the late 1920s. Strictly speaking, before the modern language reform came into full swing around the turn of the twentieth century, the concept of a standard pronunciation was rather vague. It was more of an attitudinal stance on what was supposed to be the standard language in polite society, or koine for practical purposes of interdialectal communication, rather than a reference to a specific speech form that was clearly defined, effectively promoted, conscientiously learned, and extensively used. Sound recording and transmitting devices were out of the question, and people in general did not feel the need for proper instruction in pronunciation beyond the literary reading of characters. For several centuries before modern times, what actually served as the national standard was an ill-defined, generalized form of *guānhuà*, based successively on the Zhongzhou dialect, Nanjing dialect, and Beijing dialect for most of its de facto norms and also incorporating features from a wider region.[3] Though the status of the Beijing dialect as the base of the national standard was already assumed by some scholars before the twentieth century, there was little effort on the part of Chinese scholars – other than the textbooks and dictionaries compiled mainly by missionaries for the benefits of Western learners – to provide an explicit characterization of the spoken standard. It was only later in the early twentieth century that the need for a clear definition of the standard spoken Chinese was keenly felt.

On the other hand, in the absence of efficient and convenient means of transport and oral communication, distance imposed limitations that prevented mass acquisition of the national standard before modern times. Chinese has adopted a logographic writing system in which the sound values of characters are not indicated in a way that is as direct, explicit, and decomposable as in a phonographic system. In the traditional rhyme books and dictionaries, characters are annotated in terms of categories, rather than sound values. In other words, the knowledge of the standard literary pronunciations consists of the grouping of characters according to how similar or dissimilar they sound, not according to the actual sound values of the characters. It was not until the earlier years of the twentieth century that Chinese developed a set of bona fide phonetic symbols that could be used across the country to annotate sound in a clear and dialect-neutral manner. Even though basic education ensured a knowledge of the literary pronunciation of characters that was sufficient for all literary purposes, this by no means guaranteed proficiency in Standard Spoken Chinese even at the most rudimentary level. In spite of the prestige associated with the national spoken standard, the average level of proficiency in the spoken standard was extremely low in Southern dialect areas during the final years of the Qing dynasty, even among the privileged few who had access to education. In the Mandarin speaking areas spanning vast expanses from the northeast to the southwestern part of China, the actual lingua franca in use could be any of the local varieties of Northern Mandarin, or a more generalized form known as *lánqīng guānhuà* 'impure mandarin'. Linguistic barriers constituted very serious problems in oral communication between people from different dialect areas.

While the knowledge of an ossified phonology of Chinese as represented in *Qièyùn* was effectively promoted across the country through the requirements of official examinations, there were only sporadic efforts on the part of government to promote the spoken standard. The first official effort at promoting *guānhuà* was made in the mid eighteenth century. Institutes were set up in the Yue and Min areas to teach scholars and officials to speak *guānhuà*. Those who failed the examination were disqualified from taking part in the central official examination or appointment to positions in the bureaucracy. As such training in *guānhuà* was accessible only to a very small number of privileged scholars in the Southern dialect areas, it had hardly any impact upon the overall linguistic situation in those areas, where the local dialects rather than *guānhuà* prevailed.

2.2   Establishment and promotion of Modern Standard Chinese from the late nineteenth century until 1949

2.2.1   Early efforts

The year 1840 marks a turning point in the modern history of China. In the Opium War that erupted, China suffered a traumatic defeat. For the first time, the Chinese were forced to recognize that the Middle Kingdom, for all its past glories, had lagged behind the Western powers since the Industrial Revolution. From the mid nineteenth century, tremendous efforts were exerted, on the part of both the government and the general public, to revitalize or modernize the country. Language reform was taken as one of the most urgent aspects of the undertaking.

In the face of a large number of mutually unintelligible dialects spoken in different geographic areas of the country, the establishment and promotion of a modern standard Chinese, together with the reform of the writing system, were put forward as two of the top priorities in the modernization of the Chinese language. In fact, the uniformity of the spoken language was seen as a necessary precondition for the unity of the country. In the words of Zhu Wenxiong in 1906, 'What I expect of my country's people is for us to be able to stand on our own in this competitive world. It is impossible to achieve universal education if the writing system is not easy to use, and it is impossible to attain strong unity if there is no uniform national language' (Ni 1959:152).

Inspired by the success in promoting a standard language in Japan, several influential scholars, mostly students returned from Japan, proposed the idea of *guóyǔ* 'national language'[4] which they argued should be promoted as the modern standard Chinese in China. The most influential was Wu Rulun, a famous scholar who is believed to be the first person to straightforwardly advocate 'Unification of the national language', a slogan which initiated what was later known as *Guóyǔ Yùndòng* 'National Language Movement'. According to his own account, it was prompted by what he had learned in Japan during a trip to that country. In the period of thirty years, he observed, a standard spoken language was popularized in Japan, which greatly facilitated the modernization of the country in other areas. There was no reason, he argued, why China could not attain the same results (J. Li 1935:25).

Thanks to the advocacy of high-profile language reformers like Wu Rulun, there was considerable consensus among intellectuals and bureaucrats as to the desirability of adopting a unified form of the Chinese language, i.e., *guóyǔ*, as Modern Standard Chinese. However, opinions differed with regard to the standard of the national language, and approaches to its promotion.

In spite of the fact that the Beijing dialect was the accredited *guānhuà* of the country, various proposals were put forward concerning the dialectal base of the phonology of the standard language when a precise characterization of *guóyǔ* as Modern Standard Chinese was required. The Nanjing, Wuhan, Shanghai, and Beijing dialects were among those proposed as candidates. It was also maintained by some that, rather than being based upon a single dialect, Modern Standard Chinese should assume a more generalized form.

For all the differences in opinion over the dialectal base of Modern Standard Chinese, most of the participants in the National Language Movement recognized that a modern standard Chinese would be best promoted if it was encoded in a phonetic script, which, unlike the traditional logographic writing system, would be capable of indicating the phonetic values of the language in an explicit and precise manner. As will be discussed in detail in Chapter 10, dozens of phonetization schemes were proposed, many of which were based upon varieties of Northern Mandarin. Although the main objective in the design of such phonetic scripts was to address the difficulty of learning and using the traditional script by provision of a supplementary or alternative writing system, the phonetization of the base dialect, it was argued, would also greatly facilitate the popularization of Modern Standard Chinese. As a group of earnest language reformers put it in 1903, 'if the spoken language were standardized in the form of a phonetic script, there would be uniformity from north to south' (Ni 1958:36).

Some language reformers opted for another approach to the establishment and promotion of Modern Standard Chinese. Instead of promoting a specific dialect encoded in phonetic script, they maintained that, since Modern Standard Chinese should serve as both a literary and a vernacular standard, it was preferable first to establish the norms of a national standard for literary purposes through the standardization of the pronunciation of characters in common use. The popularization of a spoken standard would follow as a natural outcome of the general acceptance of the standard pronunciation of the characters. As we will discuss shortly, such a view prevailed in the first stage of the National Language Movement.

In 1911, just before the downfall of the Qing dynasty, the *Tǒngyī guóyǔ fāngfǎ àn* 'Act of approaches to the unification of the national language' was passed at the Central Education Conference convened by the Ministry of Education, which contains the following main points (J. Li 1935; Fang 1969):

1. A *Guóyǔ Diàochá Zǒnghuì* 'General Committee for the Survey of the National Language' will be set up in Beijing, with branches set up in all provinces. It will conduct a survey of dialects with respect to vocabulary, grammar, phonology, and other related aspects.

2. On the basis of the results of the survey in all provinces, the General Committee is to decide on the standards of *guóyǔ* by selecting what is elegant,

correct, and popular with regard to vocabulary, grammar, and phonology. Textbooks and dictionaries of *guóyǔ* will be compiled in conformity with the standard.

3. A standard of pronunciation will be determined. It will be mainly based upon the Beijing dialect. The *rù* 'entering' tone, however, should be preserved. The vocabulary and grammar should be mainly based upon *guānhuà*, and meet the criteria of being correct, elegant, and logical.

4. A standard phonetic alphabet should be decided on.

5. *Guóyǔ* Instruction Schools will be set up by the Ministry of Education, which will train students from provinces. Graduates will return to their respective provinces to train more teachers. Teaching staff in schools and colleges who cannot speak *guóyǔ* must receive training in these schools. Apart from being taught as a specific subject, *guóyǔ* should gradually become the medium of instruction for all subjects.

It is evident from the above resolution that by this time consensus had been reached on several issues related to the establishment and promotion of a standard national language. First, the standardization of *guóyǔ* involved not only phonology, but also vocabulary and grammar. Second, *guóyǔ* as a standard language should be mainly based upon *guānhuà*, specifically upon the Beijing dialect, and should also meet the criteria of being correct, elegant, and logical, which were presumably characteristics of the language of educated people instead of ordinary folk in the street. Furthermore, the act suggested that, instead of basing itself exclusively upon a specific dialect or dialect group, Modern Standard Chinese was to incorporate features, including phonological features, from other dialects, which were to be selected on the criteria of being 'elegant, correct, and popular'. These assumptions and proposals constituted the basic agenda of the National Language Movement in the ensuing years. In the remainder of Part I, I will concentrate on the phonology of Modern Standard Chinese, and leave the vocabulary and grammar to Part II.

2.2.2   *Lǎo guóyīn* 'Old national pronunciation'

Language planning work resumed right after the founding of the Republic of China in 1912, pursuing the agenda set in the Act adopted at the 1911 conference with greater enthusiasm. A *Dúyīn Tǒngyī Huì* 'Commission for Unifying Reading Pronunciation' was established, which was entrusted with the task of determining the phonological standard of

Modern Standard Chinese. The Commission was composed of experts designated by the Ministry of Education, and two representatives from each province who had to meet one or more of these four requirements:

1. expertise in traditional phonology;
2. expertise in traditional philology;
3. knowledge of one or more foreign languages;
4. knowledge of Chinese dialects.

There were altogether eighty members in the Commission. Starting in February 1913, the Commission met to work on the following three major tasks:

1. to decide on the standard pronunciation of characters in common use;
2. to determine the repertoire of basic sounds in the standard language;
3. to decide on a phonetic alphabet used for sound annotation. Each basic sound in the standard Chinese should be represented by a separate letter of the alphabet.

While the Act in 1911 resolved that the national language should be mainly based upon the Beijing dialect, the view prevalent among Commission members was that the national language should be a more generalized form of *guānhuà*, incorporating features that were extensively attested in other important Chinese dialects. After more than a month's work, the Commission came to a decision on the pronunciation of more than 6,500 characters. This was achieved by voting on a case-by-case basis, with each province having one vote. Furthermore, *zhùyīn zìmǔ* 'alphabet for phonetic annotation' was chosen as the official phonetic script used for sound annotation. The outcome, however, was shelved, partly owing to the political turmoil of the period, and was not published until 1919 in a new *Guóyīn zìdiǎn* 'Dictionary of national pronunciation'. In the dictionary, the pronunciation of the 6,500 characters under review was annotated by means of *zhùyīn zìmǔ*, together with the pronunciation of another 6,000 or so characters in less common use.

The phonology of *guóyǔ* as represented in the 1919 edition of *Guóyīn zìdiǎn*, later referred to as *lǎo guóyīn* 'old national pronunciation', is a hybrid system. Although by and large based upon the phonology of the vernacular Beijing dialect, it also incorporates features that are characteristic of Northern Mandarin of an earlier period, features that are prominent in other dialects, particularly in other varieties of Mandarin and in the Wu dialects, which may not exist in the contemporary vernacular of Beijing. The phonology of *guóyǔ* presented in the form of *zhùyīn zìmǔ*, which assigns a distinct letter to each of the initials, medials, and finals, differs from that of the contemporary Beijing dialect in the following three important respects:

1. Three voiced consonant initials [v], [n], and [ŋ], are retained for some characters, although they have either disappeared or become allophonic with other sounds in the Beijing dialect.

2. Palatal initials before high front vowels in the Beijing dialect evolved from two distinct sources from Medieval Chinese, dental sibilants and velars. The former are called *jiān* 'sharp' initials, and the latter *tuán* 'round' initials. It was stipulated in the old national pronunciation that the initials that are derived from the sharp sounds should retain the previous pronunciation as dental sibilants, while those derived from the round sounds should become palatals. For example, in spite of the fact that there is no difference in pronunciation in the Beijing dialect between the corresponding characters in the two groups, 精 *jīng* 'refined', 青 *qīng* 'blue, green' and 星 *xīng* 'star' are annotated differently in the old national pronunciation from 经 *jīng* 'warp', 轻 *qīng* 'light', and 兴 *xīng* 'mood' ([tsiŋ] [tsʰiŋ] and [siŋ] vs. [tɕiŋ] [tɕʰiŋ] and [ɕiŋ]) as the palatal initials in the first three words were derived from dental sibilants in Medieval Chinese. Although the *jiān/tuán* distinction is retained in some dialects, the two series of initials have completely merged in the Beijing dialect.

3. The *rù* tone is treated as a toneme, which is supposed to have distinct phonetic manifestations, although characters belonging to this tonal group in Medieval Chinese no longer have any distinctive phonetic features in the Beijing dialect of the twentieth century.

The above features were all introduced into *guóyǔ* from outside the modern Beijing dialect. As a result, as far as its phonology was concerned, *guóyǔ* in the old national pronunciation as represented by the 1919 Dictionary was an artificial language that was not actually spoken by anyone. About 90 per cent of the characters in the Dictionary follow the Beijing dialect in pronunciation. It was decreed by the Ministry of Education in 1920 that *guóyǔ* was to be promoted across the country, and a revised edition of the 1919 Dictionary published in 1921 provided the standard pronunciation until 1932.

2.2.3 *Xīn guóyīn* 'New national pronunciation'

Immediately after the Dictionary's publication in 1919, there was some dissent over the phonological standard of *guóyǔ* (J. Li 1935). The artificiality of the old national pronunciation came under attack by Zhang Shiyi in his book *Guóyǔ tǒngyī wèntí* (*The issue of the unification of the national language*), published in 1920, in which he advocated that *guóyǔ* should take the speech of those native speakers of the Beijing dialect who have received at least a high school education as the stand- ard of pronunciation. Although this suggestion was not adopted by the Ministry of Education, it won a growing number of supporters. Two opposing groups were formed over whether *guóyǔ* should adopt a hybrid phonological system as represented in the 1919 Dictionary, or should be based entirely upon the Beijing dialect. Those in support of the hybrid system formed what was called the school of *guóyīn* 'national pronuncia- tion', and those in favor of basing *guóyǔ* entirely on the Beijing dialect, the school of *jīngyīn* 'Beijing pronunciation'. It was more than ten years before the latter prevailed.

The treatment of tones in the 1919 dictionary was most problematic for practical purposes. The dictionary only indicated the tonal category of the characters, without specifying how each of the five distinct tones was to be phonetically realized, and as dialects differ remarkably with regard to the phonetic values of the same tonal category, it left open a wide range of possibilities. It was even suggested that *guóyǔ* in the old national pronunciation should adopt the phonetic value of the *yīnpíng* 'high level' tone from the Tianjin dialect, those of the *yángpíng* 'rising', *shǎng* 'falling-rising', and *qù* 'falling' tones from the Beijing dialect, and that of the *rù* tone from the dialects in regions north of the Yangtze river.[5] Two sets of gramophone records were published right after the promul- gation of *guóyǔ* in the old national pronunciation in 1920, one recorded by Wang Pu, the other by Chao Yuen Ren. As if by prior agreement, both looked to the Beijing dialect for the phonetic realizations of all the four tones of *yīnpíng*, *yángpíng*, *shǎng*, and *qù*. To differentiate the *rù* tone from the other tones, as required in the old national pronunciation, characters of this tonal category were read with a shorter duration. Although it may be characteristic of the literary readings of the *rù* tone in the Beijing dialect of earlier periods, the differentiation is totally artificial, as the *rù* tone is phonetically no longer distinguishable from the other four tones in the modern Beijing dialect.

In comparison with a great variety of other suggestions, the recordings of Wang Pu and Chao Yuen Ren were much closer to the Beijing dialect with respect to the phonetic realizations of the tones. By this time, participants in the National Language Movement had become increasingly inclined towards the view that, rather than introducing the artificial differentiation for the *rù* tone, and between the *jiān/ tuán* initials, etc., *guóyǔ* should be exclusively based upon the Beijing dialect, not only with regard to the phonetic values of the tones, but also in all the other major aspects of phonology. In this context, the *Guóyǔ Tǒngyī Chóubèihuì* 'The Preparatory Committee for the Unification of the National Language' was convened on several occasions after 1923, with the aim of revising the standard pronunciation of *guóyǔ*. It was finally resolved in 1926 that *guóyǔ* should be based entirely upon the Beijing dialect for its standard pronunciation, with the artificial distinctions introduced into the old national pronunciation repealed. The new standard pronunciation of *guóyǔ*, called *xīn guóyīn* 'new national pronunciation', was first adopted in 1932 in the revised edition of *Guóyīn zìdiǎn*, which was renamed *Guóyīn chángyòng zìhuì* 'A Glossary of frequently used characters in national pronunciation', containing 12,219 characters including variants in graphic shapes or phonetic values. Each character is annotated with *zhùyīn zìmǔ*, now renamed *zhùyīn fúhào* 'sound annotating symbols', and with a romanized script called *guóyǔ luómǎzì* (*gwoyeu romatzyh*) 'national language romanization' (cf. Chapter 10 for details on the script).

In contrast to the old national pronunciation, the new one is based entirely upon the phonology of the contemporary Beijing dialect. Characters annotated in the 1919 dictionary in terms of syllables that do not exist in the Beijing dialect, like [ŋo], [tɕio], [tsy], and [tʂɛ], are re-annotated according to their actual reading in the vernacular of Beijing. Similarly, characters in the *rù* tone in Medieval Chinese are annotated as they are read in the Beijing dialect, with their divergence from characters of other tonal groups marked in the 1932 glossary as only of relevance to the appreciation of rhymed compositions in Old Chinese.

The replacement of the old national pronunciation by the new national pronunciation is significant in the history of the establishment of a standard spoken Chinese. Before modern times more attention had been paid to the literary pronunciation of characters used in reading and writing, which may not be the same as in the vernacular. It usually contained phonological features from an earlier period of time, or assumed a phonology that was more generalized than that of a specific contemporary dialect. It was regarded by most educated people as being more prestigious, and presumably more 'correct', than the actual colloquial pronunciation in the dialect. In fact, given that the old national pronunciation was closer to the prevalent literary pronunciation of the time than to any contemporary vernacular, the stipulation that it serve as the standard of *guóyǔ* was only the latest reflection of a tradition in which the literary standard took precedence over the vernacular. In the 1930s, for the first time in the history of the Chinese language, it was specified that, instead of retaining historical distinctions that no longer existed in modern vernaculars, or accommodating features in dialects other than the base one, the phonology of the contemporary vernacular of Beijing should be adopted as its standard pronunciation. Obviously, a standard established in this way, though first and foremost a vernacular standard, will also serve as a literary standard.

The means whereby the vernacular gained precedence over the literary standard was not a natural effortless process, as might be assumed by people half a century later. At that time, the literary pronunciation of characters, in a generalized form of *guānhuà*, commanded more respect and prestige than any local dialect. In spite of the fact that Beijing had been the capital of successive dynasties spanning hundreds of years, and that over 90 per cent of the phonological features of the literary pronunciation were the same as those in the vernacular of Beijing, the latter was no match for the former in terms of prestige. In fact, before the 1930s the local dialect of Beijing still was considered by many to be a language that was mostly used by people of lower social status such as maids and labourers.[6] In a country with a glorious literary tradition, to adopt this local vernacular as the base of Modern Standard Chinese was no simple choice. As remarked by Zhang Qingchang (1990) more than a half century later, it is much to the credit of advocates like Li Jinxi and Chao Yuen Ren that China finally broke away from the entrenched tradition, and succeeded in basing the standard pronunciation of *guóyǔ* entirely upon the contemporary Beijing dialect.

2.2.4   **Promotion of *guóyǔ* before 1949**
Concurrent with the early twentieth-century efforts to establish a standard pronunciation of Modern Chinese, administrative measures were put in place to promote *guóyǔ*, particularly in primary schools across the country. Prompted by a proposal submitted by a few high-profile language reform activists, the Ministry of Education decreed in 1920 that starting from that year, the subject of Chinese taught in Year 1 and Year 2 of primary school should switch its main content from texts in *guówén* 'national written language', which at that time referred to a classical literary style called *wényán*, to those in *guóyǔ*, which was promoted as the base of a vernacular literary style called *báihuà* (for details on *wényán* and *báihuà*, see Chapter 5). This marks a new era in the National Language Movement in China. Up until then, the Chinese language teaching in schools aimed to cultivate in students the competence to read and write in a style that was based upon Old Chinese. The decree by the Ministry of Education was meant to focus Chinese language teaching efforts on enhancing students' proficiency in Modern Spoken Chinese and Modern Written Chinese rather than in Old Chinese. The competence to speak *guóyǔ* was highlighted as one of the major objectives to be achieved through the reform. Although criticized by some as a rash action, the decree won widespread applause from academics and school teachers, and its implementation met with little resistance.

Promotion of *zhùyīn zìmǔ* constituted an important part of the promotion of *guóyǔ*. It was stipulated in the 1920 decree that *zhùyīn zìmǔ* was to be taught from Year 1 to facilitate the acquisition of the standard pronunciation of characters. *Jiàoyùbù Guóyǔ Tuīxíng Wěiyuánhuì* 'The Committee for *Guóyǔ* Promotion of the Ministry of Education' was set up in 1935, which was to coordinate the nation-wide popularization of *guóyǔ*. Among its major achievements was the design and moulding of a new matrix comprising characters in juxtaposition with the *zhùyīn zìmǔ* letters, called *zhùyīn guózì* 'annotated national characters'. The widespread use of the new type in publications, it was hoped, would greatly facilitate acquisition of literacy, and, at the same time, the popularization of the standard pronunciation among the masses. The momentum in the National Language Movement that had been built up since the 1910s was however brought to a halt by the invasion of Japanese troops in 1937.

In 1944, one year before the end of the Sino-Japanese war, the Ministry of Education intended to resume the undertaking, initiating a programme of the National Language Movement, which was composed of five major tasks (Fang 1969; B. Zhang 1974):

1. to promote the standard pronunciation of characters;

2. to promote *guóyǔ* across the country;

3. to promote the use of annotated national characters;

4. to promote *zhùyīn fúhào*;

5. to conduct research on the pedagogy of *guóyǔ*.

As the mainland was engulfed in civil war between 1945 and 1949, the initiative achieved few positive results.

2.3   Promotion of *pǔtōnghuà* after 1949

2.3.1   Definition of *pǔtōnghuà* and its promotion

After the founding of the People's Republic of China in 1949, there was much effort exerted on all the major fronts of language reform. In comparison with the situation before 1949, government in the 1950s played a much more active role, initiating and coordinating all the main activities in the undertaking. While the focus was on reform of the traditional script, a clear definition of Modern Standard Chinese also stood high on the agenda of the language planning institution. Two important conferences were convened in Beijing in October 1955, *Quánguó Wénzì Gǎigé Huìyì* 'National Conference on Script Reform' and *Xiàndài Hànyǔ Guīfànhuà Xuéshù Huìyì* 'Symposium on the Standardization of Modern Chinese', which aimed to reach consensus on some of the basic issues for language planning in the new era, including the drafting of a new phonetic scheme, and a scheme of simplification of characters, as well as the adoption of standards for Modern Spoken Chinese and Modern Written Chinese.

Following normal procedure in formulating policy on issues of national importance, the language planning institution solicited in advance comments and suggestions from the broad academic and educational community on the major issues to be addressed at the two conferences. Published records of discussions on these issues before and during the conferences show that, with regard to the standard of spoken Chinese, there was still strong argument, mainly from people from the Nanjing and Shanghai areas, in favour of the introduction of the *jiān/tuán* differentiation in Modern Standard Chinese, although no-one any longer suggested the introduction of the *rù* tone as a phonetically distinctive category (L. Wang et al. 1956:161).

General agreement was reached by October 1955. At the National Conference on Script Reform, a resolution was passed in which the standard form of Modern Chinese, called *pǔtōnghuà*,[7] was defined as being based upon the Northern dialects with the Beijing dialect as its standard pronunciation. After the Symposium on the Standardization of Modern Chinese, *pǔtōnghuà* was formally defined in 1956 as follows (J. Wang 1995):

> *Pǔtōnghuà* is the standard form of Modern Chinese with the Beijing phonological system as its norm of pronunciation, and Northern dialects as its base dialect, and looking to exemplary modern works in *báihuà* 'vernacular literary language' for its grammatical norms.

Thus, *pǔtōnghuà* is defined with respect to three aspects of language, namely, phonology, lexicon, and grammar.[8] While lexicon and grammar are covered in this brief definition for the first time, the stipulated norm of pronunciation for *pǔtōnghuà* essentially follows that of the new national pronunciation of *guóyǔ* promulgated by the Nationalist government in the 1930s. As was the case in the determination of the old and the new national pronunciations of *guóyǔ*, a special committee was established in 1956 to examine the pronunciation of words in *pǔtōnghuà*. With the consensus being that *pǔtōnghuà* should adopt the phonology of the Beijing dialect, the task was much simpler this time. What the committee sought to accomplish was mainly to settle a few cases of demarcation between what should be considered dialectalisms and what should be included as features of *pǔtōnghuà*, and to decide on a standard pronunciation for words that happened to have two or more variant readings in the Beijing dialect. Results were published consecutively, and incorporated into dictionaries, particularly *Xīnhuá zìdiǎn* 'New China dictionary' and *Xiàndài Hànyǔ cídiǎn* 'Modern Chinese dictionary'.

A note is in order on the designation *pǔtōnghuà*. The term had been used since the late nineteenth century as meaning 'general', with the connotation of being adulterated and substandard. The meaning was highlighted by Qu Qiubai and his colleagues in the 1930s, when they used it to refer to a language that stood in contrast to what was then advocated as the standard *guóyǔ* (Qu 1931a). At the two conferences in 1955, the term was assigned a new meaning that is quite different from the old one. It was redefined as meaning 'common', which is functionally equivalent to the standard language, or the earlier term *guóyǔ*. *Guóyǔ* was discarded in favour of *pǔtōnghuà*, allegedly because the former sounds somewhat Han-chauvinistic in taking the language of one ethnic group, the Han, as the national language, ignoring the fact that there are more than fifty officially recognized ethnic groups in China, which speak over eighty different languages (Atlas 1987/1991; Ramsey 1987).

After 1955, promotion of *pǔtōnghuà* proceeded across the land. A Central Working Committee on Promotion of *Pǔtōnghuà* was established which was to coordinate the nationwide promotional campaign, with sub-committees set up at the same time at the provincial and major city levels. In compliance with a series of directives issued by the state, measures were taken in the following years to ensure the successful implementation of the set policy (J. Wang 1995). Among the most important were:

1. To facilitate the learning of *pǔtōnghuà* by dialect speakers, surveys were conducted on dialects in more than 1,800 selected places. Dozens of pamphlets were compiled on the basis of the survey which highlighted the similarities and differences between the dialects and *pǔtōnghuà* in the hope that they would provide some help to the learners.

2. It was stipulated that *pǔtōnghuà* was to be the medium of instruction in all schools and teachers' colleges. It was also to be the language used in mass media across the country.

3. Twenty workshops were organized by the state to train qualified instructors in *pǔtōnghuà* who were then assigned to the provinces to serve as the backbone in the promotion of *pǔtōnghuà*.

4. People in all walks of life, especially those in the service sectors, and in the army, were encouraged to learn and use *pǔtōnghuà* in their work.

The promulgation in 1958 of *Hànyǔ pīnyīn*, a newly designed phonetic scheme, proved a useful tool in the promotion of *pǔtōnghuà*, especially in the Southern dialect areas, as it indicated the pronunciation of Modern Standard Chinese in a convenient and precise manner.

In many respects, the *pǔtōnghuà* promotional campaign was not unlike other mass movements successively launched in China since 1949. They typically started with considerable fanfare, with senior state leaders calling for popular support and participation, national conferences convened to address the main issues and set the agenda, and mass media and government bureaucracies all tuned up to promote the implementation of the agenda, etc. All these activities combined often led to a situation in which a message was quickly spread throughout the land, and a large portion of the population was mobilized into participation. However, as the whole of these promotional campaigns were conducted under the auspices of government, once the first wave of political enthusiasm was over, and the government re-directed attention to other issues, they often ran out of steam as quickly as they started. With an impressive start in 1955, promotion of *pǔtōnghuà* went into full swing within the next couple of years. Enthusiasm ebbed considerably after 1959, not so much because the goal had been achieved, but because interest faded away when the omnipresent government called public attention to other tasks. Except in a few localities, very little attention was paid to the promotional work in the 1960s and 1970s.

After the tumultuous years of the so-called the Cultural Revolution (1966–76), the promotion of *pǔtōnghuà* resumed, but seemingly with less enthusiasm and energy than in the mid 1950s. In 1982, a new clause was added to the revised Constitution of the People's Republic of China which stated that *pǔtōnghuà* was to be promoted across the country. In 1986, the National Conference on Language and Script was convened in Beijing, which reviewed language planning work since the 1950s and set a new agenda for the future. It was proposed that the following goals should be achieved by the end of the twentieth century (Proceedings 1987):

1. *pǔtōnghuà* is to become the language of instruction in all schools;

2. *pǔtōnghuà* is to become the working language in government at all levels;

3. *pǔtōnghuà* is to be the language used in radio and television broadcasting, and in cinemas and theatres;

4. *pǔtōnghuà* is to become the lingua franca among speakers of various local dialects.

There is little difference in wording between these goals and those set up in the mid 1950s. The fact that they had to be reiterated thirty years later suggests that the promotional campaign since the 1950s, for all its remarkable successes, has yet to fully attain its original goals.

2.3.2   The current situation

Several surveys were conducted in the 1980s and 1990s to ascertain the achievements of the promotion of *pǔtōnghuà* in mainland China. Based on a survey conducted in 1984, Wu Renyi and Yin Binyong (1984) report that 90 per cent of the whole population in China understand *pǔtōnghuà*, and about 50 per cent can communicate in it. It is also reported that people who can understand *pǔtōnghuà* constitute 91 per cent of the population in the Mandarin areas and 77 per cent in the other dialect areas, whereas those who can speak it make up 54 per cent and 40 per cent of the population in the respective areas. This is a considerable improvement on the situation of the early 1950s when only about 41 per cent of the whole population understood *pǔtōnghuà*, accounting for 54 per cent of the population in the Mandarin areas and 11 per cent in the other areas. The results are summarized in Table 2.1 (adapted from R. Wu and B. Yin 1984:37).[9] Table 2.1 and other reports in the literature (B. Wang 1985; Guo 1990; Z. Liu 1993; R. L. Li 1995) demonstrate that geographic localities and social groups differ greatly with regard to the extent of pop-ularization of *pǔtōnghuà*. As expected, promotion of *pǔtōnghuà* is more effective in schools than elsewhere. A survey was conducted by the State Language Commission in 1992 on the use of *pǔtōnghuà* in 851 teachers' colleges distributed over various provinces, which make up 89.9 per cent

Table 2.1 Percentage of population with comprehension and speaking proficiency in *pŭtōnghuà*

	Early 1950s	1984
Comprehension		
Mandarin areas	54	91
Other dialect areas	11	77
whole country	41	90
Speaking		
Mandarin areas	*	54
Other dialect areas	*	40
whole country	*	50

* no statistics available

of the nation's schools in this category. It shows that, generally speaking, *pŭtōnghuà* has already become the language of instruction and other campus activities, and graduates have attained a reasonable level of proficiency. There are insufficient statistics available to provide a general picture of the use of *pŭtōnghuà* in schools of other categories. Surveys based on individual cities and districts reveal an incidence much lower than what is reported for the teachers' colleges. For instance, it was reported that, of 331 primary and secondary schools under survey in a county in the mountainous area of Hubei province, 91.8 per cent use the local dialect rather than *pŭtōnghuà* as the medium of instruction (S. Wang 1992). It is also reported that only an extreme minority of primary school teachers in Shanghai and Guangzhou use *pŭtōnghuà* in class.

Results of similar surveys in various districts over the past decade suggest that, aside from the efficacy of the measures put in place for the promotion of *pŭtōnghuà*, there are several other major factors that have determined how successful the undertaking has been.

The first factor is whether there is a local dialect of high prestige which may compete with *pŭtōnghuà* as the lingua franca among speakers of mutually unintelligible dialects. Cantonese, particularly the variety spoken in Guangzhou and Hong Kong, has traditionally enjoyed a pre-stigious status in Guangdong province and adjacent areas. There is a similar situation with the Suzhou and Shanghai dialects in the Wu dia-lect areas. As a result, the promotion of *pŭtōnghuà* has met with more resistance in these areas than in those that lack such a high-prestige dialect. This partly explains why Guangdong and Shanghai are among the three districts that were identified in 1990 as in need of extra efforts in the popularization of *pǔtōnghuà* (Z. Liu 1993:64; J. Wang 1995).

The second factor is the degree of homogeneity of local dialects. Generally speaking, it is easier to popularize *pǔtōnghuà* in a linguistically heterogeneous area than in a linguistically homogeneous area. Of the areas of Southern dialects, Fujian province stands as the place where the *pǔtōnghuà* promotional campaign has achieved greatest success. It is no coincidence that it is also the place where a large number of mutually unintelligible dialects are spoken within relatively small areas. An illustrative case in point is Datian County, where *pǔtōnghuà* has effectively become the lingua franca among local residents who speak at least five major dialects that are mutually unintelligible (R. L. Li 1988, 1995).

Similarly, places where people from different dialect areas constitute a large portion of the local population are more receptive to *pǔtōnghuà* than places inhabited by people with similar dialectal background. Newly developed cities tend to have more of their residents speaking *pǔtōnghuà* than do established cities. Guo (1990) reports that Shiyan, a city in the Hubei province, has a much higher percentage of residents speaking *pǔtōnghuà* than do its adjacent cities. This is partly explained by the fact that the city grew from a town of less than 50,000 residents to one of more than 360,000 within twenty years, with most of the increase due to migration from various parts of the country. In the absence of a prestigious local dialect, *pǔtōnghuà* became the dominant language. The best example to illustrate the point is the army, where *pǔtōnghuà* has generally been used as the standard language.

The third factor is the feature of local economy. Places with a mobile population and a dynamic economy are more exposed to the outside world than places that are not easily accessible. As a result, it is easier to promote *pǔtōnghuà* in the former areas than in the latter. As observed by Li Rulong (1988:45), in the Fujian province, places along the railway have more *pǔtōnghuà* speakers than elsewhere.

The final factor is the degree of education. Generally speaking, the better the education, the higher the proficiency in *pǔtōnghuà*. As *pǔtōnghuà* is the medium of instruction in many schools, or at least promoted as the medium of instruction, it is assumed that those who received a schooling beyond primary school have attained a certain level of proficiency in *pǔtōnghuà*. In a survey of 2,372 people between the ages of seven and fifty in a mountainous area where Southern Min is the indigenous dialect, those who are proficient in *pǔtōnghuà*, accounting for 60 per cent of the subjects under survey, have all received formal school education, while those who can understand but cannot speak *pǔtōnghuà* are people who have received little or no education (R. L. Li 1995). Similar results are reported in R. Wu and B. Yin (1984:38) and S. Chen (1990). In mainland China, competence in *pǔtōnghuà* in addition to one's local dialect is generally taken as an indicator, albeit not always a reliable one, of the amount of schooling that one has received. Illiterates in non-Mandarin areas are less likely to speak *pǔtōnghuà* than school graduates.

Mainland China has entered an era of rapid economic development since the early 1980s. It is becoming easier for people in geographically remote areas to have access to all types of electronic mass media, which predominantly use *pǔtōnghuà*. While statistics are still lacking, it seems to be a safe assumption that the number of people who understand *pǔtōnghuà* is steadily increasing as more and more people have easy access to television and radio broadcasts. On the other hand, greater social and geographical mobility is also leading to increasing use of *pǔtōnghuà* as a lingua franca among speakers of mutually unintelligible dialects. All evidence indicates that mainland China is well on its way to bidialectalism where *pǔtōnghuà* is used alongside the local dialects. An optimistic estimation suggests that about 97 per cent of the whole population will comprehend *pǔtōnghuà*, and about 80 per cent will be able to speak it by 2000 (R. Wu and B. Yin 1984:38).

2.4   Promotion of Modern Standard Chinese in Taiwan, Hong Kong, and Singapore

2.4.1   Taiwan

Taiwan has always followed the mainland in terms of the standard form of Chinese. As early as the eighteenth century, as in other parts of the Guangdong and Fujian provinces, institutes were set up in Taiwan, which was part of the then Fujian province, in accordance with an edict from the imperial court in Beijing to train local officials and scholars in the use of *guānhuà*.

Taiwan was ceded to Japan in 1895. It was during the next half century of Japanese rule that language became a highly politicized issue on the island, a situation which, to a large extent, has continued ever since. Right from the beginning of the occupation, the Japanese governor set out to promote the Japanese language among the local residents at the expense of Chinese. In 1903, publications in Chinese were banned from import into Taiwan. Starting from 1920, it was stipulated that Japanese was to be the language of administration at various levels. In 1922, the Chinese language was made an elective rather than obligatory subject in schools, and was withdrawn altogether from the school curriculum in 1937. Students in school were forbidden to use languages other than Japanese. At the same time, the Taiwanese were encouraged to use Japanese for all public or private occasions, and families that used Japanese at home were rewarded. By 1944, 71 per cent of the local population were proficient in Japanese. The percentage was much higher in the middle and younger generations, with a large proportion of youngsters unable to speak any Chinese at all. Japanese was by all measures the standard language in Taiwan (Fang 1969; B. Zhang 1974; Cheng 1979; S. Huang 1993).

Given the linguistic situation, the need to promote *guóyǔ* was felt more acutely in Taiwan than elsewhere when it was returned to China in 1945. The central government Ministry of Education provided all the major resources needed for the undertaking. A special task force was sent to the island to start the work, bringing with it all the textbooks and facilities that had been used on the mainland. With the establishment of the Taiwan Provincial *Guóyǔ* Promotion Council in 1946, a vigorous movement to promote *guóyǔ* was launched, and, at the beginning, well received by enthusiastic locals. To accommodate the special situation in Taiwan, the Council drew up specific objectives and strategies which aimed to replace Japanese with Chinese as the standard language within a short period of time. In the process, however, measures were adopted which were unnecessarily harsh towards local non-Mandarin dialects, perhaps an unjustified reaction to the oppressive language policy of the Japanese occupation (Y. Wang 1991; S. Huang 1993). Except for a brief period after 1945, when local Chinese dialects were needed as a tool to promote *guóyǔ*, all dialects other than *guóyǔ* were strongly discouraged or even prohibited in schools and mass media. As reported in Young et al. (1992:13), starting from 1958, students in all teacher-training schools and colleges in Taiwan have had to pass a Mandarin proficiency examination before they could graduate. Similar measures were not initiated on the mainland until the 1990s. Up until 1987, schoolchildren in Taiwan could be penalized for speaking anything other than *guóyǔ*. The local dialects were either banned from mass media, or highly restricted in terms of time and budget allocation until quite recently. While such measures have caused serious backlashes among native speakers of local dialects, generating complaints, bitterness, or even hatred (see Chapter 4 for a detailed discussion), they appear to have been highly effective in the dissemination of *guóyǔ*. It is estimated in S. Huang (1993:117) that in 1991, about 90 per cent of the population of Taiwan spoke *guóyǔ*, a figure that is much higher than that on the mainland in the early 1980s.

2.4.2   Hong Kong

Although it is the native tongue of the great majority of the population of Hong Kong, the Chinese language did not receive much attention until 1974, when the Chinese Language Ordinance was promulgated. The term Chinese language used in Hong Kong actually comprises Cantonese in its spoken form, and Modern Written Chinese in its written form. *Pǔtōnghuà*, as a spoken language, was hardly used and understood until the mid 1980s (Miao 1989). Attitudes have changed considerably since then. A growing number of local residents, particularly those in public service, commerce and business, and education have been learning *pǔtōnghuà* in earnest since 1997, when Hong Kong was returned to mainland China.

2.4.3   Singapore

Singapore represents another place in addition to Taiwan where the promotion of Modern Standard Chinese has achieved remarkable success. In the first half of the century, the National Language Movement that started in China also made progress among ethnic Chinese in Singapore, particularly after the 1920s, although with much less impact upon the society in general. *Huáyǔ* has been the principal medium of instruction in Chinese schools since then, partly due to the fact that the local Chinese community speaks as many as six major mutually unintelligible dialects, none of which could claim a status of overwhelming predominance. Efforts to promote *huáyǔ* were mostly confined to schools, and made by individuals rather than government before Singapore became a sovereign state in 1965. From that time, with the number of students enrolled in Chinese subjects in schools on the increase, *huáyǔ* became more widespread than before. *Pīnyīn* was adopted to annotate the standard pronunciation of characters, which in theory if not in practice closely follows the norms on mainland China.

In 1979, The Singaporean government launched a *Huáyǔ* Promotion Campaign, which aims to establish *huáyǔ* as the lingua franca among the Chinese population, and in the long term as the native language of all ethnic Chinese (Kuo 1985; S. Lu 1985; Newman 1988). With the efficiency characteristic of Lee Kuan Yew's administration, the campaign achieved great success. According to a 1987 survey, 87 per cent of Chinese Singaporeans above the age of twelve speak fluent *huáyǔ* (P. Chen 1993:522).

Platt (1985:15) also reports that before 1980, 89 per cent of customers and hawkers at Chinese stalls used Southern dialects and only 1.2 per cent used *huáyǔ*, while it is reported in Q. Zhou (1990:483) that in late 1980s more and more people in these circumstances use *huáyǔ* rather other Southern dialects. It is obvious that Southern dialects are being replaced by *huáyǔ* as the most commonly used language by Chinese in Singapore (see Chapter 4 for more details).

3 Norms and variations of Modern Standard Chinese

3.1 Phonology of Modern Standard Chinese

3.1.1 Syllabic structure

Until early this century, discussions of phonological rules and changes in Chinese were couched exclusively in terms of three major component parts of syllables, called initials, finals, and tones. Even with the introduction of modern phonemics developed in the West, the traditional conceptual framework remains very popular in the analysis of Chinese phonology.[1] When analysing the phonology of Modern Standard Chinese or Chinese dialects, most present-day Chinese linguists still find it more effective to generalize in terms of initials, finals, and tones, rather than the phonemic inventory of consonants and vowels in established use with languages such as English (Li and Thompson 1981; Norman 1988).

The structure of Chinese syllables in Modern Standard Chinese is represented in Diagram 3.1:

Diagram 3.1 Syllabic structure of Modern Standard Chinese

tone	
initial	final

While the initial and final are segmental parts of the syllable, tone is supersegmental. The segmental structure of the syllable is composed of several parts, as presented in Diagram 3.2:

Diagram 3.2 Segmental structure of syllable of Modern Standard Chinese

Initial	Final		
	medial	root of final	
		main vowel	syllabic terminal
	([i])		([i])
(C)	([u])	V	([u])
	([y])		([n])
			([ŋ])

As is clear from Diagram 3.2, all finals must have a main vowel. Furthermore, some finals may begin with one of the three gliding sounds [i], [u], or [y], which are called *yùntóu* 'medial sound' in Chinese phonology. In the root of the final (known as *yùnjī* 'base of final'), the main vowel,

Table 3.1 Initials of Modern Standard Chinese

Bilabials	b [p]	p [pʰ]	m [m]	f [f]
Alveolars	d [t]	t [tʰ]	n [n]	l [l]
Dental sibilants	z [ts]	c [tsʰ]	s [s]	
Retroflexes	zh [tʂ]	ch [tʂʰ]	sh [ʂ]	r [ɹ]
Palatals	j [tɕ]	q [tɕʰ]	x [ɕ]	
Velars	g [k]	k [kʰ]	h [x]	

Table 3.2 Finals of Modern Standard Chinese

	i [i]	u [u]	ü [y]
a [a]	ia [ia]	ua [ua]	
o [o]		uo [uo]	
e [ɣ]			
ê [ɛ]	ie [iɛ]		üe [yɛ]
ai [ai]		uai [uai]	
ei [ei]		uei [uei]	
ao [au]	iao [iau]		
ou [ou]	iou [iou]		
an [an]	ian [iɛn]	uan [uan]	üan [yɛn]
en [ən]	in [in]	uen [un]	ün [yn]
ang [aŋ]	iang [iaŋ]	uang [uaŋ]	
eng [əŋ]	ing [iŋ]	ueng [uəŋ]	
ong [uŋ]	iong [yŋ]		
er [ɚ]			

called *yùnfù* 'belly of final', may be followed by what is called *yùnwěi* 'syllabic ending', which can be one of the two terminal vowels, [i] or [u], or one of the two nasals, [n] or [ŋ].

Table 3.1 presents the initials of Modern Standard Chinese in *pīnyīn* (for a detailed account of the phonetic writing *pīnyīn*, see Chapter 10), with parenthesized annotations in IPA. Syllables which do not begin with any of the consonants in Table 3.1 are said to have zero initial. There are thirty-nine finals in Modern Standard Chinese, as listed in Table 3.2.

There are four tones in Modern Standard Chinese, as presented in Table 3.3. The numbers 55, 35, 214, and 51 in Table 3.3, in accordance with

Table 3.3 Tones of Modern Standard Chinese

1st tone	high level	55
2nd tone	rising	35
3rd tone	falling-rising	214
4th tone	falling	51

Table 3.4 Rhotacized finals of Modern Standard Chinese

[ər] -i	[iər] i	[ur] u	[yər] ü
[ar] a	[iar] ia	[uar] ua	
[or] o		[uor] uo	
[ɣ] e			
	[iɛr] ie		[yɛr] üe
[ar] ai		[uar] uai	
[ər] ei		[uər] uei	
[aur] ao	[iaur] iao		
[our] au	[iour] iou		
[ar] an	[iar] ian	[uar] uan	[yar] üan
[ər] en	[iər] in	[uər] uen	[yər] ün
[ār] ang	[iār] iang	[uãr] uang	
[ə̃r] eng	[iə̃r] ing	[uə̃r] ueng	
[ūr] ong	[iūr] iong		

the traditional practice initiated by Chao (1930), serve to indicate the typical pitch contours of the four tones in Modern Standard Chinese.

Based upon *Xiàndài Hànyǔ cídiǎn* (1979), the whole syllabary of Modern Standard Chinese comprises about 420 syllables if the tonal differentiations are not counted and about 1,300 if they are counted.

3.1.2   **Phonological process of rhotacization**

The great majority of the finals in Modern Standard Chinese can undergo the phonological process of rhotacization, also known as *ér-huà*, which is characterized by the suffixation of an *ér* sound to the final and is often accompanied by changes to the sound values of the latter. The list of the rhotacized finals is given in Table 3.4. As is clear from Table 3.4, many of the finals of Modern Standard Chinese have merged in phonetic value after rhotacization.

3.2   Difference between Modern Standard Chinese and the Beijing dialect

Although Modern Standard Chinese is based upon the Beijing dialect for its phonological system, this certainly does not mean that the two are phonologically and phonetically identical. Although consensus has been reached on the general principle that Modern Standard Chinese looks to the speech of the educated Beijing residents for its standard, the line drawn between the norms of Modern Standard Chinese and the localisms of the Beijing dialect is sometimes arbitrary, and since the early days in the establishment of Modern Standard Chinese has often been open to controversy. There are certain features in the Beijing dialect that are generally not accepted as part of Modern Standard Chinese. Prominent among such features are the following.

3.2.1   Peculiar syllables

As discussed above, the initials, finals, and tones in Modern Standard Chinese can co-occur only in certain configurations, resulting in a finite number of syllables. There are dozens of syllables in the Beijing dialect, mostly representing words and morphemes peculiar to the dialect, that are not admitted to the repertoire of syllables of Modern Standard Chinese (S. Xu 1979). Following are some examples:

(1)   *biā*   'paste'
      cèi   'break'
      cěng   'break up'
      dēi   'catch'
      hǎ   'scold'

There are more syllables in the Beijing dialect than are accepted in Modern Standard Chinese. The great majority of the extra syllables in the

Beijing dialect are those which do not have conventional representation in characters. It testifies, in a revealing way, to the role that the traditional Chinese writing system plays in delimiting the scope of Modern Standard Chinese.

3.2.2   **Variations in the phonetic values of initial consonants**

There are a few phonological rules at work in the speech of some Beijing residents which change the phonetic values of certain initial consonants.

There is a tendency, particularly among young females in Beijing, to pronounce the initials j[tɕ], q[tɕʰ] and x [ɕ] as [ts], [tsʰ] and [s] respectively mainly before [i]. Examples are:

(2) *jījí*   'active'   [tɕitɕi]   →   [tsɿtsɿ]
     jīqì   'machine'   [tɕitɕʰi]   →   [tsɿtsʰɿ]
     xízi   'mat'   [ɕitsɿ]   →   [sɿtsɿ]

This phenomenon, characterized as a feature of the so-called 'school-girls' accent' in studies of the Beijing dialect, was observed as early as the 1920s. It has persisted, and is still commonly attested among young females in Beijing. However, it is seldom found among elderly women, and never found among men (Shen 1987; M. Hu 1991). The sound change is generally considered to be a feature that is peculiar to the Beijing dialect. It has never been assimilated into the standard usage of Modern Standard Chinese. Although this feature is occasionally found in the speech of news presenters on Beijing Television (BTV), it is almost never found on the China Central Television (CCTV) or the state radio broadcasting station, the Central People's Radio Station (CPRS).

Furthermore, as recorded in detail in Shen (1987), many native speakers of the Beijing dialect, particularly among the younger people, tend to read the initial [w] in some syllables as [v], as in the following examples:

(3) *wàn*   'ten thousand'   [wan]   →   [van]
     wèi   'for'   [wei]   →   [vei]

The allophonic variation between [w] and [v] in the above words is generally considered a dialectalism that has not been admitted into Modern Standard Chinese.

3.2.3   **Rhotacization**

In the Beijing dialect, rhotacized forms are used in one of three situations. First, rhotacization may serve to semantically differentiate words, as in the following:

(4) *báimiàn*   'flour'   *báimiànr*   'heroin'
     chǎomiàn   'fried noodles' *chǎomiànr*   'parched flour'
     huǒxīng   'Mars'   *huǒxīngr*   'spark'
     xìn   'letter'   *xìnr*   'message'

Second, some words habitually occur in the rhotacized form, while their un-rhotacized counterparts, although acceptable, sound unnatural and stilted. Examples are:

(5) *huā* or *huār* 'flower'
     pén or *pénr* 'basin'

Third, the rhotacized form may differ from the corresponding un-rhotacized form only in terms of stylistic effect, with the former typically confined to informal situations. The Beijing dialect, particularly in its informal usage, is characterized by an abundance of rhotacization of the last category. Anyone who listens closely to naturally occurring casual speech of local Beijing residents will be impressed by the high frequency and extent of rhotacization. Whole syllables may be found to be shortened to a *r*-sound in fast speech, as in the following examples:

(6) *bù zhī dào*   'do not know'   →   *bùr dào*
     duōshǎo qián   'how much money'   →   *duōr qián*

Modern Standard Chinese, as coded in *Xiàndài Hànyǔ cídiǎn*, is very selective in the admission of rhotacized words. Generally speaking, only those that are semantically distinct from the corresponding plain forms or those which are customarily preferred over the latter are admitted as part of Modern Standard Chinese.[2] There has been a perceptible tendency in radio and television broadcasting towards a decreasing use of rhotacized forms over the past years, especially in programmes which are targeted at audiences all over the country. An analysis I made in 1994 of the pronunciation in programmes on CCTV and BTV reveals that rhotacized words are used only half as frequently in the former as in the latter.

3.2.4   **Weak stress**

There are many words or morphemes in the Modern Standard Chinese that are normally read with what is known as the weak stress (*qīngshēng*), which is also called the neutral tone. Details of the phonetic features of the weakly stressed syllables do not concern us here. Suffice it to say that such syllables are characterized by shorter duration, and weakening of syllabic distinctness and tonal contour.

Weak stress typically falls on functional words and morphemes such as particles and affixes, and also on the second part of reduplicated nouns, verbs, or adjectives. In addition, there are some disyllabic or multi-syllabic nouns, verbs, and adjectives in which one part, usually the non-initial part, receives weak stress. As with rhotacization, syllables in weak stress in the Beijing dialect fall into three major categories according to their relationship with the corresponding stressed syllables. First, the weak stress, in contrast to the normal stress, may serve a semantically differentiating role, as in the following pairs:

(7) *dōngxi*   'thing'   vs. *dōngxī*   'east–west'
     xiōngdi 'younger brother' vs. *xiōngdì* 'brother'
     dìdao   'genuine'   vs. *dìdào*   'tunnel'

Second, the syllable in question is customarily read with a weak stress, with no semantic contrast to the corresponding stressed one which is seldom heard in the Beijing dialect. Examples are:

(8) *dòufu*   or *dòufǔ*   'tofu'
     miánhua   or *miánhuā*   'cotton'
     huánggua or *huángguā* 'cucumber'

Finally, the weakly stressed syllable seems to be used in free variation with the corresponding stressed one. A characteristic feature of the Beijing dialect is that it has a very large number of words in which the weak stress is allophonic with the normal stress, as in the following examples:

(9) *kēxue*   or   *kēxué*   'science'
     xìngfu   or   *xìngfú*   'happy'
     dāying   or   *dāyìng*   'agree'

Very few weakly stressed syllables from the Beijing dialect have been admitted into Modern Standard Chinese. Many of the weakly stressed syllables of the second and the third category occur with normal stress in Modern Standard Chinese. Zhang Xunru (1956) lists fifty-four bisyllabic words where the second syllable, according to his observation, is read with a weak stress in the Beijing dialect. Only thirteen of them are indicated as such in *Xiàndài Hànyǔ cídiǎn* (1979), with the remaining forty-one all annotated as in normal stress.

Furthermore, a weak stress may substantially affect the segmental structure of the syllable in the Beijing dialect, bringing about changes to the phonetic value of the final or initial, as illustrated by the following examples:

(10) *hútú*   [xutʰu]   →   *húdu*   [xutu]   'muddle-headed'
      gàosù   [kaosu]   →   *gàosong* [kaosɔŋ] 'tell'
      wǒmén   [wumən]   →   *wǒmen*   [wum]   'we'

Such segmental changes rarely occur in weakly stressed syllables in Modern Standard Chinese.

It must be noted that speakers of *pǔtōnghuà* from outside the Beijing area are much less likely to use rhotacized or weakly stressed syllables than those from Beijing. This is largely attributable to the fact that they mostly learn to speak *pǔtōnghuà* with heavy reliance on printed materials, where there is much less indication of rhotacization or weak stress than actually occurs in the Beijing dialect.

3.3   Adulterated *pǔtōnghuà*

There are many more people who understand *pǔtōnghuà* than those who speak it, as is clear from the statistics presented in Chapter 2. Among people from areas outside Beijing who can presumably speak *pǔtōnghuà* in addition to their native dialect, only a very tiny percentage have acquired a level of proficiency similar to native residents of Beijing. Owing to interference from the local dialects, the great majority of them inevitably speak *pǔtōnghuà* in an adulterated form, which may vary greatly in terms of the degree of approximation to the prescribed standard as coded in *Xiàndài Hànyǔ cídiǎn* (1979), or as represented by announcers of CCTV or CPBS. In recent literature, *pǔtōnghuà* in adulterated forms is labelled as *dìfāng pǔtōnghuà* 'local *pǔtōnghuà*', which, in terms of its nature and function, is similar to what was known as *lángīng guānhuà* before the 1920s.

By definition, such local *pǔtōnghuà* displays various features from local dialects and to varying degrees. It is worth noting that, of the phonological and phonetic features that differentiate the local *pǔtōnghuà* from the standard, some are more prominent than others. It is found in Yao (1989) that almost all of the local residents of Shanghai under investigation in the project speak *pǔtōnghuà* with an accent, and the typical local *pǔtōnghuà* in Shanghai displays the following features:

1. syllables historically in the *rù* tone before Modern Chinese are read with shorter duration and an abrupt ending;

2. the distinction between the finals [in] [ən] and [iŋ] [əŋ] is blurred;

3. the distinction between the dental and retroflex sibilants is blurred;

4. diphthongs are often replaced by single vowels, as [ai] and [au] changed to [ɛ] and [ɔ] respectively.

As all the above features are characteristic of the Shanghai dialect, the fact that they occur in the local *pǔtōnghuà* can no doubt be attributed to interference from the primary dialect of the speakers.

Another more illustrative case in point is provided by S. Chen (1990), which presents the results of analysis of the *pǔtōnghuà* spoken by local residents of Shaoxing, a town in Zhejiang Province. A total of twelve phonetic and phonological features which deviate from the standard are identified in the local *pǔtōnghuà*; they are listed as follows:

1. pitch contours of the four tones deviate from those in the standard *pǔtōnghuà*;

2. diphthongs become single vowels;

3. [n] as syllabic ending is lost, with the main vowel nasalized;

4. [n] and [ŋ] as syllabic endings have merged;

5. initials [tʂ], [tʂʰ], and [ʂ] become [ts], [tsʰ], and [s] respectively;

6. the velar fricative initial [x] becomes the labio-dental fricative [f];

7. the initial [r] becomes [l], or is dropped with the vowel rhotacized;

8. a glottal stop appears in the slot of zero initial;

9. the full set of voiced initial consonants in the Shaoxing dialect is preserved;

10. the glottal stop as syllabic ending in characters of the *rù* tone in the Shaoxing dialect is preserved;

11. [u] as a medial sound is sometimes lost;

12. [y] as a medial sound or main vowel changes to another sound.

All these twelve features are attributable to the interference of the local Shaoxing dialect, as they are reflections of characteristics of the latter. Although the *pǔtōnghuà* actually observed in Shaoxing during the field investigation varies greatly in the degree to which it approximates the standard, S. Chen (1990) concludes that, roughly speaking, five levels of proficiency can be established when evaluating the *pǔtōnghuà* skills of the local residents, based on how many features from the above list are observable, with Level 1 closest to the standard, and Level 5 most remote from it. The results are presented in Table 3.5.

It is clear from Table 3.5 that, among the twelve features identified as deviating from Modern Standard Chinese, some are more difficult to avoid than others. Features closer to the top of the list are more likely to occur in the local *pǔtōnghuà* than those further down the list.

While adulterated forms of *pǔtōnghuà* recorded from various speakers in various locations may deviate from the prescribed standard in a great variety of ways, extensive field investigations reveal that the following are among the most common features characteristic of non-native speakers of the Beijing dialect (J. Liang et al. 1982; Yao 1989; S. Chen 1990; Guo 1990; S. Zhang 1994):

Table 3.5 Five proficiency levels of *pŭtōnghuà* in Shaoxing

Features	1	2	3	4	5	6	7	8	9	10	11	12
Level 1	+	–	–	–	–	–	–	–	–	–	–	–
Level 2	+	+	+	+	–	–	–	–	–	–	–	–
Level 3	+	+	+	+	+	+	+	+	–	–	–	–
Level 4	+	+	+	+	+	+	+	+	+	+	–	–
Level 5	+	+	+	+	+	+	+	+	+	+	+	+

1. deviation of pitch contours of the four tones

2. merging of the nasals [n] and [ŋ] as syllabic endings

3. merging of the dental initials [ts], [tsʰ], and [s] with the respective retroflex initials [tʂ], [tʂʰ], and [ʂ]

Features (2) and (3) result in simplification of the phonology of *pŭtōnghuà*. Recent studies indicate that such a process of simplification is also in progress among native speakers of the Beijing dialect, especially among the younger generation (S. Chen 1990; R. L. Li 1995; S. Zhang 1994).

Local *pŭtōnghuà* may contain features which are neither of the standard *pŭtōnghuà* nor of the local dialect involved. For instance, it is also observed in Yao (1989) that in the *pŭtōnghuà* spoken by many people in Shanghai, the final [ai] such as in *dài* 'carry', *tài* 'too', *nǎi* 'milk', and *lài* 'rely', which corresponds to [a] in the Shanghai dialect, is often replaced by the [ɛ] sound in the local *pŭtōnghuà*.

While there can be many varieties of local *pŭtōnghuà* intermediate between Modern Standard Chinese and the local dialect, in many dialect areas specific types of local *pŭtōnghuà* have evolved which are generally accepted, and sometimes learned, in the local community as the conventionalized local standard that is appropriate for formal occasions or in communication with speakers from other dialect areas. It is characterized by pronunciation of words in the literary reading in the local dialect, as well as extensive adoption of the grammar and lexicon of *pŭtōnghuà*.

From a sociolinguistic point of view, such conventionalized adulterated forms of Modern Standard Chinese are examples par excellence of the new varieties of language that grow out of languages in contact.

Although its use has been an important part of the linguistic life of China, local *pǔtōnghuà* has until recently received curiously little attention from linguists, teachers, or language planners, and has often been brushed aside as a corrupt language that falls short of the norms of Modern Standard Chinese. Since the late 1980s, however, local *pǔtōnghuà*, in all its varieties, has attracted more and more attention, as people become more reconciled with the fact that after all, it constitutes an important feature of the actual linguistic situation in China, and deserves full attention for both practical and theoretical reasons (Z. T. Chen 1990).

Recognition of local *pǔtōnghuà* as a linguistic code in widespread use helps language teachers and language planning institutions set more realistic goals in the promotion of Modern Standard Chinese. Since the early 1990s, the State Language Commission has proposed that three levels of *pǔtōnghuà* are to be differentiated. While *pǔtōnghuà* Level 1 is Modern Standard Chinese in the most standard form, *pǔtōnghuà* Level 2 allows for some deviations. *Pǔtōnghuà* Level 3 is used to refer to varieties that may be under heavy influence from the local dialect, but can act as the lingua franca in communication with users of Modern Standard Chinese. While the criteria by which the three levels of proficiency in *pǔtōnghuà* are determined are still to be worked out in greater detail, it is suggested that learners of *pǔtōnghuà* should aim for different proficiency levels as their first goal. Level 1 is required for language professionals in mass media and the performing arts. Language teachers, especially those in primary and secondary schools, should be able to reach at least Level 2. All others should be commended if they have attained Level 3 and use it in their everyday life (J. Wang 1995).

From a theoretical perspective, the great many varieties of local *pǔtōnghuà* may provide a wealth of data on the course of development of various Chinese dialects. Historical evidence demonstrates that several major Chinese dialects, particularly Mandarin, Wu, and Cantonese, evolved mainly as people speaking different languages were brought into close contact through large-scale immigration or military occupation. A detailed picture of the linguistic aspects of the process, however, remains elusive. Comprehensive studies on the features and uses of local *pǔtōnghuà* may shed light upon the mechanisms underlying the historical process. Furthermore, as amply reported in the literature (S. Chen 1990; Guo 1990; Y. Liang 1990; H. Liu 1993; S. Zhang 1994), there have been clear tendencies during the past few decades for non-Northern Mandarin dialects to become closer to Modern Standard Chinese in the major aspects of phonology, vocabulary, and syntax. Detailed studies of the structure and use of local *pǔtōnghuà* will help us determine the role that local *pǔtōnghuà* plays in the process.

3.4   Norms of Modern Standard Chinese outside mainland China

3.4.1   Taiwan

As the mainland provided all the resources in the *guóyǔ* promotion campaign in Taiwan immediately after it was returned to China in 1945, the norms of Modern Standard Chinese formulated on the mainland, and coded in dictionaries like the 1932 Glossary, have presumably been followed in Taiwan.

Since the 1950s, the respective language planning institutions on the mainland and Taiwan have been continuously updating codification of the norms of Modern Standard Chinese, including the pronunciation of characters. As there was virtually no communication between the two sides up to the mid 1980s, discrepancies developed over the pronunciation of a large number of words, due partially to differences in the way pronunciation is codified by language planning institutions, but also as a result of natural 'drift' over decades of separation.

Q. Li (1992) reports on the result of a recent survey which aims to ascertain the differences in the norms of Modern Standard Chinese used on the mainland and in Taiwan. A comparison was made between *Xīnhuá zìdiǎn* of the mainland and *Guóyǔ cídiǎn* of Taiwan with regard to the pronunciation of 3,500 most common characters. It is found that the two sides differ on the pronunciation of 789 characters, accounting for 23 per cent of the total number of items under investigation. Following are some examples:

(14)		*Xīnhuá zìdiǎn*		*Guóyǔ zìdiǎn*
	危	*wēi*	'danger'	*wéi*
	蜗	*wō*	'snail'	*guā*
	癌	*ái*	'cancer'	*yán*

This situation obtains mainly because the language planners on the mainland and Taiwan sometimes abide by different principles when they decide on the standard pronunciation of polyphonous characters. Generally speaking, those on the mainland tend to choose the most popular pronunciation of the character in question in the present-day Northern Mandarin areas, particularly in Beijing, as the standard, while those in Taiwan are more likely to adhere to the traditional pronunciation as preserved in older dictionaries published in the 1930s and 1940s.

What is taken as representing the standard form of *guóyǔ* in Taiwan, such as the speech of broadcasters on the national television or radio stations, or of language teachers in prestigious schools, also displays other discernible features that differentiate the Modern Standard Chinese of Taiwan from that of the mainland. Most prominent is the much lower frequency of rhotacization and weak stress than is the case on the mainland (Barnes 1977; C. C. Li 1982; Cheng 1985; Kubler and Ho 1984; Kubler 1985). Other than these comparatively minor divergences, the Modern Standard Chinese of Taiwan adopts basically an exonormative standard based on the Beijing dialect, in the same way as *pǔtōnghuà*.

In addition to the above differences, several other features are prominent in the everyday speech of an overwhelming majority of the speakers of *guóyǔ* in Taiwan, including those who are well educated and well positioned in local society, which differentiate the language from *pǔtōnghuà* on the mainland. The most important are the following (Kubler and Ho 1984):

1. initials [ts], [tsʰ], and [s] tend to merge with [tʂ], [tʂʰ], and [ʂ] respectively;

2. finals [in] and [iŋ] have largely merged, and so have [ən] and [əŋ].

Both represent under-differentiation of the relevant phonological features characteristic of the prescribed standard. The phenomenon may be attributable to the fact that when Modern Standard Chinese was first introduced to Taiwan in the 1940s, the majority of the new immigrants to the island spoke an adulterated *guóyǔ* that did not make such distinctions. Such distinctions, furthermore, are absent in the predominant local dialect, Southern Min. As there are very few native speakers of the Beijing dialect on the island, pronunciations deviating from the exonormative standard are not as easily detected as on the mainland.

Sociolinguistic surveys suggest that the above features tend to become part of the de facto norm for the educated *guóyǔ* of Taiwan. Although speakers may be fully aware that the above features diverge from the norm in the Beijing dialect, they still adopt them by choice, and sometimes even consciously resist the latter as being 'foreign' or affectations.

As there are varieties of local *pǔtōnghuà* on the mainland, there are varieties of *guóyǔ* in Taiwan, subsumed under the familiar name 'Taiwan *guóyǔ*' ('Taiwan Mandarin') (Kubler and Ho 1984; S. Huang 1993). Although what is generally characterized as Taiwan Mandarin contains a much larger number of features from the local dialects (in particular Southern Min) than the unqualified exonormative or ectonormative *guóyǔ*, the two differ mainly in terms of popular attitudes towards them. *Guóyǔ*, for all the deviations from the prescribed standard discussed above, is generally taken as the norm on the island, while Taiwan Mandarin stands only as an approximation to the local standard. Following are among the most important features defining such Taiwan Mandarin (Kubler and Ho 1984:6–9; Kubler 1985):

1. the final [əŋ] becomes [ɔŋ] after a labial initial like [p], [pʰ], [m], [f], and [w];

2. the final [ɔn] is pronounced as [En];

3. the initials [n] and [l] are sometimes interchangeable, especially before finals containing a nasal sound;

4. the initials [l] and [ɹ] are collapsed, becoming a sound close to [ř];

5. the high front rounded [y] as the medial or main vowel tends to become unrounded.

As extensively observed, the above features are evident in the natural, casual speech of the majority of local residents, with the extent of deviation from the standard depending upon various social and linguistic factors, such as age, gender, level of education, profession, dialectal background, environment of usage, etc. Young, female, well-educated urbanites tend to be closer to the standard than others.

3.4.2   **Singapore**

The situation in Singapore is similar to that in Taiwan. Three major types of *huáyǔ* are identifiable, a basically exonormative *huáyǔ* that looks to the Beijing dialect for the standard, an ectonormative *huáyŭ* that is the de facto standard among local users, and a *huáyŭ* that incorporates a considerable number of features from other Chinese dialects.

The standard *huáyŭ* as used by broadcasters and some teachers is not much different from the standard *pŭtōnghuà*, only slightly diverging from the latter in the pronunciation of some words and in a much lower frequency of rhotacization and weak stress (Lock 1989). The local substandard *huáyŭ*, on the other hand, which contains an intractable mixture of features from various sources, need not concern us here. What is noteworthy is the de facto norm of *huáyŭ* used in the broad Chinese community in Singapore.

C. Chen (1983), Ng (1985), and Lock (1989) are among the recent studies that are devoted to the description of the de facto standard *huáyŭ*. C. Chen (1983) observes that in the speech of the great majority of Chinese Singaporeans, many characters belonging to the *rù* tone in Medieval Chinese and many contemporary Southern dialects are read in a special way, which C. Chen (1983) refers to as the 'fifth tone'. It is characterized by a falling pitch contour, shorter duration and increased tenseness of the whole syllable. The frequency of the occurrence of this fifth tone is found to be correlated with the dialect background of speakers, with 89.4 per cent of the Southern Min-speaking subjects under investigation displaying this feature, and lower percentages registered for speakers of the other Chinese dialects. Ng (1985) and Lock (1989), furthermore, have established that the retroflex initials have gradually merged with the corresponding dentals as the de facto local standard. It is observed in Lock (1989) that among Singaporean speakers of Modern Standard Chinese, initial retroflexion may even be evaluated negatively as 'putting it on' and regarded as a specifically Beijing pronunciation inappropriate for Singapore speakers. It is in the light of such observations, and similar observations in connection with *guóyŭ* in Taiwan, that some scholars suggest that the *guóyŭ* spoken in Taiwan and *huáyŭ* in Singapore have actually constituted another two standard varieties of a pluricentric Modern Standard Chinese which are by and large defined by the above ectonormative features (Bradley 1992).

4.1   Dialects in contact

Dialects are first and foremost geographical variants of language. Broadly speaking, when speakers of a dialect come into close contact with speakers of another dialect, three situations may eventuate with regard to the dialects involved, namely replacement, merging, or coexistence.

Replacement occurs where one of the dialects in contact is much stronger than the others in terms of number of speakers and/or prestige, gradually relegating the latter to disuse and oblivion. As a result, the geographical area in which the strong dialect is spoken expands while that of the weak one shrinks. Dialects in contact may merge, resulting in a new dialect that more or less combines the features from all the contributing dialects. Lastly, both the indigenous and the introduced dialect may remain more or less intact, with most local residents becoming bilingual either in the dialects in contact, or in their native tongue and a third dialect that has been chosen as the lingua franca of the community.

As observed by Ferguson (1959) and Fishman (1967), very often diglossia develops in a bilingual community. Diglossia, as defined by Ferguson (1959), refers to the situation in which a language has two grammatically and lexically distinct varieties, one of high status and one of low status, which are stable in a community.[1] The former is called the High variety, and the latter the Low variety. Each of them is associated with a distinct set of functions, attitudes, and values. The Low variety is usually the primary dialect, used for ordinary everyday transactions; the High variety is usually the vehicle for a large and respected body of written literature, is the only variety taught in schools, and is used for literary, scholarly, and other formal functions. As will be discussed in detail below, modern Chinese society is one which can be characterized by both bilingualism and diglossia. As people become bilingual in Modern Standard Chinese and the local dialect, what were originally geographical dialects have acquired the superimposed status of so-called social dialects, which are defined in terms of their specific social functions and values within the same community.

From a historical perspective, all of the major Chinese dialects split from the same stem and independently evolved along different paths after people migrated in large numbers to different parts of the land, sometimes finding themselves in close contact with people using different languages. The geographical distribution of the major dialects as we know them today, as well as their respective linguistic features, have been by and large stable since the Southern Song dynasty. Nevertheless, although far less extensive and frequent than before, there has been constant geographical movement and social differentiation of the dialects (W. Wu 1980; You 1992; G. Zhang 1991).

Of all the major dialects, Northern Mandarin is the epitome of a strong dialect. Its geographical area has been expanding for centuries. When native speakers of Northern Mandarin migrated to other places in large numbers, the dialect often replaced the indigenous dialects or languages as the local dominant language, as occurred in the Yunnan and Qinghai areas after the Yuan dynasty. Furthermore, recent longitudinal studies have revealed a trend for other Modern Chinese dialects like Min, Wu, and Xiang to be moving towards it, with a growing number of phonological, lexical, and even grammatical features characteristic of Northern Mandarin having been incorporated into these dialects over past decades (Guo 1990; S. Zhang 1994; R. L. Li 1995).

Cantonese is another strong dialect, although the sphere in which it is used is far smaller than that for Mandarin. It has made inroads into other dialect areas in the Southern part of China particularly in the twentieth century. Starting from the 1980s, there has been a growing number of people in other parts of the country who are eager to learn the dialect. J. Chen and W. Zhu (1992) report that 90 per cent of the residents of Shanwei, a Min dialect city, learned to speak Cantonese in a period of several years. Advertisements for Cantonese instruction are ubiquitous in large cities like Beijing and Shanghai. In overseas Chinese communities, on the other hand, Cantonese is often even stronger than Northern Mandarin, being regarded in some Chinese communities as the representative variety of the Chinese language. To be able to speak Chinese more often than not means the ability to speak Cantonese, rather than Northern Mandarin or other dialects. It is generally regarded as the only dialect that can compete with Northern Mandarin in terms of strength.

The most important factors underpinning the strength of Northern Mandarin and Cantonese are political, cultural, and economic. The strength of Northern Mandarin is derived mainly from the political and cultural clout it carries as the dialect of the seat of the capital, or of places close to the seat of the capital for many centuries. Furthermore, as will be

EDINBURGH UNIVERSITY LIBRARY
WITHDRAWN

discussed in detail in Chapter 5, it is the base dialect of Modern Written Chinese, which has contributed significantly to its strength. The strength of Cantonese, on the other hand, is to a large extent attributable to the economic success of the Cantonese-speaking area. The rising enthusiasm for Cantonese since the beginning of the 1980s is closely correlated to this area's dynamic economic development over the same period, and to its close association with Hong Kong, the main Cantonese-speaking area outside the mainland, which is also the economic powerhouse of the development of Southern China. Of all the Southern dialects, Cantonese is the only one that has a highly developed written language, which is used in many types of popular folk literature. For details, see Chapter 7.

Next in strength comes Min, including Southern Min and Northern Min. In the centuries from the Southern Song until the beginning of the twentieth century, Min had been a strong dialect expanding its geographical base to the formally Cantonese- or Wu-speaking areas, and to Hainan and Taiwan where it became the dominant local dialect. Its strength has weakened considerably since then. Instead of expanding in geographical area, it has been contracting, being displaced by Northern Mandarin or Cantonese in many places. It was reported in a survey of the school children in Sanmin, a place where Min was traditionally spoken, that nearly 50 per cent of the school children speak *pǔtōnghuà* only, and can no longer speak the Min dialect of their parents (R. L. Li 1988). A similar situation is reported for Southern Min in Taiwan, triggering an urge to protect it from further decline (S. Huang 1993).

The other four major dialects, Wu, Kejia, Xiang, and Gan, on the other hand, are weak dialects by comparison. Their areas have been dwindling, and they are seldom learned by speakers of other dialects for the purpose of enhancing their communicative competence. They are regarded as declining dialects that are, in some places, on the way to extinction. It is reported, for example, that Cantonese is becoming the most popular local language in a few places like Shaoguan and Huizhou where Kejia was traditionally the dominant local dialect (Yi 1992:62). S. Huang (1993) also observes that in Taiwan, Kejia has all but been replaced by dialects such as Northern Mandarin and Southern Min, especially in the central part of the island.

In comparison with replacement and merging, coexistence has been by far the more common situation when the various Chinese dialects since the Southern Song dynasty have been brought into contact. Bilingualism obtained in vast geographical areas where a lingua franca based upon Mandarin was learned and used for communication with speakers of other dialects, as well as for formal educational, legal, and administrative purposes, as discussed in Chapter 2. This process of bilingualization has accelerated since the beginning of the twentieth century, in which time promotion of Modern Standard Chinese has spread the standard code to all corners of the land, in particular the Southern dialect areas, on a scale unparalleled in history.

4.2   Socio-functional differentiation of Modern Standard Chinese and dialects

4.2.1   Patterns of uses for *pǔtōnghuà* and local dialects

With a growing number of people in the non-Northern Mandarin dialect areas becoming bilingual in *pǔtōnghuà* and the local dialect, a diglossic differentiation has developed between the two types of linguistic code.

As a High variety, *pǔtōnghuà* is the standard code used in television and radio broadcasting all over the country. At the same time, it must be noted, radio broadcasting in dialect areas, especially in rural areas, usually has one or two hours of programming in the local dialect, mainly for the benefit of those who do not understand *pǔtōnghuà*. Discussion panels, interviews, etc. in mass media are almost always conducted in *pǔtōnghuà* in all dialect areas. Subtitles are usually provided in CCTV programmes, which are targeted at a nation-wide audience, when interviewees speak non-Northern Mandarin dialects that may be difficult for listeners outside the local area to comprehend.

Pǔtōnghuà is also the norm in film and theatre. High proficiency in Modern Standard Chinese is an obligatory requirement for professional performers in all varieties of the field. The only exception is local opera, which, by its very nature, has to be performed in local dialects. These local operas have been a popular form of community entertainment and, as representations of local culture and heritage, have always been given all kinds of support by government at all levels. No conflict is seen between the preservation and promotion of these locally based art forms and the promotion of *pǔtōnghuà* as the standard code for other purposes.

The functional differentiation between *pǔtōnghuà* and local dialects is less clear-cut elsewhere. Recent surveys have been conducted in the major Southern dialect areas that aim to determine the patterns of usage of Modern Standard Chinese and the local dialect in various areas of everyday life. Following are the results reported for areas of three major Southern dialects, namely Wu, Cantonese, and Min. Three representative environments were chosen for the investigation: home, schools and work-places, and public places, which provide examples of situations where speakers typically communicate with people they do not know personally, such as on buses and in stores and restaurants.

Table 4.1 is adapted from S. Chen (1990:43), indicating the percentages of speakers who regularly use the local Shaoxing dialect (a Wu dialect), *pǔtōnghuà*, or a mixture of the two.

J. Su (1991) conducted similar investigations in the three major cities in the Min dialect area, Fuzhou, Quanzhou, and Xiamen. The results are summarized in Table 4.2.

Table 4.3 is adapted from Leung (1994), which concentrates on the distribution of *pǔtōnghuà* and Cantonese in the main Cantonese-speaking areas.

A comparison of the three tables demonstrates that the three dialect areas under survey display some similarities in the patterns of usage of *pǔtōnghuà* and local dialects. In all of the three dialect areas under investigation, the local dialect is by far the favourite language among family members, whereas *pǔtōnghuà* is used more often in schools and work-places than in the home or public places. It clearly demonstrates the status of the local dialect as a Low variety in contrast to *pǔtōnghuà* as a High variety. Similar patterns have been reported for other places as well (E. Chen 1989).

On the other hand, the tables also show how the three major dialect communities differ from each other. The functional separation of *pǔtōnghuà* and the local dialect in relation to the home situation and to the other two circumstances is most marked in the Min dialect area, and least marked in the Cantonese area. More people in the Min areas use *pǔtōnghuà* or a mixture of *pǔtōnghuà* and the local dialect than use the local dialect in schools, work-places, or public places, whereas in Cantonese-speaking areas, more people use the local dialect than use *pǔtōnghuà* or a mixture of the two in all three types of environments. The

Table 4.1 Patterns of uses of local dialect and *pǔtōnghuà* in Shaoxing (figures in percentages)

	Local	Pǔtōnghuà	*Mixed*
Home	88	2	10
School and work-place	34	28	38
Public places	73	15	12

Table 4.2 Patterns of uses of Min and *pǔtōnghuà* in three Min dialect cities (figures in percentages)

	Local	Pǔtōnghuà	*Mixed*
Home	54	21	25
School and work-place	8	72	20
Public places	30	35	35

Table 4.3 Patterns of uses of Cantonese and *pǔtōnghuà* in major Cantonese areas (figures in percentages)

	Cantonese	Pǔtōnghuà	*Mixed*
Home	87	9	4
School and work-place	61	32	7
Public places	78	11	11

case of the Shaoxing area stands somewhere between that of the other two areas. The majority of people use the local dialect only in the home and in public places, but when in schools and work-places, more people use *pǔtōnghuà* or a mixture of the two than use the local dialect exclusively.

Diglossia, as defined in Ferguson (1959), differs from the more wide-spread standard-with-dialects in that no segment of the speech community in diglossia regularly uses the High variety as a medium of ordinary conversation, and any attempt to do so is felt to be either pedantic and artificial or else in some sense disloyal to the community. In the usual standard-with-dialects situation, the standard is often similar to the variety of a certain region or social group which is used in ordinary conversation more or less naturally by members of the group and as a superposed variety by others. It is evident that, to the extent that *pǔtōnghuà* is being used as a family language and in public places by a certain portion of the population, as the above statistics show, diglossia in these Southern dialect areas is evolving into the standard-with-dialects situation.

The differences between the three dialect areas under investigation in patterns of usage are consistent with the remarks on the relative strengths of *pǔtōnghuà* and the dialects that are made at the beginning of this chapter. *Pǔtōnghuà* is used less frequently in an area with a strong dialect, like Cantonese, than in an area with a weak dialect, like Wu or Min.

One of the most important, if not the single most important, features that mark the diglossic distinction between Modern Standard Chinese and local dialects is the fact that the former is the base of the standard written language. Speakers of all Chinese dialects are supposed to conform to the lexical and grammatical norms of Northern Mandarin when they write. It is extensively reported by teachers that there is a strong correlation, among native speakers of Southern dialects, between an inability to speak good Modern Standard Chinese and the failure to write and comprehend written Chinese (R. L. Li 1995). I will return to this in more detail in Chapter 7.

4.2.2 **Popular attitudes towards *pǔtōnghuà* and dialects**

The differentiation of *pǔtōnghuà* and dialects in patterns of usage also correlates with differences in popular attitudes towards them in the Chinese community. As reported in the literature (Kalmar et al. 1987; Pierson 1988; H. Liu 1993; Erbaugh 1995), Modern Standard Chinese is generally regarded as the language that is associated with good education, intelligence, social sophistication, authority, and formality, whereas dialects are associated with properties such as solidarity, sociability, familiarity, closeness, sincerity, and so on.

While the widespread use of *pǔtōnghuà* befits a modernizing society, it also has the potential to reduce, or ultimately eliminate, the linguistic diversity of the various Chinese dialects. In the face of the unifying force of a prevailing Modern Standard Chinese, the specific values associated with local dialects may become even more prominent. Particularly noteworthy is their role in maintaining group solidarity among family members or members of the local community.

It is well known that regional affinity played a conspicuous role in establishing social networks in traditional Chinese society. This role has somewhat weakened in importance in modern times, but is still a factor to be reckoned with in Chinese communities. This is most evident from the large number of associations or organizations in Chinese communities which are formed according to the geographical origins of people. So long as regional identity remains an important force in modern Chinese society, the local dialect, as its most easily recognizable symbol, will always retain its status as a valuable code in the linguistic repertoire of the local community. In some places, notably in the Cantonese-speaking areas, the awareness of regional identity may be so strong that the ability to speak the local dialect is still taken as an extremely important asset for social mobility, while those who can only speak Modern Standard Chinese may find themselves discriminated against in public places (E. Chen 1989).

4.3   Language policy towards dialects

What is referred to as 'standard-with-dialects' by Ferguson (1959) was envisaged by language planning institutions from the beginning of the promotion of *guóyǔ* in the early 1920s, although the status of *guóyǔ* relative to the other dialects was not explicitly formulated until much later. *Guóyǔ* was presumably meant to serve all the functions of a standard language, such as the medium in education, mass media, and government administration, and of a lingua franca for the whole population, while other dialects were meant to serve the complementary functions, such as the language used in family and among friends and for unofficial occasions. There is no indication that the replacement of the latter by the former for all occasions was ever on the agenda.

This tolerant policy towards dialects in the promotion of standard language has been continued in the People's Republic since 1949, although it was indicated that the scope of dialect usage would be gradually reduced in the course of promoting *pǔtōnghuà*. The most explicit formulation of the official position on this issue is the following passage:

Pǔtōnghuà serves all the population whereas local dialects serve the population of specific areas. Promoting *pǔtōnghuà* does not mean intentionally annihilating local dialects, but to gradually limit their scope of use, which is in conformity with the objective rules of societal progress. Dialects will and must co-exist with *pǔtōnghuà* for a comparatively long period to come. However, the scope of the use of *pǔtōnghuà* must be incessantly expanded, and efforts should be exerted to promote the use of *pǔtōnghuà* in public places and in writing.

(*Rénmín Rìbào* (*People's Daily*) 1955:59)

It was also predicted on the basis of the then prevalent theory of language evolution that dialects will eventually converge, making it pointless to adopt measures other than those in place to put an end to the diglossic situation as a result of the promotion of *pǔtōnghuà*.

In actuality, since the early 1950s the language planning institutions have focused on positive measures to encourage the use *pǔtōnghuà*, as elaborated in Chapter 2, rather than on prohibitive measures against the use of local dialects. In comparison with the sterner measures adopted in Taiwan after 1945, mainland China has opted for a more liberal policy towards dialects. *Pǔtōnghuà* has been used in mass media more as a result of following the customary practice from the first half of the century than in compliance with the initiatives of the government. Even in schools, where *pǔtōnghuà* is promoted with the greatest enthusiasm, no attempts have been made to ban the use of dialects.

Since the mid 1980s, there has been an increase in the use of dialects across the country. More non-Northern Mandarin dialects are used in films and plays than before. Most noticeably, for some time now, almost all actors or actresses who play the role of deceased senior state leaders speak that person's local dialect on screen in imitation of the actual way in which those people spoke when they were alive. This practice, according to reports, is intended to tap into the special feelings of informality, friendliness, intimacy, etc. that are associated with the dialects as a Low language, thus achieving the special effect of strong solidarity between the stage and the audience.[2] More dramas in dialects have been included in CCTV programmes, which are supposedly targeted at a nation-wide audience.

The tendency towards increased use of local dialects is even more noticeable in the Cantonese-speaking areas than elsewhere. There are some radio stations recently established in Guangzhou and Shenzhen, such as the Traffic Station, which mainly use Cantonese instead of *pǔtōnghuà*. This obviously follows the practice in Hong Kong, which is just across the border, but stands as highly unusual both from a historical perspective, and in comparison with the norms elsewhere in mainland China.

This increased use of dialects has caused concern on the part of educators and language planning institutions at the central and local levels. Measures have been adopted since the early 1990s to arrest the spread of dialects achieved at the expense of *pǔtōnghuà*. Most noteworthy is the directive issued by the Guangdong government on 2 February 1992, which stipulates that *pǔtōnghuà*, not Cantonese, should be the standard language in the province. Accompanying the directive were the following measures adopted to implement it:

1. Radio and television stations which use the local dialect as the main language of broadcasting should reduce the time devoted to dialects and use more *pǔtōnghuà*. Programmes for school children and youngsters should be in *pǔtōnghuà* exclusively.

2. *Pǔtōnghuà* rather than local dialects should be the language of instruction in all of the province's schools by the end of 1995. The ability to speak *pǔtōnghuà* should be a compulsory requirement in the recruitment and promotion of teachers.

3. Employees in the public service sector across the province should all use *pǔtōnghuà* as the working language by the end of 1994. They must pass a *pǔtōnghuà* test before they are employed.

All of the above measures are little more than reiteration of what was advocated or stipulated by language planning institutions in 1957, aimed at maintenance of the standard-with-dialects situation. The fact that the Guangdong government resolved to make such an announcement thirty-five years after the 1957 campaign to promote *pǔtōnghuà* across the land indicates that the progress in the promotion of *pǔtōnghuà* is not fast enough in comparison with other provinces. As Cantonese is the only dialect that may match *pǔtōnghuà* in terms of geographical and social strength, and given the increasing economic clout of Southern China together with the importance of Hong Kong to the mainland, it remains to be seen how effective the directive will be in reducing the use of Cantonese in this area.

4.4   Taiwan, Hong Kong, and Singapore

4.4.1   Taiwan

The use of indigenous Chinese dialects in Taiwan has been subject to more restrictions than on the mainland. During the Japanese occupation (1895–1945), as discussed in Chapter 2, Japanese was the sole official language on the island and was promoted with the intention of replacing the local languages for all functions, formal or informal. At the end of the occupation, the local Chinese dialects were preserved as Low languages among the older population, and to a much lesser degree among the middle-aged population, while Japanese was the only language of a large portion of the younger generation. After 1945, the trend of contraction continued with Kejia, and aboriginal languages, giving way to Northern Mandarin and to some extent Southern Min.

The successful promotion of *guóyǔ* since 1945 has resulted in a bilingual society in which, according to S. Huang (1993:439), 82.5 per cent of native speakers of Southern Min are bilingual in Southern Min and *guóyǔ*, and 88 per cent of native speakers of other Chinese dialects and aboriginal languages are bilingual in *guóyǔ* and their native tongue. In much the same way as the mainland, Taiwan is characterized by bilingualism and diglossia, with *guóyǔ* as the High language and the local Chinese dialects and aboriginal languages as the Low languages.

A comparison between Taiwan and the mainland on the patterns of uses of *guóyǔ* and local dialects suggests that the diglossic differentiation is more marked in Taiwan than on the mainland. Unlike the situation in mainland China, Modern Standard Chinese is the only language of instruction in Taiwan's schools. The respective uses of *guóyǔ* and Southern Min in the home and the work-place are presented in Table 4.4 (data adapted from Z. Qiu and van den Berg 1994).

On the other hand, dialects are used much more frequently than Modern Standard Chinese in public places like markets. S. Huang (1988; 1993:285–6) and van den Berg (1988) investigated the uses of Southern Min and *guóyǔ* in marketplaces in Taipei, and four other cities in Central and South Taiwan. The results are summarized in Table 4.5. A comparison between Table 4.2 and Tables 4.4 and 4.5 shows that Southern Min is used more often in the home, work-places, and public places in Taiwan than on the mainland.

Table 4.4 Patterns of uses of Southern Min and *guóyǔ* in home and work-place in Taiwan (figures in percentages)

	Southern Min	Guóyǔ
Home	60	22
Work-place	43	42

Table 4.5 Patterns of uses of Southern Min and *guóyǔ* in market places in Taiwan (figures in percentages)

	Southern Min	Guóyǔ	*Mixed*
Taipei	53	19	26
Central and South Taiwan	95	3	2

Since the late 1980s, there has been an increased awareness of regional identity which, among other things, is most evident in the calls to enhance the status of the local dialects. Probably as a backlash to the harsh policy against local dialects, popular attitudes towards dialects, particularly Southern Min, have been much more emotional in Taiwan since the mid 1980s than is the case on the mainland. In addition to such values as sincerity, friendliness, trustworthiness, etc. that are typically associated with a Low language, Southern Min is seen as a most important, if not the most important, symbol of the cultural and linguistic heritage of the speakers of the dialect which allegedly has long been neglected and damaged in the course of promoting *guóyǔ* (Cheng 1979; 1989; S. Huang 1993). Issues surrounding the use of dialects and Modern Standard Chinese are highly politicized, with Southern Min taken to be a symbol of a local identity that separates its speakers from those speaking other Chinese dialects, and for that matter, separates Taiwan from other parts of the Chinese community. In 1987, the Ministry of Education formally abolished the penalty against school children speaking dialects at school. In 1991, time restrictions for dialect programmes on television and radio stations were lifted. The use of Southern Min is dramatically on the increase in all sectors of society. It has expanded its use from markets to areas where *guóyǔ* was traditionally the predominant code, such as the political and cultural arenas. It is reported that competence in Southern Min has become a requirement in the job advertisements of many private businesses. In public domains, the use of dialects is also evidently on the increase. As detailed in Chapter 7, the promotion of Southern Min and a written language based on the dialect is also high on the agenda of some educators, language planners, and politicians. It remains to be seen whether and how the community will deviate from the current bilingual and diglossic situation.

4.4.2   Hong Kong

Hong Kong differs from the mainland and Taiwan in that the High language is English, instead of Modern Standard Chinese. After the 1974 Official Language Ordinance which stipulated that both English and Chinese were official languages of Hong Kong, the status of Chinese was enhanced to some extent, in recognition of the fact that after all, about 97 per cent of the local residents speak Cantonese as their native tongue. Important documents and reports are published in English and Chinese. Simultaneous interpretation between English and Cantonese are provided in council meetings at various levels. Expertise in Chinese has received more attention than before in the Civil Service. Nevertheless, English was still the undisputed High language for administrative, legal, academic, and high-level trade and business purposes, while Cantonese was the everyday language used by local residents in the following decades up to the transfer of sovereignty to China on 30 June 1997 (T'sou 1986).

There have been obvious changes in practice and in policy over language issues since Hong Kong became a Special Administrative Region of the People's Republic of China in July 1997. Chinese has received much more emphasis than before, often at the expense of English. Cantonese is becoming the norm in public functions of the government, especially when the audience are mainly local Hong Kong residents. It is also stipulated that Chinese is to be the medium of instruction in the majority of secondary schools, where English, or a hybrid of English and Chinese, was used in the classroom before 1997. With increasing contact with the mainland, moreover, expertise in *pǔtōnghuà* gains in usefulness. *Pǔtōnghuà*, to some extent, is on the way to assuming a role similar to that of English, with proficiency in it a highly desirable attainment for politicians and business people at higher levels.

The linguistic situation in Hong Kong in the near future is not difficult to predict. While everyone seems to admit the importance of English to the success of Hong Kong as a dynamic international financial centre in East Asia, there is little doubt that Chinese, and particularly *pǔtōnghuà*, will play an increasingly important role in Hong Kong. Although it is unlikely that the Hong Kong government will adopt the same language planning policy as the adjacent Guangdong province, it is plausible that, in due course, *pǔtōnghuà* will be an everyday language used by the general public alongside Cantonese and English.

4.4.3   Singapore

The diglossic situation in Singapore is similar to that of Hong Kong in that English is the High language, while various Chinese dialects are the Low Languages. The *Huáyǔ* Promotion Campaign has not changed this diglossic contrast between English and Chinese. Rather, it has aimed to replace the Southern dialects with *huáyǔ* for low-level purposes among the ethnic Chinese, and keep the status of English intact. The campaign has proved to be a success. According to surveys conducted in the 1980s and 1990s, the Southern dialects are losing speakers, giving way to *huáyǔ* and English. Table 4.6, based upon a survey of the most common languages used by parents of Year 1 students in Singapore reported in Q. Zhou (1990:483), demonstrates the marked changes in the linguistic patterns of Chinese in the 1980s.

Table 4.6 Most common languages used by parents of Year 1 Chinese students in Singapore (figures in percentages)

	Southern dialects	Huáyǔ	*English*
1980	64.4	25.9	9.3
1989	7.2	69.1	23.3

Since the late 1980s, there are signs that the government intends to further enhance the status of Chinese. Addressing the International Seminar on Chinese Language Teaching in 1990, the former Prime Minister Lee Kuan Yew reiterated the official language policy according to which English is the first language and Chinese the second language. At the same time he also proclaims that (Lee 1990:8):

> Singapore made a conscious effort to substitute Mandarin for dialects, in order to make the bilingual policy of English and Chinese effective. It is succeeding. In another ten years, Mandarin will be the social language of the Chinese in place of dialects. It will be Mandarin at an effective level, effective for social and cultural communication between Chinese Singaporeans, and at a level good enough to sustain good newspapers, magazines, radio, and television.

If what Lee envisages materializes by the end of the decade, the Chinese language at the effective level described here will actually no longer be a Low language in the same way as the Southern dialects in the other diglossic Chinese communities. Rather, in the classical definition of the term it will be more of a High language than a Low language.

Part II

Modern Written Chinese

5.1   Old Written Chinese

Generally speaking, writing differs from speech to varying degrees in all languages, with the former more terse and compact than the latter. What makes Chinese outstanding in this respect is that for 2,000 years, its standard written language, *wényán* 'classical literary language', was almost completely divorced from the contemporary speech of its users.

Wényán looks to the style of writings prevalent in the period from the Spring and Autumn period to the Eastern Han dynasty for its grammatical and lexical norms. There is general consensus among Chinese linguists that, partly owing to the higher degree of independence of the logographic writing system to the phonetic details of actual speech in comparison with a phonographic writing system, and partly owing to general constraints imposed upon writing by the then available technologies, this discrepancy between spoken and written language existed from the very beginning. In its early stages, however, writing in Chinese followed speech more closely than was the case later. Detailed analysis of texts of the period demonstrates that the then prevalent written language contains a considerable number of elements of the vernacular, including those from diverse dialects of different areas. Local states and areas may also differ with regard to the script used.

After the emperor Qin Shihuang unified China for the first time in 221 BC, among the first things he did was to unify the writing system using the *xiǎozhuàn* 'small seal' style, burning books written in other writing systems, and executing scholars who disagreed with the harsh measures. This laid the foundations for the standardization of the written language across the country. In the early period of the Han dynasty, the teachings of the Confucianist school were established as the orthodox school of thought, and incentives were instituted to promote it across the land. At that time, the most enviable career for Chinese scholars was to be admitted into the imperial civil service after success in the state examinations, in which they were tested mainly on their knowledge of the pre-Qin classics, particularly those in the Confucianist school, and on their competence in composition after the model of the writing style of the classics. Educational institutions of various levels were set up where students were mainly taught the literature of the pre-Qin Confucianist school. As a result, the writings of the pre-Qin period became models both in content and in writing style, which scholars were to master in schools and emulate in examinations. The practice of selecting officials through state examination of literary achievement, which culminated later in the institution of *kējǔ*, was no doubt an effective factor in the establishment and maintenance of *wényán* as the classical standard written language for literary, scholarly, and official purposes. This status was retained up until the May 4th Movement in 1919. It was no coincidence that the abandonment of *wényán* as the standard written language occurred in less than two decades after the abolition of the state examination system.

The logographicity of the writing system is the crucial linguistic factor that facilitated the maintenance of *wényán* over such a long period. As will be discussed in detail in Part III, Old Chinese differs from Modern Chinese in that while the overwhelming majority of words in the former are monosyllabic, there is a much larger proportion of di- and multi-syllabic words in the latter. The logographic script fits Old Chinese well in that individual characters are coextensive with morphemes and words in the language. For all the inconvenience it may have caused, the lack of direct association between sound and graphic forms in the Chinese writing system gave *wényán*, as a written language encoded by such a writing system, a degree of accessibility across time and space. Logographicity largely insulated *wényán* from changes in the vernacular language, enabling it to serve as the medium whereby Chinese literary heritage was preserved and continued, and information could be spread across a land of great dialectal diversity. Had Chinese adopted a phonographic system from the beginning, there would have been much greater motivation for the written language to follow actual changes in language more closely .

5.2   Emergence of early Modern Written Chinese

In the Eastern Han dynasty, a large number of vernacular elements began appearing in writing, particularly in the translation of Buddhist texts into Chinese. By the end of the Tang dynasty, as an increasing number of words and grammatical constructions from the vernacular found their way into writing, a new type of written language, *báihuà* 'vernacular literary language' (literally 'unadorned speech'), emerged and matured.

Báihuà differed from *wényán* in that it was much closer to the contemporary vernacular. While *wényán* remained supreme as the standard written language, *báihuà* served all low-culture functions such as transcriptions of Buddhist admonitions, and scripts for folk stories and plays. By their nature, such writings required a written language that closely reflected the way less literate people spoke (Mair 1994). *Báihuà* gained in currency from the end of the Tang dynasty, providing the medium for many representative literary works of the later periods, for instance, *qǔ* 'verse' in the Yuan dynasty and novels in the Ming and the Qing dynasty. For a long period, there co-existed two types of written Chinese, *wényán* and *báihuà*. Due to the conservatism prevalent among the ruling class and the literati, *wényán* was considered refined and elegant, thus ideal for high-culture functions, while *báihuà* was despised as coarse and vulgar, suitable only for low-culture functions.

In spite of the fact that it was irrelevant to the career advancement of scholars in the bureaucracy, literature in *báihuà* was immensely popular in all sectors of society. It comprised various kinds of vernacular verse, stories, and novels which were read and enjoyed from north to south, and from one dynasty to another by emperors and school children alike. The language used in such writings, known later as traditional *báihuà* in contrast to the modern *báihuà* as used in the twentieth century, was quite well established as a written language for informal purposes such as keeping diaries and writing casual essays, and on specific occasions which required a text that approximated as far as possible what was actually being said, as in the recording of court proceedings, official negotiations, etc.

Since its early days, the traditional *báihuà* had been by and large following the national spoken standard for its grammar and vocabulary. In the early stage of the pre-modern period, it was mainly based on the Zhongzhou dialect, laying the foundation for the *báihuà* used by later writers. It is typically represented by texts such as Buddhist tracts and quotations of Buddhist masters, etc., of the period, most of which were found much later in the Dunhuang caves, as well as quotations from Neo-Confucianists and scripts of stories or operas. Later, as the written equivalent of *guānhuà*, it adopted a more generalized form based on the Jiang-Huai Mandarin and Northern Mandarin, as represented by lengthy novels such as *Xī yóu jì*, *Jīn píng méi*, *Hónglóu mèng*, *Rúlín wàishǐ*, and

Érnǚ yīngxióng zhuàn. From time to time, works in traditional *báihuà* also displayed grammatical and lexical features from other dialect areas, particularly the Wu areas, if the author was from a non-Mandarin background.

5.3   Replacement of *wényán* by *báihuà* as Standard Written Chinese

5.3.1   Earlier efforts

After the Opium War in 1840–2, there were increasing calls for the replacement of *wényán* by *báihuà* as the standard written language. It was argued that one of the most effective ways to increase the country's literacy rate was to adopt a written language which, by approximation of the spoken vernacular, would be much easier to learn and to use. As noted in Chapter 2, many of the early proponents of language reform studied or lived in Japan, and drew inspiration from that country's success in language reform. In Japan's Meiji period (1868–1912), a traditional written language that was divorced from speech in the same way as Chinese was replaced by one that was based upon the vernacular within a short period of time. The result of this reform, together with successes in other aspects of language reform, they observed, was a significant increase in Japan's literacy rate, which in turn contributed significantly to the success of political reform.

Among the first to advocate the unification of speaking and writing in explicit terms was Huang Zunxian, who in 1868 succinctly summarized his proposal with the famous line *wǒ shǒu xiě wǒ kǒu* 'my hands write as I say with my mouth'. Following him, another scholar, Qiu Tingliang, highlighted the relevance of the written language to the general education of the population when he wrote in 1898: 'there is no more effective tool than *wényán* for keeping the whole population in ignorance, and there is no more effective tool than *báihuà* for making it wise' (Tan 1956).

Around the turn of the century, most scholars and politicians with an agenda for general social and political reform realized that *báihuà* was a more effective means than *wényán* with which to propagate their ideas and win popular support. Immediately preceding and following the famous Reform Movement of 1898, more than a dozen newspapers in *báihuà* were published in the lower Yangtze river areas of Shanghai, Wuxi, Suzhou, Hangzhou, etc., and also in Beijing and the southern part of China, targeting a wide range of readership. Textbooks and dictionaries that taught *báihuà* were also published all around the country. Following the tradition of well-known vernacular literary works, more stories and novels were written in *báihuà*, enjoying the popularity of their predecessors. According to rough statistics, in the final years of the Qing dynasty before 1911, there were already dozens of newspapers and magazines, more than 50 textbooks and around 1,500 novels published in *báihuà*.

5.3.2 **New Culture Movement**

Towards the end of the second decade of the twentieth century, in spite of fierce opposition from the conservative camp of the literate elite, there was growing consensus among mainstream scholars either that *báihuà* should replace *wényán* as the standard written language for all formal purposes, such as educational, commercial, administrative, etc., or that such writing should at least include a large number of *báihuà* elements. The abundance of readily available publications in *báihuà* at that time was further evidence that the climate was ready for a comprehensive break from the situation in which *báihuà* was confined to low-culture functions.

Several factors contributed significantly to the rapid establishment of *báihuà* as the standard written language. A most important one was the abolition in 1905 of the state examination of literary attainments whereby scholars were selected for official positions in the government. As a result, students and scholars were less motivated to stick to *wényán*, which no longer served to enhance prospects of career advancement. Six years later, the Qing dynasty was overthrown, and the Republic of China was established. With the most radical change in the political system in thousands of years of Chinese history, the country was more prepared than before for drastic changes to other aspects of society.

On the other hand, earlier proposals for the wider usage of *báihuà* were typically put forward in an ad hoc manner. They were not accompanied by systematic explanation of the real significance of such a move, and failed to expound exactly what kind of *báihuà* should be used. It was only in the second decade of the twentieth century that overall reform of the standard written language was fully articulated.

Against a background of increasingly influential modern Western ideas and awakening nationalism, what has been known as the New Culture Movement started in the late 1910s. It had three major themes – the Literary Revolution, democracy, and science – which, in combination, aimed at creating a culture more consonant with modern times and the common people. The initiators of the movement, mainly Western-trained intellectuals like Hu Shi, Chen Duxiu, Liu Bannong, Qian Xuantong, Fu Sinian, and Lu Xun, advocated that democracy and science were the only correct prescription for a strong and prosperous China, and that to have democracy and science take root in China demanded that the masses of people had easy access to education (D. Chen 1917; S. Fu 1917, 1918, 1919; S. Hu 1917, 1918, 1935; B. Liu 1917; X. Qian 1918a). As the then standard written language *wényán* was divorced from actual speech, it stood as the main obstacle on the way to a higher literacy rate in the country. One of the major goals of the Literary Revolution, therefore, was to replace *wényán* with a written language that was much closer to the daily vernacular so that learning and using the written language would be made much easier for the masses. *Báihuà* was chosen as the replacement, and was meant to serve as the base for a multi-purpose modern standard written language.

Although similar proposals had been put forward several decades earlier, it was only due to the enthusiastic and effective promotion by people like Hu Shi, Chen Duxiu, Liu Bannong, Qian Xuantong, and Fu Sinian, and in the context of rapid social changes, that this proposal gained more and more support.

Hu Shi's famous article *Wénxué gǎiliáng chúyì* 'Preliminary views on the reform of literature', published in the journal *Xīn Qīngnián* (*La Jeunesse*) in 1917, initiated the first systematic discussion on the establishment of *báihuà* as the standard written language of Chinese literature. In that article, he listed eight aspects in which Chinese literature was to be improved:

1. it must have substance;

2. there is no need to emulate the ancients;

3. pay attention to grammar;

4. do not adopt a sentimental pose;

5. get rid of clichés;

6. avoid literary references or allusions;

7. there is no need to use antithetical constructions;

8. do not avoid vernacular expressions.

Strictly speaking, only (8) makes explicit reference to the use of vernacular elements, and all the other seven refer mainly to the content and rhetorical skills of writing, rather than the written language per se. Indeed, it is perfectly possible to write in *wényán* without any of the seven undesirable features listed here. The article itself, in fact, was written in *wényán*. What made many writings in *wényán* obnoxious was the fact that they were under the heavy influence of a specific rigid style of *wényán*, called *bāgǔwén* 'eight-part essay', which features the above-mentioned undesirable characteristics at their worst. By that time, *bāgǔwén* had become so entrenched that when people wrote in *wényán*, most of them tended to follow this conventionalized style in a conscious or unconscious way. Since the target of Hu's attack as articulated in the above list was customarily associated with *wényán*, it naturally led him to advocate its replacement as the standard written Chinese.

Hu made his point more explicitly and systematically in his next article *Jiànshè de wénxué gémìng lùn* 'Constructive views on literary revolution' in 1918, in which he summarized his views in the subtitle *guóyǔ de wénxué, wénxué de guóyǔ* 'literature in *guóyǔ*, and a literary *guóyǔ*'. He argued that *wényán*, as a dead language, could not serve as the medium of live literature, and live literature in China must be composed in the vernacular. Furthermore, he maintained that the language used in the best of the traditional and contemporary writings in *báihuà* provided the exemplary form of *guóyǔ*. His choice of the term *guóyǔ* in the title was intended to avoid the negative connotations of vulgarity and slanginess that *báihuà* still invoked for some people (S. Hu 1935). On the other hand, he elaborated on the importance of literary works in shaping and developing *guóyǔ*. Citing the examples of Dante, Chaucer, and Wycliff in Europe, he argued that standard Chinese can only come from great literature. The reason that there was no standard Chinese in China, in spite of the fact that quite a number of literary works in *báihuà* had appeared during the previous 1,000 years, he suggested, was that there was no one who proposed in explicit terms that the vernacular should be the base of literary language.

Hu's views were echoed by Chen Duxiu, who made even more vehement attacks on literature in *wényán* (D. Chen 1917). What had traditionally been acclaimed as classics in *wényán*, Chen argued, were nothing but flowery, extravagant, artificial, or obscure. They originated from, and at the same time contributed to, the character of the Chinese nation, which was portrayed by Chen as being servile, exaggerative, hypocritical, and pedantic. Based on these assumptions, it was claimed that political renovation should be preceded by the renovation of literature, which in turn must begin with language reform. While advocating the rejection of *wényán* as the language of literature, Hu and Chen simultaneously called for the establishment of *báihuà* as the standard written language. Their views won immediate support from other influential scholars like Fu Sinian, Liu Bannong, and Qian Xuantong, whose enthusiasm and active advocacy contributed greatly to widespread propagation of these views throughout society (cf. S. Fu 1917, 1918; B. Liu 1917; X. Qian 1918a).

In 1919, the May 4th Movement broke out in protest at the injustice inflicted on China by a few Western powers at the end of World War I. The movement imparted a sense of urgency to the need for radical domestic reforms. Against the background of the wide-spread mood for change and reform so characteristic of the China of that time, the proposal to replace *wényán* with *báihuà* achieved dramatic success within a couple of years, winning support from both the intellectual community and the government. It was decreed by the Ministry of Education of the central government in 1920 that *guóyǔ* was to be taught in Year 1 and Year 2 of primary school in lieu of *guówén*, and all the textbooks should be written in *báihuà* (see Chapter 2). A growing number of articles appeared in journals and newspapers that promoted the new status of *báihuà* as the standard for all purposes and occasions. Teaching aids and materials such as textbooks, dictionaries, grammars, and gramophones became available on the market. At least 400 newspapers and journals in *báihuà* emerged within a year.

A number of influential literary works in *báihuà* were published in the 1920s which further demonstrated that, contrary to the claims by conservatives that *báihuà* could not be the language of elegant literature, it was possible to use the new written language to compose elegant, reputable literature that rivalled and surpassed the classics in *wényán*. Among such works were Lu Xun's *The true story of Ah Q*, and Guo Moruo's first collection of poems in *báihuà*, both published in 1921. They quickly became models for a whole new generation of literati to enjoy and emulate. Thus, a movement which started with the suggestion that there should be a revolution in literature in terms of content and rhetorics in due course shifted to *wényán* as its main target of attack. Within less than a decade, *báihuà* superseded *wényán* as the basis of the standard written language.

Looking back at the articles published by Hu Shi, Chen Duxiu, and others in the late 1910s that played an instrumental role in this process, their shortcomings are not hard to find. The most serious of these seems to be the confusion of form and content. What was at issue in the beginning was the question of what should be the appropriate language of pure literature. Most of the arguments in favour of the abolition of *wényán* highlight the fact that literature in *wényán* was stilted, removed from actual life, unnatural, and fossilized. Such accusations were probably true of the majority of the then prevalent literature, but certainly not true of all literature in *wényán*. Upon closer analysis, it was the then conventionalized style of *wényán*, namely *bāgǔwén*, instead of *wényán* per se, that was really repulsive. *Wényán*, defined in terms of the grammatical and lexical norms of Old Chinese, can be used to write good literature as well as bad literature. The key to the advantage of *báihuà* over *wényán* is that the former is much easier to master than the latter, because it is much closer to speech.

Furthermore, around 1920 the term *báihuà* was used in an ill-defined way. According to S. Hu (1918), *báihuà* looks to novels like *Shuǐhǔ zhuàn*, *Xī yóu jì*, *Rúlín wàishǐ*, and *Hónglóu mèng* for its norms. The problem is that the language used in these novels is far from consistent in terms of grammar and vocabulary. They contain elements from Old Chinese and contemporary local dialects in proportions that vary considerably. As Hu Shi correctly maintained, the new standard of *báihuà* was to be gradually established on the basis of both the traditional works and the writings of his contemporaries. Other than general agreement that it should be closer to the vernacular than to *wényán*, there was not much consensus in literary circles on many aspects of the standardization of the new written language. This left the whole issue of a standard written language open to further debate in the 1920s and 1930s.

5.3.3   **To revive *wényán* or to improve on *báihuà*?**

The decade following the May 4th Movement was a transitional period in which *báihuà* gradually replaced *wényán* as the standard written language. Given the fact that *wényán* had for thousands of years been the sole written language for formal purposes, its replacement by *báihuà* could not take place overnight.

From the final years of the nineteenth century, new varieties of written language appeared as the traditional *wényán* and *báihuà* were being adapted to suit contemporary needs. The linguistic situation can be characterized as multi-glossic. As observed by Qu Qiubai (1931a), for decades there were roughly four major types of written Chinese concurrently in common use, each having its typical area of application, and each accepted by the general public as being the norm for its respective purpose:

1. traditional *wényán*

2. modern *wényán*

3. traditional *báihuà*

4. new-style *báihuà*

Traditional *wényán* continued to be the major written language used by those who were opposed to *báihuà*. It was also the norm in telegrams and writings for ritualistic purposes. While by and large following the norms of Old Chinese, what was called modern *wényán* incorporated a large amount of new vocabulary borrowed from Japanese or contemporary vernaculars. Its widespread popularity was largely due to Liang Qichao, a prolific political writer with enormous influence in the early years of the twentieth century, who favoured this particular style of written Chinese and adopted it in most of his writings. It was the conventional style used in most newspapers and periodicals, and for most legal and administrative purposes. Traditional *báihuà*, as discussed above, essentially refers to the language used in those vernacular literary works handed down from the late Tang dynasty, typically represented by several novels written in the Ming and the Qing dynasty. The new-style *báihuà*, also called May 4th style *báihuà*, which often carried a pejorative connotation, was a general name that referred to the various types of the new style that reformist writers were experimenting with at that time. It differs from traditional *báihuà* typically in that it borrows heavily from Western languages in terms of grammar. Although still mainly based upon Northern Mandarin, it was also characterized by a large amount of expressions from Old Chinese or literal translations from foreign languages. These two features in combination meant that it was still quite removed from the actual speech of any group of speakers. Qu Qiubai (1931:25) remarked that since this new-style *báihuà* could only be read and could not be spoken, it should be more aptly called 'new-style *wényán*'. The new-style *báihuà* was extensively used in literary works and for other practical applications by the advocates of language reform and their followers, who actually constituted the mainstream in the fields of literature, education, and other intellectual pursuits since the 1910s.

Following the decree by the Ministry of Education in 1920, all new textbooks in primary schools were compiled in *báihuà*, and *wényán* was explicitly banned from the early years of primary school. It was also stipulated that high school textbooks written in *wényán* must gradually be replaced by those written in *báihuà*, except for those of the Chinese language subjects, which still included some essays in *wényán*. At college level, however, students in Chinese language class exclusively studied *wényán*.

In comparison with the situation before 1920, students had far less exposure to *wényán*. On the other hand, *wényán* was still extensively used in all sectors of society. Although *báihuà* became the norm in literary compositions such as novels, poems, and plays from the early 1920s, *wényán* by and large remained the de facto standard written language in trade and business circles, as well as in government and legal institutions. As mentioned above, the typical style found in most newspapers was still a form of *wényán*, adhering to a tradition that began well before the New Culture Movement. Even in the college entrance examination in Chinese language subjects, the proficiency of students was assessed in terms of their competence in composition using *wényán* rather than *báihuà*. *Wényán* was also the standard language used in examinations for the civil service.

It was reported that the proficiency in Chinese writing of students trained in the new curriculum was far from satisfactory. Xu Maoyong (1934) reported on his findings as examiner of the compositions of more than thirty students of Year 3 in senior high school. Of the more than thirty essays written by students, he did not find a single one that was satisfactory with respect to grammar, in spite of the fact they were all fairly short articles, with the longest not exceeding 500 characters.

The fact that students fell short of the expected proficiency level in written Chinese was ascribable to several factors. A most important one was that *báihuà*, still in the process of development, was in many ways not well equipped to serve all the functions expected of a modern written language. The writers of the May 4th style *báihuà* were mostly well trained in *wényán*. When they started to write in *báihuà*, many simply replaced the function words in *wényán* with their equivalent expressions in the vernacular, while leaving the other parts largely unchanged. This resulted in an awkward mixture of styles. Others wrote in a heavily Europeanized style, producing texts that read like literal translations from a foreign language. One of the most serious problems of *báihuà* at that time was its paucity of vocabulary. While expressions conventionally used in *wényán* had been discouraged since the beginning of the language reform, it was far from clear to what extent words from various dialects should be incorporated in the new *báihuà*. This issue did not come to the fore until the 1920s. Before then, what was generally referred to as *báihuà* was only a written approximation of the lingua franca, serving only the most basic of written communicative needs among speakers of mutually unintelligible dialects. The need for higher expressivity was felt more acutely when *báihuà*, at least in theory, became the basis of a new written language that was required to fulfil all the functions of a standard written code in a modernizing society. For example, as observed by Xia Mianzun (1934), *fùqin* 'father' and *mǔqin* 'mother' were in common use in the new-style *báihuà*. In actual everyday life, however, a variety of other words were used, such as *bàba*, *diē*, *yé*, or *mā*, *māma*, *niáng*, etc. Curiously, only *fùqin* and *mǔqin* were favoured by writers of *báihuà*, and found their way into the school textbooks, in spite of the fact that they were seldom used in everyday speech. Falling short of the goals of its proponents, who envisaged a *báihuà* as plain as vernacular speech, the typical May 4th style *báihuà* was a highly artificial one that was detached from speech.

Given the gap between what was taught in schools and what was actually required of students after graduation with respect to skills in written Chinese, it was not surprising that Chinese language teaching, particularly the teaching of written language, became an issue of concern and debate in the late 1920s and early 1930s, with arguments for improvement taking two opposing directions.

One proposed solution to the problem was to revive *wényán*. Arguing against the directives from the Ministry of Education that *wényán* was to be gradually reduced in high school, it was proposed that more, instead of less, *wényán* should be taught in high school, and, furthermore, that it should be reintroduced into primary school (Ren 1934).

The advocates of the revival of *wényán* had in mind issues that went beyond improvement of the writing skills of school graduates. When *wényán* was denounced in the New Culture Movement, as discussed above, what was involved was not a simple matter of language reform. *Wényán* was denounced by Hu Shi and his associates less for its inconvenience in use than for its position as the medium of what they saw as a moribund literature representing traditional culture, which in turn was regarded as the major culprit responsible for the problems facing China in modern times. As the literature that *wényán* had been used to write was rejected as being inappropriate for a modernizing China, *wényán* as a medium was also discredited at the same time as being too closely related to the content to be redeemable. While *wényán* was taken to be synonymous with traditional Chinese values, after the May 4th movement *báihuà* was assumed to be the only appropriate linguistic vehicle for the whole set of new, mostly imported Western concepts subsumed under democracy and science. After more than a decade, it was felt by conservatives that the promotion of *báihuà* had not only proceeded at the cost of skills in written Chinese, but had also resulted in the attrition of traditional Chinese values and ethics as embodied in such pre-Qin classics as the *Analects, Mencius, Shī jīng*, etc., which, they believed, should constitute the basic training of every Chinese student. As a remedy, they proposed the strengthening of *wényán* teaching, which would on one hand enhance the written Chinese skills of school graduates, and on the other ensure more exposure to traditional Chinese values and ethics through a greater use of Chinese classics in *wényán* as teaching materials (M. Wang 1934; Yu 1934).

In the intellectual climate of the 1920s and 1930s, where there was an overwhelming sense of the need for drastic changes to all aspects of traditional Chinese society, such proposals found little sympathy among the liberal intellectual mainstream, which was still under the sway of the anti-traditionalist sentiments initiated in the New Culture Movement. Efforts to reverse the replacement of *wényán* by *báihuà* were viewed as reactionary, and rejected out of hand. Such proposals found little favour among school teachers, editors, and publishers either, who generally gave warm support to the new written language out of such practical considerations as ease of acquisition and increase in readership.

The majority of those concerned with the development of modern written Chinese opted for improvement of the May 4th *báihuà*, instead of retreating to a re-implementation of *wényán* as the standard written Chinese. Initially, Hu Shi suggested that the new literary language should be modelled after the traditional *báihuà*. Later it was suggested by scholars like Fu Sinian and Qian Xuantong that the new *báihuà* should be based upon the living vernacular, and at the same time incorporate grammatical constructions from European languages in order to accommodate the need to convey complicated thoughts (S. Fu 1918; X. Qian 1918b). Not satisfied with the results of more than a decade of evolution, a group of language reformers in the 1930s, with Qu Qiubai and Chen Wangdao as their more articulate spokespersons, suggested that the excessive number of elements from foreign languages and Old Chinese in the new-style *báihuà* disqualified it as a candidate for the new standard written language that was conceived at the beginning of the movement. It was suggested that the new-style *báihuà* should be replaced by what they called *dàzhòngyǔ* 'language of the masses', a language that was actually spoken by ordinary people and understood by them. The promotion of such a *dàzhòngyǔ* represented the most serious efforts so far to push the written language as close as possible to the vernacular of the general public (W. D. Chen 1934; Z. Z. Chen 1934; Q. Hu 1990).

Two issues stood out in the advocacy of *dàzhòngyǔ*. One related to the dialect base of the written standard, and the other to the relationship between the written language and the writing system. While some proposed that the written language should be mainly based upon Northern Mandarin, others argued that speakers of various dialects, especially those of the Southern dialects, were entitled to a written standard based on their own dialect. According to the latter view, as there was at that time no generally accepted spoken standard, *dàzhòngyǔ* in the true sense of the word was possible only if there were various varieties of written language based upon the major dialects. On the basis of these varieties of *dàzhòngyǔ* a single standard written language accepted by speakers of all dialects might ultimately emerge. Although only espoused by a few participants in the debate, this view was enthusiastically echoed half of a century later in Taiwan by advocates of a standard written language based on the predominant local dialect. For details, see Chapter 7.

It was also argued that the establishment of a true vernacular-based written language must be accompanied by reform of the writing system. In such a view, the new-style *báihuà* is a half-baked version of the ideal written language, as it still retains a large portion of expressions not found in actual speech. This situation, it was argued, is inevitable due to the conservative nature of the traditional writing system. The logographic script suits *wényán*, not *báihuà*. When distinctions not apparent in speech can be clearly indicated by the graphic shapes of characters, people are less motivated to abandon expressions from *wényán*. As long as this writing system is retained, it is impossible to expect the written language to be truly as plain as speech. Furthermore, there are quite a few expressions in dialects that do not have conventional representation in characters. As a result, it would be unrealistic to expect people to write as easily as they speak. The best approach to achieve the unification of speech and writing, it was argued, was through adopting a phonographic writing system. As the promotion of *dàzhòngyǔ* was almost contemporaneous with the promotion of a phonographic writing system called *latinxua sin wenz* 'latinized new script', the relationship between the reform of the written language and the writing system received more attention than ever before (see Chapter 9 for a detailed description of *latinxua sin wenz*).

The views in favour of a multi-standard *dàzhòngyǔ*, preferably coded by a phonographic writing system, were not shared by all language reformers. In the course of the debate, the majority of participants agreed that the real difference between the new-style *báihuà* and the proposed *dàzhòngyǔ* was that the latter was closer to the living speech of the masses (Ni 1949). The development of modern *báihuà*, namely Modern Written Chinese, continued from the 1920s. While based upon Northern Mandarin, modern *báihuà* has been undergoing steady enrichment in its linguistic repertoire, incorporating whatever useful elements it finds necessary from Old Chinese, non-Northern Mandarin dialects, and foreign languages. With respect to the norms in grammar and vocabulary, the *báihuà* used in the early 1920s is remarkably different from the present-day Modern Written Chinese.

5.4   Sources of and avenues of influence upon Modern Written Chinese

5.4.1   Dialects other than Jiang-Huai and Northern Mandarin

As remarked above, traditional *báihuà* before modern times is by and large based upon Jiang-Huai Mandarin, and particularly since the late Qing dynasty, upon Northern Mandarin. This is true not only of writers from the Jiang-Huai and Northern Mandarin areas, but also of writers from the other dialect areas. On the other hand, features peculiar to their own dialects are also found in the writings of those from other dialect backgrounds, which is only to be expected of writers that presumably adopted a variety of language that was closer to their speech than *wényán*. Dialectal features in grammar and vocabulary are taken to be important evidence in establishing the identity of the authors of some *báihuà* writings.[1]

It was pointed out earlier that the major goal for the written language reform in the 1910s was to eliminate, or at least reduce, the gap between speech and writing. The proposal to write what one says, if put into practice in a literal sense, could have given rise to serious problems in a situation where the spoken standard was far from being extensively mastered. Written texts exclusively based on Southern dialects are hardly intelligible to readers unfamiliar with the dialects.[2]

Many factors prevented Modern Written Chinese from diversifying into several distinct codes, each based upon a Chinese dialect. The most important is the strong influence of the exemplary literary works in traditional *báihuà* mentioned earlier, the popularity of which had ensured the continued familiarity of literates. Speakers of dialects other than Jiang-Huai or Northern Mandarin had to conform to the grammatical and vocabulary norms of the traditional *báihuà* as much as possible if they intended their writings to reach a readership across dialectal barriers. For them, the norms they followed in writing were acquired not via speech, but from exemplary writings based upon a dialect they had not yet learned how to speak.

On the other hand, no matter how strong the normative force of these exemplary works, it was very difficult for writers to eradicate the influence of their own dialect from their writing. While this situation held for writers in *báihuà* from previous centuries, it was especially so in a period when it was felt that the all-purpose functions demanded of *báihuà* left it in need of improvement. As the concept of the standardization of Modern Written Chinese was not raised until later, the writers of other dialect backgrounds in the early days of the New Culture Movement, as well as in the 1920s and 1930s, were actually quite free in their choice of grammatical and lexical devices, constrained only by the concern that their work should remain intelligible to a wide range of readership. A substantial proportion of the most influential writers in the 1920s and 1930s were native speakers of the Wu dialect, such as Lu Xun, Zhou Zuoren, Yu Dafu, Xu Zhimo, Mao Dun, and Ye Shengtao, to name but a few.[3] All of their writings displayed features characteristic of the grammar and vocabulary of their native tongue. Owing to the popularity of these writers, many of these features subsequently became part of the established norms of Modern Written Chinese.

While basically following the norms formed in mainland China from the 1910s up to the late 1940s, Modern Written Chinese in Taiwan, Hong Kong, and Singapore has also been under the influence of the local dialects, mainly Southern Min in Taiwan and Singapore and Cantonese in Hong Kong. As a result, the grammatical and lexical norms of Modern Written Chinese differ somewhat among the four major Chinese communities. We will return to this point in Chapter 6.

5.4.2   Old Chinese

Old Chinese constitutes another major source of influence upon the formation of the norms of Modern Written Chinese. The situation with Chinese in this century is usually assumed to be similar to what happened to the Western European languages more than four centuries ago, in that the range of functions of a written vernacular was extended to include that of the high culture, which until then had been served by another literary written language, namely Latin in Western Europe, and *wényán* in China. However, Chinese differs remarkably from the

European languages in that, whereas Latin virtually became a dead language after its replacement by the Modern European languages, *wényán* continues to exist in Modern Written Chinese to an extent unparalleled in European languages.

As explained earlier, *wényán* is based upon Old Chinese, while *báihuà* is close to contemporary Northern Mandarin. So far as the relationship between Old Chinese and contemporary Northern Mandarin in Modern Written Chinese is concerned, it is better to view them as two poles along the parameter of formality in styles, with the former suitable for extremely formal and frozen texts and the latter for casual, informal occasions. Between them may be many intermediate positions that combine features from Old Chinese and the contemporary vernacular in various proportions. Although most writings taken to be models of Modern Written Chinese are closer to the vernacular end, there are quite a few which are closer to the other end. The syntactic, morphological, and lexical features of Old Chinese are extensively preserved in words, phrases, sentence patterns, and the numerous so-called *sì zì chéngyǔ* 'four-character set expressions' that are in active use in Modern Written Chinese. This situation is to be ascribed to merits of Old Chinese that are unmatched by the vernacular-based traditional *báihuà*. First, owing to its continuous use for more than two millennia, *wényán* had accumulated a richer repertoire of morphemes, words, and expressions than was available in *báihuà* at the beginning of this century. As a result, writers of Modern Written Chinese regularly turn to Old Chinese as a fountain-head of linguistic resources. Second, *wényán* is superior to *báihuà* in terms of compactness and terseness, capable of conveying more information than the latter in the same space of text, often resulting in a highly refined style. Finally, *wényán*'s remoteness from actual speech, and its function as the medium used in Chinese classics, help to impart a tone of formality, derivatively an aura of authority, to present-day readers. By virtue of these merits, features of Old Chinese constitute an essential part of the norms of Modern Written Chinese, characteristic of the styles that indicate qualities like succinctness, refinement, and formality. As a matter of fact, *wényán* writings still make up from one third to half of the content in the textbooks of the Chinese language subject in high schools in mainland China, Taiwan, Hong Kong, and Singapore. A good knowledge of Old Chinese is considered to be vital for mastering the whole range of styles in Modern Written Chinese.

In spite of the passionate calls to eradicate all traces of Old Chinese from the new vernacular-based Modern Written Chinese since the 1910s, *wényán* seems to die hard. Aside from the above-mentioned merits that make *wényán* functionally useful, it is the continued use of the logographic script that makes it at all possible for words and expressions from Old Chinese to be extensively employed in Modern Written Chinese. As noted above, Old Chinese is basically a monosyllabic language, with one word represented by one syllable in the form of one character in the overwhelming majority of cases. The inventory of syllables was drastically reduced as Old Chinese evolved into Modern Chinese.[4] With syllables becoming less and less differentiated, many monosyllabic words which were pronounced differently in Old Chinese later became homonymous in speech. As a compensating mechanism for this phonetic attrition, a large number of words underwent a process of di- or multi-syllabification, substantially reducing the number of homonyms that could lead to ambiguity in speech.[5] On the other hand, although the presence of a large number of homonymous words makes it rather difficult to understand *wényán* in speech, those homonyms are much easier to process in the written language because they are represented by characters with differentiating graphic shapes.[6] This is the fundamental reason why words and expressions of Old Chinese occur much more frequently in Modern Written Chinese than in Modern Spoken Chinese. If Chinese characters are abolished in favour of a romanized script, as has been advocated for more than a century, it would be extremely difficult, if not impossible, to resort to the features of Old Chinese as freely and extensively as is presently attested in Modern Written Chinese.

5.4.3   Foreign languages

Foreign languages are the most important source of influence upon the evolution of the norms of Modern Written Chinese. To meet the demand for new terms in the fast-growing fields of humanities, social sciences, and modern science and technology, Chinese has absorbed a large number of loans mainly from European languages and Japanese. The process of large-scale lexical expansion started in the middle of the nineteenth century, and accelerated towards the turn of this century. First used in *wényán*, the loan words continued their use in *báihuà* after it replaced *wényán* as the base of Modern Written Chinese. It is estimated that in comparison with the situation before 1840, more than half of the expressions in common use in present-day Modern Written Chinese are loans from foreign languages (L. Wang 1979).

Aside from being sources of new terms, foreign languages, especially European languages like English, French, and Russian, have also constituted the most important influence upon the evolution of the grammatical norms of Modern Written Chinese since the 1910s. The most remarkable difference between the present-day Modern Written Chinese and the traditional *báihuà* lies in grammatical norms, which are much more Europeanized today than eighty years ago. Discussing the Europeanization of Modern Written Chinese, Wang Li (1954) observed that, as a result of the notable development of Chinese in its overall grammatical structure, well-written articles in present-day newspapers and magazines can be translated into Russian or English almost in a word-for-word manner without substantial alteration of the structure. This tendency towards the Europeanization of Modern Written Chinese has been growing ever since the 1950s, with no sign of decline.

Three major factors have underlain the rapid Europeanization of the grammatical norms of Modern Written Chinese. First, the expressiveness of traditional *báihuà* left much to be desired, especially where accuracy or explicitness as required in scholarly and scientific writings was concerned. Second, the great majority of the intellectual elite that led the New Culture Movement held traditional Chinese culture in all its major aspects in abhorrence. This included the character script and, consequently, the Chinese language. The extreme radicals among them advocated that the Chinese language should be replaced in toto by another language, such as Esperanto or English, in order to modernize the whole nation (X. Qian 1918b; S. Fu 1919). Failing that, they argued, Modern Written Chinese should at least be Europeanized as much as possible.[7] In translating from European languages into Chinese, they proposed as a matter of principle that the structure of the original text should be followed as closely as possible. Third, a large number of translated works that were, and have been, on the market were done by people who were, strictly speaking, unqualified for the task. It is certainly easier for them to follow the grammar of the source language dogmatically, resulting in a highly Europeanized Chinese rendition, than to bring the product more in line with the idiomatic usage of Modern Chinese. These sloppy translators and adherents of the direct-translation school have combined to create what has been referred as translationese, a highly Europeanized Chinese style.

Given the thirst for Western ideas that has permeated intellectual circles, and through them the whole of Chinese society during the past 150 years, the influence of such translationese upon the shaping of the norms of Modern Written Chinese cannot be underestimated. As a matter of fact, the great majority of the leading scholars in all disciplines in China since the turn of this century have at some time engaged in translation from Western languages or Japanese as part of their academic activities. It is almost impossible for an educated Chinese to avoid translated works in his or her daily intellectual life.

There were two periods when translated works constituted an especially important part of the daily reading of educated Chinese. The first period was in the 1920s and 1930s, when translated works provided the main source of information for scholars more interested in fresh Western ideas than in traditional Chinese scholarship. The second period started during the 1950s, when the teachings of Marx and Lenin were revered as the guiding ideology in mainland China. It was advocated, and sometimes stipulated by the government, that political writings by the ideologues, often in very poor translationese, were to be read by every literate Chinese. For decades it was the vogue in mainland China for political leaders and mass media writers to cite these coarsely translated political writings in their directives, articles, and books, which were in turn studied and quoted by the masses. The language used in these writings, which typically is highly Europeanized in grammar and vocabulary, has played a modelling role that is imitated by writers of Modern Written Chinese.

5.5   Uses of *wényán* and *báihuà* since the 1940s

Following the definition of *pǔtōnghuà* in 1956, there is now more consensus than in the first half of the century concerning what constitutes the standard of Modern Written Chinese. It is generally agreed in theory that, as the written counterpart of *pǔtōnghuà*, Modern Written Chinese should be a literary language based upon contemporary Northern Mandarin, while at the same time absorbing elements from Old Chinese, other Chinese dialects, and foreign languages. It must be noted, however, that Modern Written Chinese in actual use is far more heterogeneous than many language reformers have hoped for, as will be discussed in detail in Chapter 6.

The use of *wényán* was greatly reduced on the mainland after 1949. Luo Changpei and Lü Shuxiang (1956) maintained that it was only after 1949 that *báihuà* won a comprehensive battle over *wényán* as the standard form of Modern Written Chinese. A campaign was launched on the mainland in the 1950s to reform the language used for business purposes, which aimed to establish *báihuà* firmly as the norm of written Chinese in the domains where *wényán* had maintained a stubborn presence. These efforts proved to be largely successful. Although *wényán* expressions still abound in modern writings, texts have rarely been written completely in *wényán* in mainland China since the 1950s. Only occasionally do we read books written by contemporaries that are composed exclusively in traditional *wényán*.[8]

Wényán maintains a more persistent presence in the other Chinese communities. Written Chinese for legal, business, and administrative purposes in Hong Kong typically features a mixture of *wényán* and *báihuà*, with features of the former outweighing the latter in the majority of cases. Practically the same situation is found in Taiwan, where most legal and business documents display a mixture of *wényán* and *báihuà*, very much in the tradition of the mainland of the 1920s–1940s. Also noteworthy is the fact that in Taiwan some important official and administrative documents, particularly those of a ritualistic nature like credentials of appointment, and laudatory discourse on special occasions are still composed in *wényán*. Although there is a lack of statistics on the relative frequency of expressions characteristic of Old Chinese in the Modern Written Chinese used in mainland China, Taiwan, and Hong Kong, the general impression is that the proportion is higher in Taiwan and Hong Kong than on the mainland.

5.6   Establishment of Modern Written Chinese and status planning

Two major types of language planning are recognized in the literature, status planning and corpus planning. The former refers to the allocation of languages or language varieties to given functions, whereas the latter refers to activities that aim at developing a single language or variety of a language with respect to its phonology, grammar, lexicon, writing system, etc. (Christian 1988; Cooper 1989).

The replacement of *wényán* by *báihuà* as the base of Modern Written Chinese since the 1910s is a typical case of status planning, whereby a vernacular-based written variety of Chinese was promoted as a substitution for the established standard for all literary and scholarly purposes. As we have seen, it has achieved remarkable success, but in a way notably different from the case of Latin, in so far as the motivation of the activity and the status of the replaced language are concerned.

The replacement of Latin by vernacular languages in Western Europe was a direct reflection of the raising of national consciousness, whereas in China, the replacement of *wényán* was first and foremost prompted by the desire to reduce widespread illiteracy as an integral part of the drive to modernize the nation. China at the turn of the century was characterized by surging nationalism just as Western Europe was around three hundred years earlier. However, instead of being looked upon as a sacred symbol of nationalism or statehood, the Chinese language as a whole was treated more as a culprit that should be held responsible for the misery of the nation. *Báihuà* finally won over *wényán* as the basis of Modern Written Chinese, not because it was a better symbol of the nationalism or statehood, but mainly because it was easier to learn and to use.

Furthermore, when Latin gave way to the modern European languages, it essentially became a dead language. By contrast, in China, instead of being relegated to disuse after it gave way to *báihuà*, *wényán* still plays an important role in Modern Written Chinese, providing for special stylistic effects that otherwise could not be obtained. According to the formal definition, Modern Written Chinese should look to *báihuà* as the model for its lexical and grammatical norms. Just as Cooper (1989:134–5) observes, however, people are more likely to agree that an all-purpose model exists than to use it for all the purposes for which they feel it appropriate, if in fact they use it at all. One of the reasons for this, following on from Cooper (1989), is that we have to move from style to style or from variety to variety to suit our communicative context – casual or formal, sacred or secular, and so forth – as well as to suit our communicative content. In Cooper's words, 'because the style or variety we employ is itself part of the meaning we convey, we cannot restrict ourselves to a single style without restricting our ability to implement our communicating content'. As a style indicative of formality, terseness, and refinement, *wényán* is still alive and well in Modern Written Chinese. To the extent that *wényán* represents a tradition that was held in veneration for more than two millennia, the present status of *wényán* indicates how strong the bond of traditionalism is in the Chinese community.

6.1   Newly developed grammatical norms in Modern Written Chinese

6.1.1   Features of non-Northern Mandarin dialects in Modern Written Chinese

Some of the new grammatical norms in Modern Written Chinese originated in dialects other than Northern Mandarin. As a large proportion of such features are characteristic of several non-Northern Mandarin dialects, it is often impossible to pin down their origin in terms of a particular dialect. Following are some of the most conspicuous examples.

Patterns (1) and (2) are both used for yes–no questions, as in (3) and (4):

(1)   *yŏu méiyŏu* + VP

(2)   VP + *méiyŏu*

(3) a.   nĭmén *yŏu méiyŏu* kànjiàn tā chūqu?
you   have not:have see   he out
'Did you see him go out?'

   b.   nĭmén kànjiàn tā chūqu *méiyŏu*?
you   see   he out   not:have
'Did you see him go out?'

(4) a.   tā hòulai *yŏu méiyŏu* huílai?
he later   have not:have return
'Did he come back later?'

   b.   tā hòulai huílai le   *méiyŏu*?
he later   return PFV not:have
'Did he come back later?'

Pattern (1) was originally confined to dialects in the Southern areas, mainly Wu, Min, and Cantonese, and was not found in Northern Mandarin, which normally uses Pattern (2). In Modern Written Chinese, however, (1) has been extensively used as a freely interchangeable alternative to (2).[1]

Pattern (6) represents a usage in traditional *báihuà*, where the normal position for the place of destination in relation to verbs of movement is in a prepositional phrase that precedes the verb, as in (7)b and (8)b below.

The Southern dialects normally use Pattern (5), where the place of destination follows the verb, as in (7)a and (8)a. In Modern Written Chinese, both patterns are equally acceptable.

(5)   *lái/qù* 'come/go' + place of destination

(6)   *dào/shàng* 'to' + place of destination + *lái/qù*

(7)a.   nǐ   zuótiān   *lái*   *zhèr* le   ma?
        you yesterday come here PFV Q
        'Did you come here yesterday?'

   b.   nǐ   zuótiān   *dào/shàng zhèr lái*   le   ma?
        you yesterday to   here come PFV Q
        'Did you come here yesterday?'

(8)a.   tā *qù yóujú*   jì   yì   fēng xìn.
        he go post:office mail one CL   letter
        'He went to the post office to mail a letter'

   b.   tā *dào/shàng yóujú*   *qù* jì   yì   fēng xìn.
        he to   post:office go mail one CL   letter
        'He went to the post office to mail a letter'

Another feature involves extension of the verbal measure word *yíxià* 'a bit'. In traditional *báihuà* this word was used only with a small number of verbs, usually those related to the meaning of hitting. Now, following the usage of the Southern dialects, the use of *yíxià* has been extended to other verbs in Modern Written Chinese such as *kàn* 'look', *shì* 'try', etc. as in (9)a and (10)a. More specialized measure words, *yì yǎn* 'one eye' for *kàn*, and *yí shì* 'one try' for *shì*, would be required in Northern Mandarin, as in (9)b and (10)b (J. Chen 1989:148):

(9)a.   Ràng wǒ lái   *kàn yíxià*
        let   me come look a:bit
        'Let me have a look'

   b.   Ràng wǒ lái   *kàn yì   yǎn*
        let   me come see one eye
        'Let me have a look'

(10)a.   Qǐng nǐ *shì yíxià*
　　　　 please you try a:bit
　　　　 'Please have a try'

　　 b.   Qǐng nǐ *shì yí shì*
　　　　 please you try one try
　　　　 'Please have a try'

As has been widely reported in the literature (E. Chen 1989), some of the features originating in Southern dialects, like those discussed earlier, have found their way not only into Modern Written Chinese, but also increasingly into the speech of native speakers of Northern Mandarin. These speakers use them just as naturally as the indigenous forms, without being aware that such expressions would have grated on the ears of their grandparents back in the 1910s. This situation can undoubtedly be attributed to the extensive presence of such features in Modern Written Chinese, which exerts a strong influence upon the speech of its readership, whatever their dialectal background may be.

6.1.2   **Europeanization of grammar of Modern Written Chinese**

Some of the newly emerged grammatical norms in Modern Written Chinese are clearly outcomes of the Europeanization process that has been in progress since the 1910s. Following are a few remarkable examples.

　　One of these is the extension of use of *bèi* as a passive marker. In traditional *báihuà*, this marker was almost always used for undesirable events, as in (11) and (12).[2]

(11)   Lao Wang zuótiān   *bèi* lǎobǎn xùn le   yí   dùn.
　　　 LW   yesterday BEI boss   scold PFV one CL
　　　 'LW was scolded by the boss yesterday'

(12)   Xiao Li lǎoshì bù jiāo   fángzū, jiēguǒ *bèi* fángdōng gǎn   le   chūlai.
　　　 XL   always not submit rent   finally BEI landlord throw PFV out
　　　 'XL never paid rent, and in the end was thrown out by the landlord'

Since the 1910s, however, its usage has been extended beyond undesirable to neutral or desirable situations, more or less like a pure grammatical marker for passive voice, as exemplified in (13) and (14).

(13) wǒ chángcháng *bèi* pài   dào nèi ge dìqū   qù jiǎnchá gōngzuò
      I   often   BEI assign to that CL district go inspect work
      'I am often assigned to that district for work inspection'

(14) tā *bèi* dàjiā guāngróngde xuǎn wéi dàibiǎo
      he BEI all   honourably   elect as representative
      'As an honour, he was elected by all as the representative'

Such extension of the use of *bèi* was first considered a distinctive feature of translationese, with its origins in the imitation of passive markers in European languages. Gradually, it made its way into the norms of Modern Written Chinese, and is now extensively used by writers.

Another feature involves lengthy and complicated modifiers. Traditional *báihuà* tends to have short sentences, because of its stylistic resemblance to actual speech; this also reflects the intrinsic constraints on lengthy constructions that were characteristic of Chinese at the various phases of its development prior to its close contact with European languages. In present-day written Chinese, however, lengthy sentences are very common, especially in texts of the expository or argumentative genres; most examples involve long and complex pronominal modifiers that are connected to the head noun by the function word *de*. As reported in J. Chen (1989:145), in a 4,500-character-long article by Mao Zedong, whose writings are taken as exemplars of Modern Written Chinese in mainland China, *de* occurs 123 times, introducing various kinds of pronominal modifiers that result in lengthy and convoluted constructions. In contrast, a 5,520-character-long speech by a labourer contains only 43 tokens of *de*. This marked discrepancy between the written and spoken modes shows the influence that foreign languages, via translationese, have exerted on Modern Written Chinese. One characteristic is that all modifiers of nouns are located in front of the modified noun and strung together with the aid of *de*. The following example is from Mao (1969:1151):

(15) Xīnmínzhǔzhǔyì guójiā shǒulǐ yǒu-zhe   cóng guānliáo   zīchǎnjiējí
      new-democratic state   hand:in have:DUR from bureaucrat capitalist:class

      jiēshōu guòlái de kòngzhì quān guó   jīngjì   mìngmài de jùdà de
      take   over   DE control whole country economy lifeline DE huge DE

guójiā qǐyè,   yòu yǒu cóng fēngjiàn zhìdù jiěfàng chūlái, suīzé
state   enterprise also have from feudalist system liberate out   although

zài yí   ge pō   cháng shíjiān nèi   zài jīběnshàng réngrán shì fēnsàn de
in one CL quite long   time   within in basically   still   be scatter DE

gètǐ   de, dànshì zài jiānglái kěyǐ zhúbùde yǐn xiàng   hézuòshè
individual DE but   in future   can gradually lead towards co-operative

fāngxiàng fāzhǎn de nóngyè   jīngjì
direction develop DE agriculture economy

'The new democratic state will possess huge state enterprises taken over
from the bureaucrat-capitalist class and controlling the economic lifelines
of the country, and there will be an agricultural economy liberated from
feudalism which, though it will remain basically scattered and individual
for a fairly long time, can later be led to develop, step by step, in the
direction of co-operatives.'

The two object NPs, *guójiā qǐyè* 'state enterprises' and *nóngyè jīngjì*
'agricultural economy', each have lengthy and complex modifiers in front
of them, bound to the head by *de*. For all their seeming clumsiness,
constructions of this type, while never found in traditional *báihuà* or the
contemporary vernacular, abound in Modern Written Chinese – especially
in scientific, political, and journalistic writings. The extensive acceptance
of such constructions in Modern Written Chinese is facilitated by the
functional contribution they have made to the expressive power of the
language. In traditional *báihuà*, attributes to nominals usually follow
the head noun, unless they are quite short, as in (16).

(16)   tá mǎi le   yí   liàng hóngsè de pǎochē,   1991 nián chūchǎng   de
       he buy PFV one CL   red   DE sports:car 1991 year out-of-factory DE
       'he bought a red sports car, which was made in 1991'

Lengthy pronominal modifiers, although grammatical, were actually
very seldom used. The functional deficiency involved here is that post-
nominal modifiers, like *1991 nián chūchǎng de*, are normally subject to
the non-restrictive interpretation only. In translating restrictive relative
clauses of European languages into Chinese, there was often little choice
but to put the modifiers in front of the head noun so as to distinguish

them from those of the non-restrictive interpretation. Since restrictive clauses in European languages can be lengthy and complicated, so are the corresponding pronominal constituents in Chinese translation. Such usage has spread very rapidly since the 1920s. Now, in contrast to the short, mostly post-nominal modifiers typically used in traditional *báihuà* and the present-day vernacular, constructions involving long and complicated pronominal modifiers have become the norm in Modern Written Chinese for sentences that have modifiers in restrictive use. This is a welcome development: the pattern certainly enhances the explicitness and precision of the text, making Modern Written Chinese a more effective tool for a modern society.

Finally, we find proliferation of affix-like morphemes. Since the 1910s, there has emerged in Modern Written Chinese a group of morphemes that serve functions like those of the prefixes and suffixes of European languages, e.g. English non-, -ness, -tion, -cal, -ize. Imitating the use of such European affixes, the Modern Written Chinese morphemes are attached to other words, modifying their meanings and changing their parts of speech. Among the most commonly used are *fēi-* 'non-', *-xìng* '-ness', '-tion', *-huà* '-ize':

(17)   *fēi* 'non' + *huìyuán* 'member' > *fēi-huìyuán* 'non-member'
(18)   *tán* 'rebound' + *xìng* '-ness, -tion' > *tán-xìng* 'elasticity'
(19)   *fùzá* 'complex' + *xìng* > *fùzá-xìng* 'complexity'
(20)   *xiàndài* 'modern' + *huà* '-ize' > *xiàndài-huà* 'modernize'
(21)   *jīxiè* 'machine' + *huà* > *jīxiè-huà* 'mechanize'

Morphemes used in this way are still increasing in number, and tend to match all the important affixes in European languages, particularly English. The emergence and proliferation of these affix-like morphemes in Chinese, especially in Modern Written Chinese, is another important feature that has developed since the 1910s under the influence of European languages.

It is worth noting that almost all of the Europeanized grammatical innovations in Chinese, as exemplified above, have evolved within the structural constraints of Chinese grammar. They either involved the extension of the usage of words and expressions existent in traditional *báihuà*, assigning them the same range of functions as that of the corresponding elements in European languages which they were used to translate for, as in the case with *bèi* and those affix-like morphemes. Or they represented the full development of the potential that is allowed by Chinese grammar, but had previously been left largely unutilized, as in the case of the multiple embedding of pre-nominal modifiers by means of *de*. From this perspective, Europeanization of Chinese grammar in modern times involved innovative employment of indigenous resources after the pattern of European languages (cf. Gunn 1991; Peyraube 1995).

6.2   Regional variations in the grammatical norms of Modern Written Chinese

What were discussed earlier as newly emerged norms in Modern Written Chinese are established not only in mainland China, but also in the other three principal Chinese communities: Taiwan, Hong Kong, and Singapore. As speakers in these areas usually turn to mainland China for the standard of *pǔtōnghuà* (or *guóyǔ*, *huáyǔ*), especially in terms of pronunciation and grammar, their Modern Written Chinese has inherited almost all the grammatical features that developed in mainland China since the 1910s. At the same time, however, each place has also developed its own norms.

6.2.1   Taiwan

As the majority of the population are bilingual speakers of *guóyǔ* and Southern Min, it is inevitable that some Southern Min features have entered Modern Written Chinese grammar and vocabulary, constituting a subset of norms that is not attested in the Modern Written Chinese of mainland China. With regard to deviation from the grammatical norms in mainland China, the most noteworthy is the use of *yǒu* and *méiyǒu*.

Yǒu and *méiyǒu* function as verbs in Modern Chinese. In addition, *méiyǒu* is used as the negative counterpart of the perfective aspect marker *le*, indicating the non-completion of an action. However, the two verbs fulfil more functions in the Modern Written Chinese of Taiwan than in that of mainland China: both can also be used as markers to indicate the occurrence or non-occurrence of an action, or to indicate the existence or nonexistence of a situation, as exemplified in (22):

(22) Q: nǐ *yǒu méiyǒu* qù kàn tā?
           you have not:have go see he
           'Did you go to see him?'

     A: wǒ *yǒu* qù kàn tā
           I   have go see he
           'I went to see him'

Yǒu in the answer is used as the affirmative counterpart of *méiyǒu*, indicating the occurrence of the action. This usage is very common in the Modern Written Chinese in Taiwan, but is not allowed in that of mainland China, where *le* is normally used for such purposes, as in (23):

(23)   wǒ qù kàn *le*   tā.
        I   go see PFV he
        'I went to see him'

Consider also (24)–(26):

(24)   wǒ zǎoshàng *yǒu* zài jiālǐ.
        I   morning have at home
        'I WAS at home in the morning'

(25)   Lao Luo niánjì *yǒu* dà yìdiǎn, dànshì yě bú tài lǎo[3]
        LL   age   have old a:bit but   yet not too aged
        'LL IS a little old, but not too old yet'

(26)   wǒmén xiànzài dōu shì xuéshēng, *méiyǒu* zhuànqián
        we   now   all be student   have:not earn:money
        'At present we are all students, and don't have any income'

Here *yǒu* and *méiyǒu* are used to stress the existence or nonexistence of a situation. Such use is not accepted in the Modern Written Chinese of mainland China. This is a typical example of the influence of Southern Min on Modern Written Chinese in Taiwan. According to Cheng (1985, 1989), two words *ū* and *bô* in Southern Min are used for the functions served by *yǒu* and *méiyǒu* in (22) and (24)–(26). When native speakers of Southern Min speak or write in *guóyǔ*, they tend to express the cognitive semantic content that is actually constructed in the mind in terms of their native dialect. As *ū* and *bô* are distinctively non-Mandarin, *yǒu* and *méiyǒu* have been chosen as the formal substitutes.

6.2.2   **Hong Kong**

The written Chinese of Hong Kong is supposedly based on Northern Mandarin, in conformity with the standard in mainland China. Given the role of Cantonese as the lingua franca among the local Chinese, and also given the fact that English has long been the language for high-level administrative, commercial, legal, and educational purposes, Modern Written Chinese norms in Hong Kong inevitably deviate somewhat from those in mainland China. Although the most remarkable differences lie in the vocabulary, there are also some variations in grammatical norms. Compare the word order of the verb and the adverb *duō* 'more' in (27):

(27) a.   tā huì zài zhèr zhù *duō* jǐ   tiān.
          he will in here live more several day
          'He will live here for a few more days'

      b.   tā hùi zài zhèr *duō* zhù jǐ   tiān.
          he will in here more live several day
          'He will live here for a few more days'

The adverb precedes the verb in North Mandarin, but follows it in Cantonese. Under the influence of Cantonese, both word orders are frequently attested in the Modern Written Chinese of Hong Kong.

6.2.3   **Singapore**

As in Taiwan, Modern Written Chinese of Singapore inevitably comes under the influence of the locally dominant Southern Min dialect. As observed in several research reports (C. Chen 1986; Lock 1989; Y. C. Wu 1990; X. Zhou 1989), almost all of those grammatical features that are generally accepted as the norm in the Modern Written Chinese of Taiwan, but not in that of mainland China, are also extensively used in Singapore.

6.3   **Newly developed lexical norms in Modern Written Chinese**

Along with grammar, the vocabulary of Modern Written Chinese has also undergone a process of elaboration since the 1910s. New words and expressions have entered Modern Written Chinese from three major

sources, namely, Old Chinese, non-Northern Mandarin dialects, and foreign languages. We are concerned here with the last two.

6.3.1 Borrowings from non-Northern Mandarin dialects

While based upon Northern Mandarin for its core vocabulary, Modern
Written Chinese has borrowed many words from other dialects. Such borrowings either fill lexical gaps, expressing notions that had no names in
Northern Mandarin that could be appropriately used in Modern Written
Chinese, or they provide the users of Modern Written Chinese with alternative expressions that encode more or less the same kind of semantic
notions, but differ as regards stylistic nuances. For instance, the word for
'rubbish' in Northern Mandarin, as represented by the Beijing dialect, is
zāng-tǔ 'dirty soil'. If the word were used in Modern Written Chinese,
readers who do not speak Northern Mandarin would probably interpret it
in terms of the literal meaning of the component characters, which is
quite different from the specialized meaning of the expression in the
spoken vernacular. The Wu dialect word *lājī* nicely fills the gap. By contrast, the word *bǎxì* 'acrobatics, trick', which was also borrowed from the
Wu dialect, is now used in Modern Written Chinese, with a deprecatory
connotation, side by side with words from Northern Mandarin like *zájì*
'acrobatics' and *huāzhāo* 'trick'. Other common examples include *gāngà*
'awkward', *mòshēng* 'unfamiliar', *biéjiǎo* 'shoddy', and *míngtang* 'what
lies behind something, result', etc. These are mostly from the Wu dialect,
further testifying to the influence of a large number of prominent writers
of Wu background on the evolution of Modern Written Chinese during its
formative periods in the 1920s and 1930s (see Chapter 5).

6.3.2 New words from foreign languages

The most important source of new words in Modern Written Chinese is
from other languages. There were three times in which Chinese imported
words and expressions from other languages on a large scale. Translation
of Buddhist canons since the Eastern Han to the Song dynasty brought
into Chinese hundreds of new words, many of them having been part of
basic vocabulary since then, such as *shìjiè* 'world' and *yìshì* 'consciousness'. The Jesuit missionaries in the late Ming and early Qing dynasty, in
addition to their religious activities, introduced modern Western learning to the imperial court and the literati. Works they wrote or translated in

Chinese included a large number of titles in astronomy, mathematics, physical sciences, metallurgy, anatomy, biology, cartography, and military science, as well as in humanities and social sciences. Among the Chinese converts were many prominent scholars and court officials, like Xu Guangqi, who were keenly interested in Western science and technology, and also took an active part in translation in collaboration with the missionaries. They coined words like *jǐhé* 'geometry' and *dìqiú* 'the earth', which have been in common use since that period.

The past 150 years surpassed any previous periods in terms of the volume and scope of influx of new concepts and expressions from other languages into Chinese. It was a harsh awakening to the military strength of the Western nations by virtue of advanced sciences and technology when China was defeated in the Opium War. The nation felt an urgent need to know more about the invaders, and to acquire modern sciences and technology originating in the West. Schools were founded in Beijing, Shanghai, Guangdong, and other cities where foreign languages were taught to Chinese students. Meanwhile, institutions were set up respectively by western missionaries, the Chinese government, and Chinese businessmen which were devoted to translating from European languages and Japanese. Between 1811 and 1911, 2,291 titles were translated and published. Before 1900, most of the books on western learning were translated directly from English, French, German, and other European languages, whereas after 1900 more were translated via Japanese.[4] According to Xiong (1994:13), of the 533 titles translated between 1902 and 1904, 60 per cent were from Japanese. In contrast to the late Ming and early Qing time, most of the works translated during this period were in the fields of social sciences and humanities, reflecting the growing recognition of the need to initiate reform in political, social, and economic institutions and in the prevailing traditional values in ethics and ideology.

The Japanese started large-scale importation of Western concepts and institutions during the Meiji period. Books were translated into Japanese in large quantities. Earlier in the period, according to Masini (1993), the Japanese borrowed from Chinese a certain number of new words first used by Chinese or Westerners to translate from European languages into Chinese. Some of them were later borrowed back into Chinese, referred to as 'return loans' by Masini. Examples are *pànjué* 'judgement, judge' (Ja. *hanketsu*) and *jǐhuì* 'opportunity' (Ja. *kikai*).

Chinese, on the other hand, borrowed much more from Japanese. The Japanese coined many new words by using kanji, the Chinese characters, frequently with reference to their meaning in Old Chinese. Broadly speaking, these new words in Japanese fall into two groups. The first is composed of words that were used earlier in the Chinese classics, but were now assigned a new, though often somewhat related meaning in order to serve as Japanese equivalents of European expressions. Examples are *jīng-jì* (Ja. *keizai*) and *bǎo-xiǎn* (Ja. *hoken*). Used in the Chinese classics for more than a millennium, the two words meant 'to govern and to help', and 'to safeguard places that are strategically located and difficult of access', respectively. During the Meiji period, the Japanese used these two words to translate 'economy' and 'insurance', thus assigning new meanings to the old forms.

The second group contains words that were newly coined by the Japanese, with the component characters often used in the meanings of Old Chinese. Examples include *dú-cái* 'alone-decide' (Ja. *dokusai*) for 'dictatorship', and *zhé-xué* 'wisdom study' (Ja. *tetsugaku*) for 'philosophy' (for a detailed account, cf. Ma 1984; Coulmas 1989; L. Wang 1980b). A large number of these kanji words were later borrowed into Chinese, constituting an important proportion of the new words and expressions that have appeared since the end of the nineteenth century. As the Japanese kanji are almost the same as Chinese characters, they are easily assimilated into the Chinese language. Many have made their way into the basic vocabulary of Modern Chinese, including such frequent words as the following:

(28)	Japanese	English	Chinese
	eisei	hygiene	*wèishēng*
	rekishi	history	*lìshǐ*
	kenchiku	build	*jiànzhù*
	keiken	experience	*jīngyàn*
	futsū	common	*pǔtōng*
	kagaku	science	*kēxué*
	jōken	condition	*tiáojiàn*
	ginkō	bank	*yínháng*

Few Chinese today realize that these expressions are actually borrowings from Japanese.

Since the 1910s, the Chinese have again increasingly translated and borrowed directly from European languages, mainly English. This trend continues to the present day. Since Chinese has a logographic script, words in the roman script must be transformed into expressions in Chinese characters when they are introduced into Chinese. Generally speaking, there are five possible methods of introducing a new notion from the European languages.

(a) Loan translation: the foreign term is translated in a literal way, with a morpheme-for-morpheme match between the two languages. This method is most frequently used in translating compounds or phrases.

(29) *mì-yuè*   'honeymoon'
       mǎ-lì   'horse power'
       lán-qiú   'basketball'
       shēngmìng-xiàn 'lifeline'

(b) Semantic translation: a new Chinese word is coined using indigenous morphemes in a way that attempts to capture the most characteristic feature of the foreign concept. The literal meaning of the Chinese words may not match that of the original, as can be observed in these examples.

(30) *qì-chē*   (steam vehicle)   'car'
       gāng-qín (steel musical instrument)   'piano'
       yóu-piào (post coupon)   'stamp'
       dǎ-zì-jī (hit character machine)   'typewriter'

(c) Phonetic transcription: by this method, words are directly borrowed from the source languages, with Chinese characters used to simulate their original pronunciation.

(31) *shāfā*   'sofa'
       mǎdá   'motor'
       tǎnkè   'tank'
       qiǎokèlì 'chocolate'

(d) Juxtaposition of (b) and (c): a Chinese morpheme is added to the transliterated word to indicate the semantic category, thus facilitating the intelligibility of the new lexical item.

(32) *chē-tāi*   (car-)   'tire'
      jiŭ-bā   (liquor-)   'bar'
      bāléi-wŭ   (-dance)   'ballet'
      pí-jiŭ   (-liquor)   'beer'

(e) Combination of (b) and (c): while matching the sound of the original word as in transliteration, the combination of the characters also has its own semantic meaning that is intended to be indicative of the semantic content of the foreign word.

(33) *mí-nĭ*   (enchanting you)   'mini'
      Ài-zī   (generated by love)   'Aids'
      léi-dá   (thunder arrive)   'radar'
      wéi-tā-mìng (safeguard his life) 'vitamin'

Throughout the evolution of Modern Written Chinese, vocabulary has been the domain where norms have differed most remarkably in terms of time and place. There was a period, mainly in the 1920s and 1930s, when it was very common for a single notion from the West to be given two or more names in Chinese, frequently as a result of the term being introduced into Chinese by different methods. Furthermore, dialect areas may differ as to the preferred form, even when the same method of translation or borrowing is used. Following are some examples (letters in parentheses indicate the methods used in coining the word):

(34) microphone   *huà-tŏng* (speech tube) (b)
                   mài-kè-fēng (c)

(35) engine   *fādòng-jī* (launch machine) (b)
                   yĭn-qíng (draw lift) (e)

(36) cement   *shuĭ-mén-tīng* (c)
                   yáng-huī (foreign dust) (b) – prevalent in the Wu dialect area
                   shuĭ-ní (water mud) (b) – prevalent in the Northern
                       Mandarin area

(37) rifle   *bù-qiāng* (footstep gun) (b)
                   láifù-qiāng (-gun) (d)

(38)   vitamin   *wéi-tā-mìng* (safeguard his life) (e)
                      wéi-shēng-sù (safeguard life element) mainly (b), except for
                      the first character, which reflects (e)

As a rule, the situation in which functionally undifferentiated terms for the same referent coexist in the same language community will not last long. There has been competition between the alternatives for the status of the norm of Modern Written Chinese. Generally speaking, two principles are at work throughout the evolution of norms among competing items.

First, preference is given to loan translation and semantic translation over transliteration. For instance, with regard to the examples given above, the standard names for 'microphone', 'engine', 'rifle', and 'vitamin' are *huàtǒng*, *fādòngjī*, *bùqiāng*, and *wéishēngsù*, respectively.

Second, preference is given to the name prevalent in Northern Mandarin areas over other areas. Thus, for 'cement', *shuǐní* (rather than *yánghuī* or *shuǐméntīng*) has been established as the norm.

The explanation for the resistance to transliteration lies in the logographic nature of Chinese script, and the traditional importance attached to reading rather than speaking in the Chinese world. In addition to their sound value, most Chinese characters used in texts have their own semantic content as well. Chinese readers tend to pay more attention to the meaning conveyed by the graphic forms of the characters than to their phonetic values; it is not uncommon for Chinese readers to recognize the semantic content of characters without being able to pronounce them. Although much controversy still surrounds the cognitive mechanisms underlying the processing of texts in Chinese characters, most researchers seem to believe that the Chinese script indicates meaning more directly that do alphabetic or syllabic scripts, which are connected to the meaning completely via sound (see Hoosain 1991 for details). Since characters in transliteration are used for their sound value only, the string of characters that constitute a word does not make much sense when reference is made to the inherent meaning of the graphic forms, and thus requires more processing effort on the part of readers. When alternatives exist, Chinese readers who tend to read meaning into the graphic forms of a text would prefer words in which each character makes sense as opposed to those coined purely through transliteration.

Table 6.1 Lexical variations among mainland China, Taiwan, Hong Kong, and Singapore

	Mainland China	*Taiwan*	*Hong Kong*	*Singapore*
'taxi'	*chūzū qìchē*	*jìchéngchē*	*díshì*	*déshì*
'petrol'	*qìyóu*	*qìyóu*	*diànyóu*	*diànyóu*
'folk-dance'	*mínjiānwŭ*	*tŭfēngwŭ*	*tŭfēngwŭ*	*tŭfēngwŭ* or *mínjiānwŭ*
'film'	*jiāojuăn*	*jiāojuăn*	*fēilín*	*jiāojuăn* or *fēilín*
'motorcycle'	*mótuōchē*	*jīchē*	*diàndānchē*	*mótuōxīkă* or any of the other three
'disabled'	*cánjí*	*cánzhàng*	*shāngcán*	*cánquē* or any of the other three

6.4   Regional variations in the lexical norms of Modern Written Chinese

As lexical norms vary with time, they also vary with place. Indeed, the four major Chinese communities differ considerably with regard to the lexicon of Modern Written Chinese. Such variations constitute a main source of difficulty and misunderstanding when Chinese read publications from the other areas (Hsu 1979; G. Huang 1988; C. C. Li 1982; S. Lu 1990; H. Wang 1990; X. Zhou 1989). Table 6.1 presents some examples.

Variation is at its greatest with the transcription of proper names from European languages. Very often the same referent assumes different Chinese names in the four Chinese communities, composed of different characters that have the same or similar pronunciations. It is reported that Mrs Thatcher appeared in twenty-seven different forms of transcription in Chinese publications (Ho 1989).

6.4.1   Mainland China and Taiwan

Discrepancies between these two areas can be ascribed to three factors. First, because of the long period of separation, the two areas have developed separate lexical norms, although the lexical terms involved are all constructed from indigenous sources in Northern Mandarin, as exemplified by the following expressions:

(39)   Mainland China   Taiwan   English

    chŭbèi   *cúndǐ*   'reserve'
    lìjiāoqiáo   *jiāoliúdào*   'overpass'
    yŭhángyuán   *tàikōngrén*   'astronaut'

Second, nearly half a century's rule of Taiwan by the Japanese had an effect on the Modern Written Chinese used there. Some borrowings from Japanese that became the norm in Taiwan, but not in mainland China, are the following:

(40)   Taiwan   Japanese   Mainland China   English

    biàndāng   *bentō*   *héfàn*   'meal in box'
    fúzhǐ   *fukushi*   *fúlì*   'welfare'
    chēzhăng   *shashō*   *shòupiàoyuán*   'conductor'

Third, some expressions from the local Southern Min dialect have acquired the status of the norm in Taiwan, as follows:

(41)   Taiwan   Mainland China   English

    fānshŭ   *báishŭ*   'sweet potato'
    bàibài   *jìbài*   'hold a memorial ceremony for'
    shuāi   *dăoméi*   'bad luck'

6.4.2   Hong Kong

The distinctive characteristics of Modern Written Chinese in Hong Kong mainly result from the strong influence of English and Cantonese. The vocabulary of written Chinese in Hong Kong contains a larger number of borrowings from English than in either mainland China or Taiwan, as exemplified in Table 6.1. Furthermore, as Cantonese is the predominant spoken language among Hong Kong's Chinese residents, many Cantonese words have replaced their Mandarin counterparts as the norm. Following are some examples:

(42)   Hong Kong   Mainland China/Taiwan   English

    huīchūn   *chūnlián*   'New Year couplets'
    suŏchí   *yàoshi*   'key'
    xuěguì   *bīngxiāng* 'refrigerator'

6.4.3   **Singapore**

Singapore is unique in that the lexical norms of written Chinese used there are not as well established as in the other three places, displaying more variation within the community. In many cases, variant forms from mainland China, Taiwan, and Hong Kong show stable coexistence in Singapore, with the frequency of use differing from case to case. This situation is also illustrated in Table 6.1. Whereas each of the other three communities has a single normal term for each of the notions, Singapore often has several alternatives. As remarked by Wang Huidi (1990:356), it seems that Singaporeans have not yet made up their minds whether to establish a set of distinct standards for their own community, with regard to the grammar and vocabulary, or to adhere to the set of standards adopted in mainland China or Taiwan.

6.4.4   **Tendency towards reducing variation in lexical norms**

For several decades the vocabulary of Modern Chinese in mainland China was different enough from that of Taiwan, Hong Kong, and other overseas Chinese communities for people to identify the source of a publication on the basis of the words used in the text. The situation has changed somewhat since the end of the 1970s, when mainland China started adopting an 'open door' policy: this has led to some changes in the lexical norms of Modern Chinese. On the one hand, a large number of new expressions have rushed into mainland China through the open door. For example, *pìlìwǔ* 'break dancing' and *chǎo yóuyú* 'fire, sack' have been adopted from Hong Kong, and *gòngshì* 'consensus', *xīntài* 'mentality', *gòuxiǎng* 'idea' from Taiwan. Such words have gained currency in mainland China, sometimes used side by side with the traditional norms, such as *guǎndào* (vs. *qúdào*) 'channel', *shuǐzhǔn* (vs. *shuǐpíng*) 'level'. On the other hand, as expected, closer contacts between the Chinese communities have also introduced certain expressions, formerly peculiar to mainland China, into Taiwan, Hong Kong, Singapore, and other overseas Chinese communities. Words such as *cùjìn* 'promote, accelerate', *jǐnzhāng* 'in short supply', *guàshuài* 'be in command', which were rarely heard outside mainland China a few decades ago, are becoming increasingly popular in newspapers and magazines throughout the entire Chinese-speaking world.

6.5   Efforts of corpus planning in the development of Modern Written Chinese

Ferguson (1968) describes three basic types of corpus planning. Graphization refers to activities which establish and/or refine the writing system of a language. Modernization refers to efforts to expand the resources of a language, particularly its vocabulary, to meet the new functional demands placed upon it by the modern world. Standardization means development of a norm which overrides regional and social dialects. Graphization will be treated in detail in Part III, and here I will discuss the other two aspects in relation to the development of Modern Chinese.

In the exercise of corpus planning, modernization is usually accompanied by standardization. This, according to Rubin (1977), is composed of six interrelated parts. The first three are (a) isolation of a norm, (b) evaluation of the norm by some significant group as 'correct' or 'preferred', and (c) prescription of the norm for specified contexts or functions. For standardization to take effect, the prescribed norm must then (d) be accepted, (e) be used, and (f) remain in effect until another norm replaces it. As observed by Haugen (1983) and Cooper (1989), a common, if not absolutely essential, feature of this process is codification, the explicit statement of a norm.

As mentioned earlier, the expansion of the Chinese vocabulary started after the Opium War in 1840, and after the turn of the century was accelerated to accommodate the fast growing number of new notions in a rapidly changing and modernizing society. An official institution, the National Bureau of Compilation and Translation, was established in Nanjing in 1932. One of its major functions was to set up standard terminologies in all educational and academic institutions, similar to that of the Hebrew Language Council reported by Cooper (1989:123). This institution has been in operation since 1932 both in mainland China and in Taiwan, although under other names in mainland China since 1949 (Y. Liu 1986; Tse 1986). At the same time, semiofficial translation institutions, publishing houses, and individuals have also been coining new words and expressions, mainly in translations from foreign languages, with varying degrees of acceptance by the wider community.

Alternative names may still be found for the same notion in Modern Chinese, especially in the domains of the humanities and social sciences.

The first serious attempt to standardize the grammar and lexicon of Modern Chinese in a comprehensive way was launched in mainland China by Lü and Zhu (1952), which was originally serialized from 6 June to 5 December 1951 in *Rénmín Rìbào*, the most important newspaper in mainland China. Targeted at what was described as a chaotic situation with regard to the use of Modern Chinese in its grammatical, lexical, and stylistic aspects, the work analysed major types of 'wrong and ungrammatical usages' as exemplified by a large number of sentences collected from contemporary publications; and it prescribed the appropriate forms. It is interesting to note that, of the emerging features that originated in non-Northern Mandarin dialects and foreign languages, very few were labelled as substandard. Most of the errors pointed out were ascribable to negligence or incoherence in matters of grammar and logic. The work was greeted with great enthusiasm across the country, and served as the standard 'writer's manual' for many years to come. Not all of its admonitions and suggestions have been accepted, however. For instance, the use of morphemes like *-xìng* and *-huà*, as Chinese equivalents of the Western suffixes -ness and -ize, seems to have become more and more popular during the past decades in spite of the objection raised in Lü and Zhu (1952).

As discussed in Chapter 2, the first explicit statement of the standard of Modern Chinese was made at the First National Conference on Script Reform convened in Beijing in 1955. Although considerable consensus had existed with regard to the standard of pronunciation of Modern Chinese since the 1930s, opinions still differed as to the standards of the vocabulary and grammar. Some maintained that not only pronunciation but also vocabulary and grammar should be based exclusively on the Beijing dialect; given the historical fact that the dialectal basis of *báihuà* extends beyond the Beijing dialect, some believed that the vocabulary and grammar of *pǔtōnghuà* should also be built on a wider dialectal basis. In the end, the latter viewpoint prevailed, as demonstrated by the final definition of *pǔtōnghuà*. Following the conference, a campaign to standardize Modern Chinese was launched in mainland China, together with the other two stated tasks of language reform, promoting the speaking of *pǔtōnghuà* and reforming the script.

The Symposium on the Standardization of Modern Chinese held in Beijing in 1955 set forth several tasks that had to be accomplished in the endeavour to standardize Modern Chinese; among them was the compilation of a standard reference grammar and an authoritative dictionary of Modern Chinese. Efforts directed towards the latter goal have culminated in *Xiàndài Hànyǔ cídiǎn*, whereas the grammar project has not yet started.

Generally speaking, the following principles have been invoked in establishing lexical norms from alternative expressions in Modern Chinese in mainland China:

1. Words that were confined to the local Beijing dialect were rejected in favour of equivalent expressions that had wider circulation in the Northern Mandarin area. For example, *bàngwǎn* 'dusk' and *kǒushuǐ* 'saliva', rather than the Beijing localisms *cāhēir* and *hālázi*, were chosen as norms.

2. Words peculiar to the non-Northern Mandarin areas gave way to the corresponding expressions in the Northern Mandarin area. Some examples illustrating this point have been given earlier.

3. With regard to translations or borrowings from other languages, when there were alternatives, transliterations gave way to words formed by the other methods, preferably by the method of semantic translation. As the eminent Chinese linguist Wang Li put it, semantic (rather than phonetic) translation reflects the national self-esteem of the Chinese-speaking people (L. Wang 1954).

4. Proper names should be transliterated with combinations of characters which do not convey any unintended connotation that might arise out of the inherent meanings of the characters used. A good example is the Chinese transliteration of Mozambique. It was *Mò-sān-bí-jī* (not-three-nose-supply) in the 1950s, which was later replaced by *Mò-sāng-bǐ-kè* (not-mulberry-than-can). Obviously, the combination of the four characters in the first name has an undesirable meaning, whereas it is not the case with the second name. A corresponding list of English sounds and Chinese characters was promulgated by the official Xinhua New Agency in the 1950s, followed by a handbook that contained the standard transliterations of the most frequently used proper names.

Efforts to standardize the lexical norms in Modern Chinese according to the above listed principles have been quite successful in mainland China. Actually, few people in the 1990s understand the meaning of phonetically

transcribed words that were prevalent before the 1940s, such as the
following:

(43)   Earlier forms   Present forms   English

       yānshìpīlĭcún   *línggǎn*   'inspiration'
       démòkèlāxī   *mínzhǔ*   'democracy'
       pǔluólìètǎlìyà   *wúchǎnjiējí*   'proletariat'
       bùěrqiáoyà   *zīchǎnjiējí*   'bourgeois'
       yĭndé   *suǒyĭn*   'index'

In addition, many natives of Beijing, especially the youngsters, do not
even understand such former localisms as *qǔdēngr* for *huǒchái* 'match',
yízi for *féizào* 'soap', let alone use them in writing.

However, little has been achieved in the way of ridding Modern
Chinese of the elements of Old Chinese, as has been advocated by some
language planners since the 1910s. So long as the character script is still
used as the writing system of Chinese, as discussed in Chapter 5, such
proposals may well continue to prove fruitless.

In contrast to the considerable success with the lexicon of Modern
Chinese, there is far less consensus with regard to which grammatical
features in Modern Chinese should be granted the status of 'standard',
and which should be labelled 'substandard', especially when dialect
features are involved. The official documents of the National Conference
on Language and Script that was convened in January 1986, as well as
articles in journals of language planning, made little mention of standardization for the grammatical norms of Modern Chinese. Actually, grammatical features that deviate from the vernacular Northern Mandarin are
much less obtrusive to the general users of Modern Chinese than lexical
deviance, and thus much more likely to be incorporated into the norms
of Modern Chinese.

A similar situation exists in Taiwan. Standardization efforts have
been concentrated on the vocabulary of Modern Chinese, especially with
regard to translated terms, and little attention has been paid to the grammatical aspect. Up to 1974, according to Tse (1986:29), sixty-six lists of
scientific and technical terms had been authorized by the Ministry of
Education through the National Bureau of Compilation and Translation.
With increasing contacts between mainland China and Taiwan, calls

arise on both sides to reduce terminological discrepancies, especially in the fields of modern science and technology.[5] Whether this will materialize seems to hinge upon the future political relationship between the two sides.

Corpus planning of Modern Written Chinese was less active in Hong Kong than in mainland China and Taiwan, largely because, until 1974, English was the sole written language for almost all formal occasions in Hong Kong, whereas written Chinese was relegated to marginal status, used mainly for informal purposes among local Chinese. The situation changed somewhat in 1974. In dealing with the ensuing tremendous amount of translation of government documents and laws from English to Chinese, government agencies have compiled handbooks to standardize the terminologies involved. Curiously, these manuals are circulated only within a small circle, and are not easily available to the public (Ho 1989). As matters stand, lexical terms and grammatical usages are not very consistent in the Modern Written Chinese of Hong Kong; they are dependent upon the personal language background or preference of writers, and little effort has been exerted on the part of the official institution to set up grammatical or lexical norms.

Officially speaking, Singapore looks to mainland China for the standard form of *huáyǔ* in its phonological, grammatical, and lexical aspects. As discussed above, however, the influence from the local Chinese dialects and other languages upon the evolution of the norms of Modern Chinese is obvious. There is a Panel for Standard Chinese Vocabulary under the Ministry of Education, which monitors the actual use of lexical items in Singapore, but it has not yet promulgated a list of standard lexical items for general consideration (S. Lu 1990). With regard to the grammatical standard, it has been observed by Wu Yingcheng (1990) that a large proportion of teachers and students can recognize grammatical patterns that deviate from those of Beijing, and in some cases brand them as substandard; however, they use these patterns regularly. What we see is a typical case of attitudinal rather than behavioural characterization of the assumed grammatical norms. No local language planning agency has taken a stand upon grammatical features of this kind.

Single standard written language for dialects

None of the major Chinese dialects other than Northern Mandarin has an established writing tradition, in spite of the fact that they represent very large populations and are distributed over very large geographical areas – often much larger than is the case with most of the Modern European languages. As a result, the acquisition of literacy for native speakers of the non-Northern Mandarin dialects was normally in *wényán* before the New Culture Movement, and since then has been in Modern Written Chinese.

The uniformity provided by Modern Written Chinese as a written code for all Chinese is achieved at the expense of non-native speakers of Northern Mandarin. It is more difficult for Southern dialect speakers to acquire Modern Written Chinese than it is for native speakers of the base dialect of Modern Written Chinese. Actually, this difficulty was raised as an important objection to the replacement of *wényán* by *báihuà* as the standard written language (J. Li 1935). It was argued that, as *wényán* was dissociated from all of the contemporary dialects, the dialectal background of learners does not make any difference in its acquisition; with *báihuà*, on the other hand, southerners are at a linguistic disadvantage in comparison with native speakers of Northern Mandarin. This concern, as it turned out, was overridden by the urgent need for a written language that was closer to the vernacular of the majority of population and thus more suitable for a modernizing society. As discussed in previous chapters, one of the major goals of language reform in China has been to achieve the unification of speech and writing, and the replacement of *wényán* by *báihuà* as the base of a standard written code is considered to be the decisive achievement in that direction. However, as Modern Written Chinese differs remarkably from Southern dialects in its lexical and grammatical norms, there is little positive import in its establishment for speakers of Southern dialects, unless they have become bilingual, speaking Northern Mandarin in addition to their native dialect.

Some of the Southern dialects do have a literature of sorts, particularly Cantonese, Wu, and Southern Min, but this is mostly confined to writings serving popular cultural functions, such as records of folk drama scripts, folk songs, stories, and other literary genres that approach the vernacular speech.[1] Aside from such literature that has been handed down from earlier times, there are also contemporary publications in dialect writing.

In comparison with the other Southern dialects, Cantonese has a written form that is more conventionalized, and, theoretically at least, is capable of fulfilling all of the functions expected of a written medium. As will be discussed shortly, however, Cantonese writing, like other dialect writing, is generally held to be low in prestige, often appealing to dubious taste and inappropriate for more formal purposes.

Western missionaries in China in the nineteenth century were the first to adopt a totally different approach to dialect writing. Primarily in avoidance of the difficulty of learning the traditional script, but also in view of the mismatch between characters and Southern dialects (I will return to this point later), they chose to design phonetic scripts that were used exclusively to write the major Chinese dialects, especially the Southern coastal area dialects. As discussed in the literature (Ni 1948a, 1948b; Y. G. Zhou 1979, 1992), distinct writing systems were designed for each of the major Southern dialects. Literature in these phonetic scripts included the translation of the Bible, catechisms, and other religious tracts. People acquainted with the writing systems also used them for secular purposes. [2]

7.2   Causes of the under-development of dialect writing

7.2.1   Under-development of dialect writing

In comparison to literature in *wényán* and *báihuà*, texts in other dialect writings account for a negligible fraction of the traditional Chinese literature, much less influential in terms of the number of publications, and range of functions. While in Europe Dante opted to write his masterpiece in the Tuscan vernacular rather than the standard literary language, Latin, and Chaucer chose to write in the Southeastern English dialect of his time, rather than Latin, the language of the church and courts, or French, the language of polite literature, no Chinese writers of any prominence in Southern dialect areas deviated from the established literary tradition and produced vernacular literature to rival that of the North. Partly because of its scarcity, and partly because of reasons to be discussed below, literature in dialects other than Northern Mandarin has almost been ignored by history. In the volume on literature in *Zhōngguó dà bǎikéquánshū* (*Encyclopedia Sinica*) (Y. Zhou 1986), which represents the most up-to-date and comprehensive scholarship on the study of literature in China, non-Mandarin literature does not even receive a passing mention.

The under-development of dialect writing, and its failure to gain wider usage are mainly attributable to the inadequacy of the Chinese writing system in representing Southern dialects, and to questions of prestige and policy.

7.2.2 Inadequacy of the traditional script

Since vernacular writing developed on a Mandarin base from its inception, the Chinese script has been much less adapted for writing Southern dialects than for writing Northern Mandarin. When the script is used to render the Southern dialects in writing, there are many words and expressions that do not have adequate representation in characters. As observed by Cheng (1978, 1989), J. Xu (1992), and S. Huang (1993), among the most commonly used words in Southern Min, about 25 per cent do not have conventional representation in the traditional Chinese script. When they choose to write in these dialects, writers usually resort to the following devices to solve the problem of inadequate representation (Bauer 1988; Fan and Wu 1992; Cheng 1978).[3]

1. *Běnzì.* Some words in dialects did once have representation in characters, but these characters, called *běnzì* 'original characters', have long since fallen into disuse, and are preserved only in dictionaries handed down from ancient times. Not all the words in dialects can be uncontroversially traced to their original representations. In most cases, there is a lack of consensus among scholars as to which character correctly represents a particular word.

2. *Phonetic borrowing.* This method consists of borrowing characters of similar pronunciation to write the words in dialects, and is preferred by people whose educational level is not very high. The shortcoming of this device is that the dialect words in question may have no characters with the same pronunciation. Furthermore, as each character is usually associated with an intrinsic semantic meaning, it is not always easy for readers to tell when the characters are used for their original meanings and when they are borrowed for their phonetic values only.

3. *Semantic borrowing.* Characters representing the corresponding words in Modern Written Chinese may be borrowed to write words of the same meaning, but with different pronunciation in Southern dialects. This is called

xùndú, or 'diglossic paraphrasing' by Bauer (1988:247). This method is mostly resorted to by people with a high level of education.

4. *Coining new characters.* Occasionally, new characters are coined to represent dialect words. Very few have gained acceptance by people other than the inventors.

Disagreement among writers as to which device to choose in particular cases is an important reason for the present pre-standardized status of dialect writings.

7.2.3   Popular attitudes toward dialect writing

Dialect writing has always been held in low esteem by both the literati and the general public. On the one hand, it lacked the prestige that had been accorded to *wényán* before the twentieth century. On the other hand, it did not enjoy the popular usage of *báihuà*. When even the borrowing of vernacular expressions into *wényán*, or dialectalisms into *báihuà* met with disapproval, it is only to be expected that general attitudes towards dialect writing over the past centuries ranged from indifference, through contempt, to opposition. Even in present-day Hong Kong, where over 90 per cent of the population speak Cantonese, and Cantonese literature is read and written more than anywhere else in the world, dialect writing is to a certain extent looked upon with contempt by most educated Chinese, and is sometimes referred to as 'low-class' Chinese, as reported in Bauer (1988:285–7).

Actually, as a linguistic issue, dialect writing received little attention until the second half of the nineteenth century. Almost from the very beginning there have been two opposing attitudes towards dialect writing. The group in favour of it demanded that more effort should go into the design and promotion of writing systems for each of the major dialects, which could be used by native speakers of the dialect in question either as the sole written code or as one that was supplementary to the standard written language. The group opposing it maintained that there should only be one standard written language, and that dialect writing should be discouraged or prohibited in the interests of the uniformity of written Chinese within Chinese society. The opposition of the latter group appears to have been the major non-linguistic factor responsible for the current under-development of dialect writing.

As discussed in previous chapters, in addition to script reform, the language reform in progress in China during the past century has had two major goals: unification of speech and writing, and the unification of the national language. The former demands easy access to literacy via a written language that approximates actual speech as much as is practically possible, and the latter aims at the establishment of a standard language, in the spoken and written modes, that is to be used across dialectal barriers for all formal purposes. The controversy over dialect writing to a great extent hinges upon whether to assign primacy to the unification of speech and writing, or to the unification of the national language.

Opponents of dialect writing have been mainly motivated by concerns for the uniformity of written Chinese, which they believe has served a most important role in Chinese history – that of a unifying bond between speakers of mutually unintelligible dialects. To develop distinct writing systems based on various dialects, whether in the traditional script or a phonetic script, would serve to weaken the bond, and strengthen regional identity in a way that could have negative impact upon the unity of the Chinese nation-state.[4] The first to point out the potential negative impact of separate writing systems for dialects (in phonetic script) is S. Wells Williams, an American missionary who was in China for more than forty years from 1833 onwards. The following passage is quoted from Williams (1883:608):

> Local, unwritten phrases, and unauthorized characters, are so common, however, owing to the partial communication between distant parts of so great a country and mass of people, that it is evident, if this bond of union were removed by the substitution of an alphabetical language, the Chinese would soon be split into many small nations. However desirable, therefore, might be the introduction of a written language less difficult of acquisition, and more flexible, there are some reasons for wishing it to be delayed until more intelligence is diffused and juster principles of government obtain.

While scholars may dispute the extent to which the written language has served as a bond of union for distinct dialectal regions in Chinese history, it seems that the point made by Williams was not lost on the language planning institutions of successive Chinese governments, as will be discussed shortly.

Furthermore, it has been maintained that one standard language for the whole country, in both its spoken and its written modes, would greatly facilitate communication among Chinese, contributing substantially to the cause of modernization of China. Granted that dialect writing systems are effective tools of communication among speakers of the same dialect, the learners of such writing systems would have only limited access to specific parts of the Chinese community. Rather than learn a written language that has only restricted use, and is confined to a limited readership, native speakers of Southern dialects should learn what is taken as the standard language by the majority of the Chinese population, with the consequent benefits more than compensating for the extra effort demanded by its acquisition. In the words of a commentator from around the turn of the century, for the long-term benefits of learners and the state, it was necessary to *qiáng Nán jiù Běi* 'to force the South to follow the North' (Ni 1958:59).

On the other hand, the proponents of separate writing systems for each of the major dialects have given priority to ease of learning. Assuming that it is much easier for children or adults to gain literacy in a writing system that is close to their speech than in one that is far removed from it, those in favour of dialect writing have maintained that distinct writing systems for Chinese dialects, especially those in a phonetic script, enable native speakers to acquire literacy with the expenditure of far less time and effort than is the case with *wényán* or Modern Written Chinese. This is particularly true for Southerners, as it would remove the disadvantage that is entailed by the dialectal base of Modern Written Chinese.

7.2.4   Language policy toward dialect writing

It has to be pointed out that while scholars may differ in their personal opinions on the issue, successive Chinese governments, be it that of the Qing dynasty, the Nationalist in the Republic of China, or the Chinese Communist Party (CCP) in the People's Republic, have been conspicuously consistent in discouraging or proscribing any form of dialect writing, either in the traditional Chinese script or in a phonetic script.

In the initial stages of the language reform movement that began towards the end of the nineteenth century, when attention was mainly devoted to the drastic reduction of an illiteracy rate of at least as high as 90 per cent, the approach of designing separate phonetic writing systems for different dialects was very popular. As recorded in the literature (Y. G. Zhou 1979; Ni 1948b), the more than twenty schemes proposed during that period were designed first and foremost to make it easier to acquire literacy. Some of these schemes were for Northern Mandarin, but more were for the various Southern dialects. Around the turn of the century, concomitant with the growing advocacy of a national spoken standard based upon Northern Mandarin, the trend shifted away from the approach of distinct writing systems for different dialects. In fact, devising phonetic scripts for Southern dialects was viewed with the suspicion that it could impact negatively upon the goal of nation-wide uniformity of language. Lao Naixuan, an ardent advocate of dialect writing who designed separate alphabetical schemes for writing Southern Min, Cantonese, and Wu in addition to Mandarin, was snubbed by the relevant institutions of the imperial court each time he approached them for official recognition of his schemes (J. Li 1935). As observed in an article in 1906, such efforts were condemned as actually encouraging the further diversity of language in China (Ni 1958:59). In so far as easy access to literacy for non-Northern Mandarin speakers was still a concern, the attention was re-directed to providing aids that would enable all speakers to learn the traditional characters.

On the mainland before 1949, the Nationalist Government was very articulate in its opposition to writing based on non-Northern Mandarin dialects. Chen Guofu, the long-time senior government official with the cabinet portfolio for education and culture, was unmistakably clear about the reasons for such an attitude when he asserted that 'China's ability to achieve unity is entirely dependent upon having a unified written language' (DeFrancis 1950:222). The design or standardization of writing systems for non-Northern Mandarin dialects disappeared from the official agenda of language reform. Two phonetic schemes for Chinese, *zhùyīn zìmǔ* published in 1918 and *guóyǔ luōmǎzì* published in 1926, were renamed *zhùyīn fúhào* 'sound-annotating symbols' and *yìyīn fúhào* 'transcription symbols' respectively in 1930 and 1940 in order to make it clear that, contrary to the expectations of their original designers, they were not intended by the government to serve as bona fide writing systems for Northern Mandarin or other dialects. *Latinxua sin wenz*, which was designed to write the major dialects, was ruthlessly banned. This official policy towards dialect writing has continued ever since the Nationalist government regained control of Taiwan in 1945. It is reported that Western missionaries were expelled for using dialect writing systems in phonetic script in church (Cheng 1989; W. Hong 1992a, 1992b; J. Xu 1992; S. Huang 1993).

Most interesting is the change of attitude towards dialect writing on the part of the CCP, and its left-wing liberal intellectual supporters. Before it became the party of government, the CCP and its followers were adamant in their theoretical and practical support for separate writing systems for dialects. At the First Congress of the Chinese New Writing convened in the Soviet Union and organized by Chinese scholars and Soviet linguists, which adopted *latinxua sin wenz*, it was proclaimed (Ni 1949:54–5):

> The congress is opposed to the so-called 'Movement for Unification of the National Language'. No single dialect can be treated as the standard pronunciation of the whole country. The accents of the various geographical areas of China fall roughly into five groups . . . Distinct writing systems should be developed for these accents for the purpose of developing the respective local culture.

After the CCP became the party of government on the mainland in 1949, it was first anticipated that the principles espoused by the proponents of *latinxua sin wenz* would be implemented as government policy. However, the policy articulated in the above proclamation was abandoned in favour of a single standard spoken and written language, in spite of the fact those holding important positions in government language planning institutions were basically the same group of people that had earlier advocated distinct dialect writing systems (Proceedings 1957). The last article that could be found that still subscribed to the old view was published in the mid 1950s. Since then, there has been no further mention of developing dialect writing.

7.3   Current endeavours in Taiwan towards dialect writing

7.3.1   Schemes for writing in Southern Min

Since the mid 1980s, the endeavour to develop dialect writing has been continued in Taiwan, where there has been an upsurge of interest in the design and promotion of a standard writing system for Southern Min.

The participants have the same objective in mind – to design and promote a standard writing system based upon the dominant local dialect rather than Northern Mandarin – although they differ in regard to the type of script that should be used for the writing system. As reported in the literature (Cheng 1989; W. Hong 1992a, 1992b; S. Huang 1993), there are two major groups of schemes for Southern Min writing in Taiwan.

The first group is composed of schemes that mainly use the Latin script. Most of them are modified versions of the writing that has been used by the church for about one and a half centuries, with some opting to indicate tones with letters rather than superimposed diacritics. While some employ the Latin script exclusively, others also make occasional use of traditional Chinese characters to enhance clarity. The other group includes schemes that mainly adopt the traditional script. Many also use a phonetic script to write common grammatical morphemes or words that have no conventional representation. For instance, several articles in Cheng (1989) are written in this way.

There are also people, like Hong Weiren (1992a, 1992b), who are not satisfied with either of the two major groups, particularly with respect to the inclusion of the Latin script in the same text as the traditional Chinese script, which they regard as an incongruity. What they suggest for words without conventionalized representation in Chinese characters is a new script modelled on Korean which is phonetic and assumes the square shape of the traditional Chinese script. However, no details have yet been released concerning such a script. Dialect writers write mainly in either the Latin script or the traditional Chinese script, with the other script frequently employed as a supplementary device.

7.3.2 **Motivating factors**

The current movement to develop a standard writing system for Southern Min represents the most intense interest yet shown towards activities of its kind in non-Northern Mandarin areas. It shares with previous efforts the concern for easier access to literacy for the native speakers of dialects. On the other hand, it is unique in that it aims at objectives beyond mere native language literacy. Correlated with an increased assertion of regional identity of which language is an important defining feature, the current linguistic undertaking constitutes a very important part of the overall effort to elevate the status of the language and the culture, and to advance the political interests of the dialect's speakers, who constitute the majority of the island's population. In other words, it is mainly triggered by, and contributes to, a political cause.

Since the 1970s, and particularly after the formation in 1987 of the Democratic Progressive Party (DPP), which appeals strongly to the rising awareness of regional identity, the language policy the government has held since 1945 came under attack. This may be seen partly as a backlash against the stern language planning measures, best understood in the context of the heightened assertion by a large number of local residents of an identity based not on Northern Mandarin but on their native dialects of Southern Min and Kejia. Language has become a highly politicized issue on which the DPP fights against the ruling Nationalist government. The long-standing policy of stipulating *guóyǔ* as the standard language is denounced as an act of linguistic imperialism that is unfair to native speakers of non-Northern Mandarin dialects. It is argued that the success in promoting *guóyǔ* on the island has been achieved at the expense of local dialects, which are allegedly on the way to extinction. Among the objectives of the language policy in the programme of the DPP are bilingual education, and equal rights for all dialects in mass media and public life, although details of the policy issues, such as how to reconcile different opinions on dialect writing, how to achieve the goals, and how to deal with the negative consequences of the policy, etc., have yet to be furnished. It is also proposed that *guóyǔ* should ultimately be replaced by Southern Min, the native tongue of the majority of the local population, as the lingua franca on the island. Essential to achieving this goal is the standardization and promotion of a written language based upon the dialect.

With local dialects, Southern Min in particular, taken to be the defining feature of regional identity, the linguistic issue of dialect writing has become the symbol of a wider political and cultural cause. Promoting the dialects to the status of languages (in every sense of the word) through the standardization of a written code is seen as an integral part of the cause to preserve and promote the local culture that is represented in the dialects, and to protect and advance the interests of the people who speak the dialects. As explained in the relevant literature (Cheng 1989; W. Hong 1992a, 1992b; J. Xu 1992; S. Huang 1993), the special emphasis placed on dialect writing is motivated on the following grounds.

First, on the assumption that dialects are an important medium of the sentiments that bind the local people together, it is maintained that they play an essential role in fostering and strengthening the sense of regional identity. As discussed in Chapter 2 and Chapter 4, at present in Taiwan, *guóyǔ* is the High language, used for almost all formal functions, such as education and administration, and, until recently, as the sole language in mass media except for some commercials, while the native dialects are for use in everyday life. Unless the Southern dialects become as fully standardized in terms of a well-developed written code as Northern Mandarin, they will always be viewed as Low languages. To some people, the status quo of the local dialects, and the inequality that exists between their native tongues and Northern Mandarin are unacceptable. As they see it, to develop and standardize a written language based upon the local dialect constitutes the first step toward fundamental change in the situation. This is also generally attested in studies of similar situations elsewhere in the world (Haugen 1966, 1983; Ferguson 1968; Fishman 1968; Cooper 1989; Coulmas 1989; Clyne 1992).

Furthermore, as dialects are regarded as a component part of the cultural heritage of native speakers, a written language is seen as essential for the preservation of the dialect-unique culture, and the preservation of regional identity. As estimated by Huang Shuanfan (1993), if the current language policy in Taiwan continues for a certain number of years, *guóyǔ* will emerge as the dominant language of the island, not only in terms of the major functions, but also in terms of the number of native speakers. Needless to say, many find it unacceptable that the local dialects, as the most important means by which much of the local culture has been preserved, and as a defining feature of the regional identity, should be replaced by a non-indigenous language.

7.3.3   Responses to writing in Southern Min

The movement to develop a standard writing system for Southern Min has met with mixed responses from the academic and educational communities, and the general public on the island.

Among its most enthusiastic participants and supporters are some linguists in Taiwan and abroad who are native speakers of Southern Min. While they may disagree on issues such as the intended functions of dialect writing, or argue over the technicalities of proposed schemes, they have been devoted to the study of the major aspects of Southern Min as a foundation for the design and standardization of an optimized scheme for the writing of the dialect, and to the promotion of dialect writing in the wider community. Dictionaries of Southern Min, textbooks and readers in the dialect writing have been compiled with the aim of providing the orthographic norms for the language in the process of standardization.

The entertainment sector and the literary circle echo this enthusiasm for dialect writing. Concurrent with the increasingly widespread use of Southern Min in all sectors of society, there are large numbers of films, songs, and television shows in Southern Min which have proved to be very popular among the general public. Script writers for these productions find it much more effective and convenient to write directly in dialect, adopting one of the schemes most familiar to co-workers in the field. Meanwhile, the number of dialect writers of other literary genres is increasing. More and more stories, poems, essays, etc. written in dialect or containing a large amount of dialectalisms are published regularly in the print media alongside writings in Modern Written Chinese. Publications exclusively in dialect writing have also increased remarkably in recent years. Many literary works originally written in Modern Written Chinese are being translated into the local dialects.

Responses from schools and other sectors of the community towards dialect writing have been much more cautious. So far, the teaching of Southern Min writing in various schemes is mainly conducted in an ad hoc way, depending mainly upon the efforts of enthusiastic individuals. It is mostly confined to non-accredited institutions or programmes, and has not been included in the regular curriculum of the formal educational system in Taiwan or abroad. Writings of a formal nature, whether by individuals, the government, or non-government institutions, customarily use Modern Written Chinese instead of the local writing. While the gradual replacement of Mandarin by Southern Min as the common speech has been a topic of heated debate that attracts widespread attention, dialect writing, at least for the time being, has failed to draw much interest from any part of the community other than the relatively small linguistic and literary circles.

Lack of a standardized, or widely recognized, writing system is just one reason for the fact that dialect writing has not been as successful as its promoters have wished. Given the present momentum, however, it may not be long before Southern Min is fully standardized in terms of a written code that represents the consensus of linguistic opinion in the community, and is regularly used by those opting to write in the dialect instead of Modern Written Chinese.

A more important factor underlying the under-achievement of dialect writing in Taiwan, in my view, is that the wider community is not yet prepared to accept efforts to standardize and promote a separate orthography for Southern Min. Whether these efforts will ever be accepted depends on how the pros and cons surrounding dialect writing are weighed by the general public in connection with other educational, social, and political factors in the community.

7.4   Implications of standardization of dialect writing

If the current endeavour in Taiwan were to be emulated in other major non-Northern Mandarin speaking areas, like the Cantonese or Wu dialect areas, it would also be just a matter of time before the situation emerges where there are distinct standardized written languages in Chinese communities, representing the dominant dialects that are used in these areas. Full standardization of the non-Northern Mandarin dialects in the form of generally accepted and extensively used written codes would have major implications for the educational, cultural, social, and political aspects of life in the non-Northern Mandarin speaking regions, and for Chinese society as a whole. I do not expect that the current movement in Taiwan will win extensive support from the wider community before it is convincingly demonstrated that the costs of a separate standardized orthography for Southern Min are outweighed by the benefits.

As discussed above, what the proponents of dialect writing are aiming for, according to their own accounts, is a society characterized by multilingualism in the full sense of the word – the coexistence of several languages each having its own standardized written literature. It remains then to be seen what type of interrelationship these languages would form. Two possible situations could emerge in the major Chinese-speaking communities, if the process of the standardization of the regionally dominant, non-Northern Mandarin dialects is fully completed in the form of a well-developed, and widely used written code. In either scenario, there will be so many foreseeable problems that the majority of the population may decide that they prefer the present linguistic situation to the brave new world painted by the language reformers.

It is possible that the multilingual community will be characterized by diglossia, not only in speech, but also in writing (see Ferguson 1959; Fishman et al. 1968; Fasold 1984; P. Chen 1993, 1994, 1996a). Given the fact that the written language based upon Northern Mandarin has for a long period of time been used as the sole written code for all geographical areas, it will most likely retain its position as the High language in all of the bilingual Chinese communities. Actually, this is what was envisaged by the early promoters of dialect writing. As Lu Zhuangzhang (1892) and Qu Qiubai (1931b) indicate, the writing systems of the local dialects were intended to be used for book-keeping in everyday life. People who were literate in the local dialect writing system could, if they had the time and economic means, then go on to learn the written language of wider acceptance, presumably the one based upon Northern Mandarin, as a tool for the acquisition of science and arts, and for participation in political and social activities at the national level. As a result, most students would have to learn two separate written languages. That extra effort must be added to the educational costs to the diglossic community, which may turn out to be higher than those presently faced.

It is also possible that the languages concerned will not differ with regard to High or Low socio-cultural functions, but with regard to the targeting of the intended readership. As proposed in Cheng (1989:86), whether materials be in the fields of politics, administration, literature, or news reporting, those that are important will be published in all three languages, namely *guóyǔ*, Southern Min, and Kejia, in the case of Taiwan, and those that are unimportant will be published in a language that is learned by the majority of the people in the community. Such measures would in effect dampen the motivation to acquire literacy in another language. While it may save people the trouble of learning to speak or write in a language other than their own, there are obviously substantial disadvantages. Their communicative competence will be severely restricted if their native language happens to be relatively minor in terms of speakers. In the meantime, written communication between the major linguistic groups within and across communities could become a serious problem, if each group only learns writing in its own dialect. This may further lead to undesirable social and regional fragmentation along linguistic lines, as reported in the literature (Fishman et al. 1968).

For thousands of years of Chinese history, there was a standard written language for speakers of all dialects, and dialect writing as an issue did not arise until comparatively recently. The least we can say about this is that, in spite of the remarkable differences between dialects, the fact that there has been a single written standard makes the Chinese language less of a disintegrating factor than would otherwise be the case.[5] Those who cherish the time-honoured literary tradition of the Chinese community, and value the role of Modern Written Chinese as an important unifying force between different dialectal regions will most likely, if only for that reason alone, be ill disposed to any efforts to promote dialect writing at the expense of Modern Written Chinese. To judge from the lack of enthusiasm for dialect writing from the general public, it seems that, at least for the time being, and possibly also for the foreseeable future, the majority of the Chinese population, even in Taiwan, are not convinced that standardization of dialect writing and its widespread use will bring them great benefits.

Part III

The modern Chinese writing system

8.1   Typological characterization

The Chinese character script is one of the oldest writing systems in the world, and is the only one that has been in continuous use for more than three millennia. While the great majority of modern languages have adopted phonographic writing systems, Chinese is conspicuous as the most important language to retain a logographic writing system. Tremendous efforts have been made during the past century to simplify the traditional script, and to design and promote a phonetic writing for Chinese. In fact, nowhere in the world has there been a writing reform comparable in magnitude to the Chinese endeavours to shift from a logographic writing system to a phonographic one. Before I discuss in detail the efforts at script reform, let us consider some basic features of the traditional Chinese writing system in relation to the language it encodes.

Writing systems in the world can be differentiated along two dimensions. First is the size of the speech segments that are represented by the basic graphic units, and second is whether the graphic units encode speech sound only, or both speech sound and meaning.

Following DeFrancis (1989:54), I use the term grapheme to refer to the basic graphic unit in a script that corresponds to the smallest segment of speech represented in the writing. English graphemes are letters, whereas Chinese graphemes are characters. Writing systems differ with regard to whether it is phoneme or syllable that is represented by the grapheme. Graphemes in languages like English and Finnish represent phonemes, which may assume the form of a letter or group of letters. Graphemes in languages like Chinese and Japanese, on the other hand, represent a syllable, encoded by a character in the case of Chinese and a kana symbol in the case of Japanese.[1] Thus, the writing systems of languages like English and Finnish are said to be phonemic, whereas those of Chinese and Japanese, in the form of characters or kana respectively, are syllabic.

Furthermore, graphemes differ with regard to whether they encode pure phonetic values, or phonetic values together with meaning. As is generally recognized in the literature (Gelb 1963; Haas 1983; Hill 1967; Trager 1974; Pulgram 1976; Sampson 1985; Coulmas 1989, 1992), those used as pure phonetic symbols devoid of any meaning are called phonographic or cenemic, whereas those encoding phonetic value together with meaning are called logographic, pleremic, or morphemic. The former are exemplified by letters in languages like Finnish, and kana symbols in Japanese, and the latter by characters in Chinese. Writing systems are characterized as phonographic or logographic, depending upon whether they are mainly composed of phonographic or logographic graphemes. As observed in Bolinger (1946) and Sampson (1985, 1994), however, the distinction drawn here between phonography and logography is a relative one, in the sense that many writing systems, including those of English and Chinese, while mainly phonographic or logographic, also display features of logography or phonography to varying degrees. The writing system of English, for example, is more logographic than that of Finnish, although both are generally recognized as phonographic.

On the basis of the above definition, the writing system of Chinese is characterized as logographic, and its graphemes, i.e., characters, as morpho-syllabic.

8.2   Brief history of the Chinese script

The Chinese script as a well-developed system dates back to the four-teenth century BC, although individual characters may have an even longer history (Jiang 1987; X. Q. Li 1985:156; X. Qiu 1988:22). The script at its earliest stage of development is represented by *jiǎgǔwén*, with charac-ters inscribed or painted on ox bones and tortoise shells, and mostly recording divinatory outcomes. It evolved into *jīnwén* 'bronze script' in the Zhou dynasties, which was used in inscriptions on bronzeware dur-ing the period. The next major development is represented by *xiǎozhuàn*, which was stipulated as the standard script in the Qin dynasty. Another script that was simpler in graphic structure, known as *lìshū* 'clerical script', was in popular use in the Qin and Han dynasties alongside *xiǎozhuàn*. While *xiǎozhuàn*, referred to as *zhèngtǐ* 'standard style', was the formal writing system, *lìshū*, referred to as *sútǐ* 'vulgar style', served an auxiliary role, mainly for occasions where ease of writing outweighed consideration of formality. *Xiǎozhuàn* was gradually replaced by *lìshū* as the norm in the Han dynasty. While scripts before *xiǎozhuàn* belong to the so-called old scripts in literature of Chinese linguistics, *lìshū* marks the beginning of the Modern Chinese writing system. *Lìshū* was in turn replaced by *kǎishū* 'model script' in the Southern and Northern dynasties, which since then has been the standard form of the Chinese script.

As is the case with two other ancient writing systems, Sumerian cuneiform and Egyptian hieroglyphs, most Chinese characters during the initial phase are logographic signs, indicating both the sound and meaning of the morphemes they represent. In the literature of traditional Chinese philology, these characters fall into three major groups according to the principles underlying their graphic structure, *xiàngxíng* 'pictographic', *zhǐshì* 'ideographic', and *huìyì* 'compound indicative'. *Xiàngxíng* characters bear a physical resemblance to the objects they indicate. Examples are familiar characters like 日 *rì* 'sun', 月 *yuè* 'moon', 山 *shān* 'hill', 水 *shuǐ* 'water'. Supplementary to the principle of pictographic resemblance is *zhǐshì*, which refers to a more diagrammatic method used to create characters that represent more abstract concepts. Examples are 上 *shàng* 'up', and 下 *xià* 'down'. On the basis of *xiàngxíng* and *zhǐshì* characters evolved the third method *huìyì*, which combines graphs of the first two categories on the basis of their semantics to create new characters that imply a combination of the meanings of the component parts. A good example is 从 *cóng* 'follow' which is made of two 人 *rén* 'person', with one after the other.

All of the three groups share the feature that the characters were shaped in a way that attempted to capture the semantic content of the morphemes they represent in a more or less iconic fashion. Characters formed on the iconic principle constitute the bulk of the early stage of the Chinese writing system represented by *jiǎgǔwén* (Guan 1988; X. Qiu 1988:32).

It is obvious that the iconic principle has severe limitations. There are words indicating complicated concepts which are difficult to map onto graphic shapes. Furthermore, the most fertile imagination would find it difficult to use iconic means to represent words that serve purely grammatical functions. To meet the growing demands for graphemes in the writing system to record increasingly complicated texts, Chinese did what the Sumerians and Egyptians did by turning to the method of phonetic borrowing, whereby the originally logographic characters are used as pure phonetic signs, representing homophonic or near-homophonic morphemes that have no or little semantic relation to the original characters. It is reported that even among the characters in *jiǎgǔwén*, many were found to have been used as cenemic syllabograms only, although the percentage of these phonetic loans is quite small in comparison with characters which were used as pleremic logograms.

With more and more pleremic logograms simultaneously serving as cenemic syllabograms, as discussed in Coulmas (1989, 1992:225), it became increasingly necessary to introduce some sort of differentiation into the writing system, usually in the form of some markers that are attached to the grapheme to indicate, or hint at the phonetic or semantic value of the sign for the particular occasion. The same process is attested in all of the four major ancient writing systems, namely Egyptian, Sumerian, Maya, and Chinese (Gelb 1963; Haas 1976:177; X. Qiu 1988:151). In Chinese, some graphs are attached to cenemic syllabograms as semantic determinatives, and some are attached to pleremic logograms as phonetic determinatives. The addition of the semantic or phonetic determinatives serves to enhance the clarity of the writing system by reducing the possibility of ambiguity, either through the reduction of the number of polysemous graphemes by the addition of semantic determinatives to cenemic syllabograms, or through the differentiation of graphically similar characters by the addition of phonetic determinatives. When it comes to the positioning of the determinatives in relation to the root characters, however, it seems that the aesthetic consideration that characters be of equidimensional shape led Chinese to pursue an approach different from that adopted in Egyptian and Sumerian. Instead of preceding or following the grapheme in question as a separate sign, the determinative in Chinese was incorporated into the root grapheme as an integral part of a new character, constituting what is called *xíngshēng* 'phonetic-semantic' compound. As discussed in the literature (Coulmas 1989; 1992; X. Qiu 1988), the Chinese would most probably have evolved into a phonographic writing system, in the same way as the other writing systems in the world, if the characters initially created on the iconic principle had been used increasingly as cenemic syllabograms, instead of becoming a component part of *xíngshēng* characters.

Xíngshēng characters are typically composed of two parts, a phonetic component and a semantic component.[2] Although they are more complex in graphic shape, the *xíngshēng* characters hold an advantage over the pleremic logograms in that they carry more information in terms of phonetic or semantic value, and over the purely phonetic borrowings in

Table 8.1 Number of characters in Chinese history

Number of characters	Dictionary	Period	Date
3,300	Cāngjiépiān, Yuánlìpiān, Bóxuépiān	Qin	221–206 BC
9,535	Shuōwén jiězì	Eastern Han	100AD
16,917	Yùpiān	Liang	543
26,149	Guǎngyùn	Northern Song	1011
32,200	Hóngwǔ zhèngyùn	Ming	1375
47,043	Kāngxī zìdiǎn	Qing	1716
48,000	Zhōnghuá dà zìdiǎn	ROC	1916
56,000	Xiàndài Hànyǔ dà zìdiǎn	PRC	1986–90

that they carry more semantic information. From the way in which their writing system developed, it appears that the Chinese opted for clarity over economy. *Xíngshēng* provided an efficient method to create a large number of characters on the basis of the current stock, and consequently after the *jiǎgǔwén* period it became the major principle by which new characters were made, bringing about a sharp increase in characters in the following two millennia. Table 8.1 demonstrates the number of characters contained in the major dictionaries of different periods (Norman 1988; Z. M. Zhou 1988:198).

According to several statistics, *xíngshēng* characters constitute only about 37 per cent in *jiǎgǔwén*, but more than 80 per cent in *Shuōwén jiězì*, and around 90 per cent in dictionaries after *Guǎngyùn* (Guan 1988:109; X. Qiu 1988:32). As observed by Qiu Xigui (1988:32), however, the percentage is lower with commonly used characters, with *xíngshēng* characters constituting 74 per cent of the list of 2,000 common characters published in 1952.

Another group of character components other than the phonetic or the semantic part found in characters of the *xíngshēng* category and elsewhere is known as *jìhàofú* 'symbolic mark' . They do not indicate any phonetic or semantic value of the containing characters, and are used merely as differentiating symbols serving mnemonic functions. They are mostly derived from pictographic or ideographic characters as a result of the attrition of the original graphic shape.

8.3   Correlation between script and language

Much discussion on Chinese script reform has been based upon an impressionistic assessment of the complicated interrelationships between characters, syllables, morphemes, and words in Chinese, and this is partly responsible for some of the gross misunderstanding and shaky argumentation once prevalent in the field. Since the 1980s, a number of quantitative studies have been undertaken which aim to establish the basic facts regarding the major phonological and morphological features of characters in Modern Chinese. The findings that have been reported provide the basis for a proper understanding of the important issues involved in the Chinese script reform.

8.3.1   Number and structure of common characters

Although around 56,000 characters have been accumulated in Chinese, only a few thousand are needed to write Modern Chinese. Two important lists have recently been published in China that contain characters in common use in Modern Chinese.

One is a List of Common Characters in Modern Chinese published by the State Language Commission and the State Education Commission in January 1988, which is composed of two parts. Part 1 contains 2,500 common characters, and Part 2 contains 1,000 less common characters. The other is a List of Regular Characters in Modern Chinese published by the State Language Commission and the State Press and Publication Administration in March 1988, which contains 7,000 entries (Y. Fu 1989a). The coverage rate of the commonly used characters in modern publications is given in Table 8.2 (data from Chang 1989; P. Su 1992:7; Yin 1991:19).

Literacy in Chinese is measured by the number of characters a learner has acquired, rather than words, as is the case with Western languages. The threshold is generally set at around 2,000 characters. Graduates from primary school are expected to have learned around 2,500 characters, and the number increases to 3,500 for college graduates.

The primary part in the graphic structure of characters is called the stroke, of which the average number per character for the 7,000 or so most common characters is eleven (Wu and Ma 1988:50). Strokes in turn combine to form one of the three types of component parts of characters,

Table 8.2 Coverage rate of characters in publications in Modern Chinese

Number of characters	Coverage rate (per cent)
500	80
1,000	91
2,400	99
3,800	99.9
5,200	99.99
6,600	99.999

Table 8.3 Number of characters pronounced as *ji*

Tone	Number of characters
1	47
2	33
3	12
4	45

namely phonetic components, semantic components, and symbolic marks as explained above. When a character is composed of two or more of the three types of components, it is called *hétǐzì* 'composite character'. It is called *dútǐzì* 'simple character' when it has just a single component.

8.3.2   Characters, syllables, and morphemes

Given the monosyllabicity of Chinese characters, and the tremendous discrepancy between the number of characters and the number of syllables, it is only to be expected that there are a large number of characters that are homophonous. For example, In *Xiàndài Hànyǔ cídiǎn* under the syllable *ji* are listed a total of 137 distinct characters (excluding variant forms of the same character), which encode different morphemes, as shown in Table 8.3.

Furthermore, let us consider the 3,500 characters in the List of Common Characters in Modern Chinese published by the State Language Commission and the State Education Commission in 1988. In the list

Table 8.4 Correspondence between characters and morphemes

Character–morpheme correspondence	Number of characters	Percentage
1:1	3,686	87.5
1:2	429	10.2
1:3	73	1.7
1:4	18	0.4
1:5	6	0.1

only 31.5 per cent of the tonal syllables are represented by only one character; 68.5 per cent are represented by at least two homophonous characters, with 15.8 per cent by six or more. Needless to say, homophony increases when a larger number of characters are counted. Obviously, the distinctive graphic shapes of characters play a most important disambiguating role in writing.

The correspondence between characters and morphemes is much closer than is the case between characters and syllables. As estimated in Yin (1988:255; 1991:17), there are about 4,800 morphemes in common use in Modern Chinese. Table 8.4 displays how they are represented in terms of characters.[3] As Table 8.4 shows, the great majority of characters encode one morpheme, and only little more than 10 per cent represent two or more. Moreover, it is also established that about 95 per cent of morphemes in Chinese are monosyllabic, and represented by single characters (L. Lin 1980; Yin 1988, 1991; N. Qian 1990:546; Fan 1993). The close match between characters and morphemes underlies many of the other features of the Chinese writing system, which will be discussed later.

8.3.3   Morphemes and words

In Old Chinese, the majority of the monosyllabic morphemes are simultaneously words. A remarkable distinction between Old Chinese and Modern Chinese is that many of the free morphemes in Old Chinese have become bound in Modern Chinese, used only in combination with other morphemes as component parts of words and other types of expressions. Statistics reveal that while words in Old Chinese are overwhelmingly

Table 8.5 Percentage of monosyllabic words in Chinese history

Date	Period	Percentage of monosyllabic words
before 221BC	Pre-Qin	96
618–1279AD	Tang–Song	93
1368–1911	Ming–Qing	90
1910s–1930s	ROC	62
1950s–1980s	PRC	46

monosyllabic, there was a substantial increase in the number of di- or polysyllabic words as Old Chinese evolved into Modern Chinese. In the literature of Chinese historical linguistics, this is generally known as the drift towards di- or multi-syllabification (L. Wang 1980b). Table 8.5 presents the percentage of monosyllabic words in prose of different periods. The percentage of di- or multisyllabic words in the whole vocabulary of Modern Chinese is even higher. Of the 50,000 or so entries contained in *Xiàndài Hànyǔ cídiǎn*, about 2,500 are monosyllabic, accounting for only 5 per cent of the total, and about 40,000 are disyllabic (M. Chen 1981). It is generally believed that the drift towards di- and multisyllabic words was largely an outcome of functional compensation for attrition in the differentiation of syllables due to the drastic reduction of the syllabary through these periods, as discussed in Chapter 5.

It has to be emphasized that, far from falling into obsoleteness, a large number of bound morphemes which were free words in Old Chinese are still very active in Modern Chinese, constituting the important stock of components in word formation. Many of them are quite versatile in their capacity to combine with other morphemes to form words or nonce words.

8.4   Merits of the Chinese script

As a writing system that has been serving the Chinese language for thousands of years, the traditional script does have its own strengths, in terms of suitability for the language, which have enabled it to survive as the sole major logographic system in the world. From a purely linguistic perspective, the Chinese writing system has two major advantages in comparison to the various phonographic writings which have been proposed for the language. First is its capacity to differentiate homophonous morphemes, and second is its versatility in bridging time and dialects, although it has to be pointed out that both claims have to be qualified to some extent, as will be discussed in detail later.

8.4.1 Differentiation of homophonous morphemes

As Table 8.4 demonstrates, the great majority of Chinese morphemes are monosyllabic, and, owing to the limited number of syllables in Chinese, there are many homophonous morphemes. When morphemes are represented by characters, there is little danger of ambiguity, as distinct characters serve the important function of differentiating the homophonous morphemes. This function is essential for writing Old Chinese, where most monosyllabic morphemes are independent words which would be hardly differentiable if encoded in a typical phonographic system. Homophony, on the other hand, is much less of a problem with a written language based upon the vernacular of Modern Chinese, largely because of the presence of a much higher percentage of di- or multisyllabic words, as shown in Table 8.5, which are less likely to be homophonous than monosyllabic. It is no coincidence that the advocacy of a phonographic writing either to replace or to co-exist with the traditional characters rose in concomitance with calls to bring written Chinese closer to the present-day vernacular, instead of relying on the classics of 2,000 years ago for its lexical and grammatical norms. As observed in Chapter 5, however, Modern Written Chinese still retains many features from Old Chinese in spite of the attempts to get rid of them. To the extent that features of Old Chinese persist in Modern Written Chinese, homophony would pose a serious problem for any attempt to devise phonographic writing for Chinese. However, the problem would be less serious if Modern Written Chinese were closer to colloquial speech in Modern Chinese, which, being subject to the constraints of oral communication, is unlikely to contain a large number of homophonous words.

8.4.2 Use across times and dialects

One of the most lauded merits of the Chinese script is its ability to span times and dialects. As characters can have different phonetic values in different times and at different places, they can be used to represent the Chinese language spoken in different periods and in different geographic areas. It is largely by virtue of this feature that it is much easier for present-day Chinese to read the writings of more than 2,000 years ago than it is for the users of a phonographic system, such as English, to read texts from very early times. To a certain extent, it is also by virtue of this feature that the Chinese people can sometimes communicate in writing even if they speak mutually unintelligible dialects.

Some caveats are in order here with regard to the use of characters across dialects. Strictly speaking, as discussed in Chapter 7, the Chinese script has been much better adapted to write Mandarin, especially Northern Mandarin, than the Southern dialects of Cantonese, Wu, and Min. The fact that more effort is needed on the part of native speakers of Southern dialects to acquire literacy in Modern Chinese, as well as the problems that are encountered in the representation of these dialects in characters, demonstrate that the alleged versatility of the Chinese script in bridging dialects needs to be viewed with some reservation.

8.5   Motivation for reform

8.5.1   Difficulty of learning

First, it is maintained by many that characters are difficult to learn to read and write.

As mentioned above, over 90 per cent of characters in Modern Chinese belong to the *xíngshēng* category. It must be pointed out that the phonetic determinatives of *xíngshēng* characters are not to be treated on a par with the sound-indicating symbols like kana in Japanese, or letters in Finnish or English. While the number of basic phonetic symbols in a phonographic system is usually no more than a few dozen, an analysis of the *xíngshēng* characters in Modern Chinese shows that there are around 1,300 distinct symbols that are used as phonetic determinatives, and 250 as semantic determinatives. Not counting the characters in the other categories, the number of the basic phonetic symbols in *xíngshēng* characters alone is already much higher than that in English or Japanese, demanding strenuous effort on the part of learners.

Furthermore, contrary to what is generally assumed, a large portion of these phonetic and semantic determinatives provide only a vague hint as to the phonetic value and semantic category of the characters that contain them. Due to historical sound change, more often than not there is considerable discrepancy between the Modern Chinese pronunciation of the phonetic determinatives and their pronunciation at the time when they were first incorporated into the *xíngshēng* characters in question. The syllable represented by a Chinese character, as discussed in detail in Chapter 3, is traditionally analysed into three parts: initial, final, and tone. Recent investigations reveal that, out of the 5,990 common *xíngshēng* characters in Modern Chinese, only 1,578 are pronounced exactly the same as the phonetic determinative with regard to the initial, final, and tone, accounting for 26.3 per cent of the total. The percentage is even lower with the *xíngshēng* characters that are most commonly used. The indicative ability is higher with semantic determinatives. Out of the most commonly used 2,522 *xíngshēng* characters, 2,082 have semantic determinatives that indicate the thesaurus-like category of the containing characters in a way that ranges from precise to remotely suggestive (C. Ye 1965; P. Su 1992:8).

With characters other than the *xíngshēng* type, there is no clue in the graphic structure as to the phonetic value. As a result of attrition in the graphic structure, a large number of the graphemes of the *xiàngxíng*, *zhǐshì*, and *huìyì* categories discussed earlier have lost all traces of the iconicity of the original shape, and become mere mnemonic symbols, namely symbolic marks. The same happened to a large number of graphs that were originally incorporated into *xíngshēng* characters as phonetic or semantic determinatives. According to the latest statistics, characters that comprise such symbolic marks constitute at least 20 per cent of the characters in common use in Modern Chinese (X. Qiu 1988:36). Needless to say, students can do little with these characters beyond rote memorization.

As mentioned above, in Modern Chinese there is an average of eleven strokes per character. In order to differentiate between characters, the configurations of these strokes are necessarily complex. Since the graphic shape of the characters provides little indication of their pronunciation, learning to read and write thousands of graphically complex characters becomes a massive mnemonic task. The success of this task demands a large amount of time and energy on the part of Chinese school children, which could be used in learning other subjects. It is estimated that 30 per cent of the total class hours in Chinese primary and secondary schools are devoted to learning the Chinese language, and much of that time is spent on learning characters. A comparative study shows that the reading materials in language class up to Year 4 in Chinese schools are only about one sixth of the length of those at the comparable level in countries that use phonographic writing systems (Y. G. Zhou 1979). It also shows that while it takes only three to four months of intensive learning for people in countries using phonographic writing systems to achieve literacy, the process takes much longer in China. It is estimated that in order to learn this difficult writing system, the Chinese, on average, spend two years more than people who use phonographic writing (Wu and Ma 1988:74–5). This is generally taken as one of the reasons for the comparatively high illiteracy rate in China, especially in rural areas where peasants can hardly afford the time and money required for such an enormous task. Before the 1950s, illiteracy in China reportedly reached 90 per cent, and it was recorded at 30 per cent around 1980 (DeFrancis 1950; W. Z. Chen 1988). The latest statistics report that in 1996 there were still 140 million illiterates. Admittedly there are many factors that contribute to a nation's literacy rate, but, given the extra time needed to learn the Chinese script, it seems sensible to guess that China would enjoy a much higher literacy rate if it used a phonographic writing system.

8.5.2   Difficulty of use

The use of such a large number of characters as basic graphemes makes the Chinese writing system a very clumsy tool for many purposes. Owing to the complicated nature of the graphic structures, the Chinese script is much less convenient than a phonographic system when it comes to indexing and retrieving, such as in cataloging, dictionary compilation, etc., where the ordering of the writing symbols is involved. Indexing systems of Chinese are divided into the following four major types:

1. radical and stroke number system
2. beginning stroke system
3. four corner system
4. phonetization system

Type (1) is the time-honoured system that has been most extensively used. It is based upon the so-called *bùshǒu* 'radical', a term used to refer to the distinguishing component parts of characters on the basis of which characters are arranged. Characters containing the same radical are arranged together, which are further differentiated according to the number of strokes of the remaining part of the character. An alternative method is to group together characters with the same number of strokes, which are further differentiated on the basis of radicals. The problem with this indexing system is that dictionaries may differ with regard to the type of radicals and number of strokes. Take some most important Chinese dictionaries for illustration: radicals number 243 in *Kāngxī zìdiǎn*, 189 in *Xīnhuá zìdiǎn*, 188 in *Xiàndài Hànyǔ cídiǎn*, 250 in *Cíhǎi*, and 200 in *Hànyǔ dà zìdiǎn* and *Hànyǔ dà cídiǎn*. Characters grouped in one place in one dictionary may be scattered in another dictionary. Furthermore, in cases where a character contains several component parts each of which can be a radical by itself, dictionaries may differ with regard to which of them is taken for indexing. Furthermore, when a character does not have any part that is easily recognizable as a radical, arbitrariness is inevitable with regard to where it belongs in a dictionary. According to the statistics of Zhou Youguang (1992:181), of the 7,000 common characters in modern Chinese, about 10 per cent do not have a radical by which they can be readily arranged in a dictionary. Given such uncertainties, it is no wonder that there are scarcely two Chinese dictionaries which have exactly the same indexing of entries on the basis of the graphic structure.

Since strokes of a character are written in an orderly way, (2) arranges characters on the basis of their initial strokes, which fall into five to seven types. Characters with the same beginning stroke are ordered according to the number of strokes they have. As the number of characters beginning with the same stroke and with the same number of strokes may be very large, users have to spend quite some time before they locate the character in question.

Devised by Wang Yunwu in the 1920s, (3) is based upon the shape of the four corners of the tetralateral characters. A number is assigned to each of ten groups of distinctive shapes, which are differentiated along lines similar to the identification of radicals. Characters are arranged according to the four numbers that are assigned to them in this way. Some variant forms of the system have been derived from the original one which assign numbers to characters on the basis of the graphic shape in three corners instead of four, or on the basis of the graphic shape of the top and the bottom of character. The same remark on the uncertainty inherent in (1) applies to (3). Besides, users have to memorize the numbering method, which often differs from author to author, before they are able to use the indexing system with ease and convenience.

In (4), characters are arranged according to the order of the phonetic symbols that are used to transcribe or represent the characters, following the same principles as dictionaries in phonographic languages. In comparison with the other systems, this is the most efficient and convenient way to order characters. The only problem with this method is that users must first know the phonetic value of the character before they can locate it. Given the poor cues provided by the graphic shape as to the pronunciation of the character, that is on many occasions precisely the information that users are looking for when they consult a dictionary.

The deficiencies of the Chinese script become even more apparent and serious in the present-day information age with its widespread use of computers and communication networks. The input and output facilities of the computer as we know it today best suit the phonographic writing that makes use of a relatively small number of basic units which are combined in a systematic way to represent the language. Near the end of the 1980s there were more than 700 input schemes for the Chinese script, which testifies to the tremendous amount of effort that has gone towards solving the problem. In spite of all the time and money invested in the endeavour, we have yet to see a scheme that is truly satisfactory and widely adopted.

The inconvenience of the script has imposed severe restrictions on the use of Chinese in computer network communication (see Mair 1991). Although one can read Chinese on the Internet with the help of some software packages, English is still much more convenient to use than Chinese in computer communication, mainly owing to the inefficiency of the traditional Chinese writing system in encoding and decoding. The working language of CHINESE, an Internet discussion group dedicated to the promotion of communication among teachers, researchers, and students of the Chinese language, ironically, is English rather than Chinese. To the dismay of many, the overwhelming majority of private communications in the Internet among native speakers of Chinese, both in China and in the English-speaking world, are conducted in English. Coupled with other factors, the ever-increasing popularity of information retrieval and exchange via the Internet is prompting a large number of people in China, particularly of the younger generation, to place a higher value on proficiency in English than in Chinese. The full impact of these trends upon the Chinese language, and Chinese culture in general, remains to be seen.

8.5.3   Contribution to dialectal diversity and the discrepancy between writing and speech

It is generally maintained that the logographicity of the script is a contributing factor to the dialectal diversity of the Chinese language. As characters have different phonetic values in different dialects, the writing system does not encourage the promotion of a spoken lingua franca among the speakers of dialects in the same way as a phonographic system does.

The traditional writing system, as discussed in detail earlier in this book, is an important factor underlying the discrepancy between writing and speech in Chinese. The fact that expressions which are unintelligible in speech due to excess homophony can be clearly differentiated in the traditional writing system is largely responsible for the inertia of Old Chinese in Modern Written Chinese, standing as it does in the way to the true uniformity of speech and writing. On the other hand, there are many expressions which are used in vernacular speech that have no appropriate characters to represent them, which is particularly the case with many Southern dialects, as discussed in Chapter 7. Many scholars maintain that the traditional logographic script fits best with *wényán*, and that it is not very compatible with an ideal vernacular written Chinese, which is only possible when encoded in a phonographic system (Qu 1931b; J. Li 1935; L. Wang 1940; K. Wang 1992).

8.6   Approaches to script reform

Script reform as an issue did not attract serious attention until after the Opium War, and gained momentum at the turn of the twentieth century. It was and has since been argued that the written language encoded in the traditional Chinese script is to a large extent responsible for the country's high illiteracy rate and poor performance in comparison with the Western countries, and stands as an impediment to the process of modernization.

Two main approaches have been pursued in order to address the problems of the traditional script. One is to simplify the script, and the other is to adopt a phonographic writing system that would play an auxiliary, supplementary, alternative, or superseding role in relation to the traditional system. Let us discuss the respective approaches in the following two chapters.

9.1   Approaches to simplification

Simplification of the traditional Chinese writing system proceeds mainly in two ways. One is through reduction of the number of strokes per character. This is effected when a component of a character is replaced by another with fewer strokes, or when the whole character is represented by one of its components, or replaced by a homophonous character that is simpler in terms of graphic structure.

The other approach to simplification is through the reduction of the number of characters in common use. When a character was used in different geographical places, through different times and for different purposes, it often underwent changes in its graphic shape, giving rise to variant forms of the same character, which are called *yìtǐzì* 'character in variant shape' in Chinese linguistics. The number of *yìtǐzì* accumulated in Chinese is huge, accounting for 40 per cent of the total characters in *Kāngxī zìdiǎn*. The writing system as a whole is simplified through choosing one of the variant forms of the same character, usually the one that is simplest in graphic structure, as the standard, and relegating all the others to disuse.

9.2   Simplification before the twentieth century

As two counteractive processes, complication and simplification have been at work throughout the evolution of Chinese script. The script passed through the process of complication more or less as a natural development in the course of being used in different times and places, and for increasingly complicated purposes. Simplification, on the other hand, was effected both as a result of a natural tendency towards ease of effort, and as an outcome of meticulous exercises of planning and implementation.

Characters displayed variation in graphic shape as early as in *jiǎgǔwén*. It is found that the same character may have as many as forty variant forms (Jiang 1987:227), which presumably represent forms used in different places and at different times. The same is true of the descendent *jīnwén*. In the Eastern Zhou period, when the central authority was relatively strong, there was an official in the central government whose main duties included promoting a standard writing system across the country. The weakening of the central authorities and the emergence of the many rival local powers in the following Western Zhou warring period was, not surprisingly, accompanied by greater diversity in the scripts used in various states. Indeed, a script prevalent in one state might have been hardly intelligible to people in another state.

The composition of characters of the *xíngshēng* category represents another major route to complication. The graphic structure was made more complex when another grapheme was added to the root grapheme as a phonetic or semantic determinative. As characters of the *xíngshēng* category proliferated, the Chinese script became increasingly complicated both in terms of the graphic structure of many characters, and in terms of the total number of characters in the system.

As noted in Chapter 5, it was the emperor Qin Shihuang who put an end to the diversity of script in different parts of the country. After unifying China by conquering all other rivals, one of the first things he set out to achieve was to the unify the writing system of the country by stipulating that the writing system used in the previous Qin state, *xiǎozhuàn*, be adopted as the standard system across the country, and by abolishing all the other variant scripts.

The establishment of a standard script did not prevent the existence of variant styles within the same system. As mentioned in Chapter 8, there was a so-called *lìshū*, which is the simplified form of *xiǎozhuàn*, that was used for informal purposes, Several other variant styles, most notably *cǎoshū* 'cursive script', *kǎishū*, and *xíngshū* 'running script', developed from *lìshū* after it replaced *xiǎozhuàn* as the formal style. While *kǎishū* later replaced *lìshū*, and became the standard up to the present times, *cǎoshū* and *xíngshū* have also been in continuous use for informal purposes, such as personal correspondence, diaries, or in the recording of popular literature.

It must be noted that, generally speaking, simplification was the mechanism underlying the succession of *xiǎozhuàn*, *lìshū*, and *kǎishū*, each of which was replaced by a style that was more simplified in graphic structure. Simplified variations appeared immediately after a certain style was established as the standard.

At the same time, the substitution of characters by homophonous ones was a common practice. Many words were represented by more than two distinct characters in classical literature, with some by as many as more than a dozen. Characters borrowed to replace homophonous ones were treated on a par with those used to represent words that had no ready representing characters. Described as *jiǎjiè* 'borrowing', the method stood as one of the six major ways in which characters were made and employed. Obviously, when a character might assume several diverse forms and a word might be represented by several distinct characters, there must have been rather loose criteria for defining correctness in the use of script.

The criteria tightened up at the beginning of the Tang dynasty, when serious attempts were made to establish and promote a standard writing system. Requirements that the standard style and the 'correct' characters be used on formal occasions, such as state examinations, and in official documentation became increasingly rigorous. Scholars would be penalized, sometimes quite severely, for using the simplified forms for formal purposes. The concept of correctness was further strengthened in the following Song dynasty when the newly invested printing technology made copies of books more easily available.

Styles other than the standard one were known by various names, such as *sútǐ, pòtǐ* 'broken style', *biétǐ* 'variant style', *èrtǐ* 'second style', etc., most carrying pejorative connotations. There was a great reduction in the substitution of homophonous characters, with most new instances found only in the handwriting of the poorly educated. The distinction between the 'correct' characters in the standard style and those in the vulgar, simplified style was strictly observed by the literati for more than 1,000 years, well into the twentieth century.

9.3   Simplification in the twentieth century

9.3.1   Before 1949

Starting from the second half of the nineteenth century, simplification of the writing system took on a new dimension as an essential part of an overall reform of the Chinese language. On the one hand, there was a growing consensus that the writing system constituted an obstacle to the achievement of a higher literacy rate. On the other hand, with the abolition of the state examination for bureaucratic appointments in 1905, and the ultimate overthrow of the imperial Qing dynasty in 1911, the aura surrounding the traditional writing system was greatly diminished, preparing the way for a more drastic reform of the script that would benefit the great mass of users.

The early stage of script reform in the final years of the Qing dynasty was marked by its high enthusiasm for phonetization of the script, in preference to the less radical approach of simplification. The prevailing feeling about the traditional script among language reformers around the turn of the twentieth century was that it was so incompatible with a modernizing China that it would be better to replace it with, or at least supplement it with, a phonographic writing system. About two decades passed before it was generally realized that replacement of the traditional writing system by a phonographic one was not achievable in the immediate future, if at all. Furthermore, phonetic writing was still considered by many scholars, including some proponents of phonetic writing, to be appropriate only for low-culture functions (He 1923). Close attention was then directed to simplification as a practical approach to the improvement of the traditional script.

Qian Xuantong (1923) published a most influential article which elaborated on the motivation and agenda for the reform of the script. He maintained that unless the traditional script underwent a revolution, universal education in China would be impossible. Neither would it be possible to have a uniform national language, or a fully developed written language which could be used as a convenient and effective medium for the new knowledge already shared by people in other countries. This, he argued, was because the Chinese script, as a moribund writing system, was ill equipped to encode expressions from everyday vernacular, or to express new concepts from other languages.

What he meant by revolution was phonetization. Qian Xuantong asserted that it was not only necessary, but also feasible to write the national language in a phonetic script. According to Qian, the Chinese script was actually only a step away from being phonetic at a certain stage of its development. The widespread use of the method of borrowing before the Song dynasty displayed an important feature characteristic of a phonetic script. If all words with the same sound had been represented by a single character, and characters of the *xíngshēng* category had done away with differentiating semantic components, Chinese would have had a phonetic script. Its failure to take this crucial step was attributed to the pedantry and stupidity of the literate elite.

It was suggested by Qian Xuantong (1923) that the traditional script should be replaced by a phonetic writing system within a decade. As characters still had to be used during the period, some improvements were highly desirable. Following were his main proposals:

1. to select from variant forms of character the one that has the most simple graphic structure;

2. to use characters with simple graphic structure to replace homophonous ones with a more complicated structure;

3. to use phonetic symbols for vernacular words that have no existing characters to represent them;

4. to write loan words from other languages in their original form;

5. to promote *zhùyīn zìmǔ*, a newly designed phonetic script, as an autonomous, bona fide writing system (see Chapter 10 for more details).

Qian's suggestion proved to be programmatic for all script reform since then, although of the above five proposals, only the first two have been implemented on a large scale. As discussed earlier, (1) and (2) had actually been the main methods adopted in the simplification of the traditional script for thousands of years. One year before, Qian Xuantong (1922) had analysed the simplified characters that were in popular use at that time. He found that about 70–80 per cent of them had been in use since the Song and Yuan dynasties. They fall into eight major groups according to the method of simplification:

1. deduction of most of the character strokes, leaving only an outline of the original shape, as 寿 *shòu* 'longevity' for 壽, and 关 *guān* 'close' for 關

2. adoption of the cursive form, as 东 *dōng* 'east' for 東, and 会 *huì* 'meeting' for 會

3. adoption of a portion of the original character, as 声 *shēng* 'sound' for 聲, and 条 *tiáo* 'note' for 條

4. replacement of a complicated part of the character by a simple part, as 观 *guān* 'look' for 觀, and 凤 *fèng* 'phoenix' for 鳳

5. adoption of a character's ancient form that is simpler in graphic structure, as 礼 *lǐ* 'ritual' for 禮, and 云 *yún* 'cloud' for 雲

6. replacement of the phonetic determinative with a simpler component with fewer strokes, as 远 *yuǎn* 'far' for 遠, and 灯 *dēng* 'lamp' for 燈

7. invention of a new character, as 灶 *zào* 'cooking stove' for 竈, and 响 *xiǎng* 'loud' for 響

8. replacement of the character with a homophonous one, as 姜 *jiāng* 'surname' for 薑 *jiāng* 'ginger', and 几 *jī* 'small table' for 幾 *jī* 'nearly'

On top of proposals to replace *wényán* by *báihuà* as the base of Modern Written Chinese, it was now suggested by Qian that formal recognition should be given to characters that had been simplified in these manners, which during the Ming and Qing dynasties were forbidden by official institutions, despised by the literati, and confined to informal and low-culture uses. The simplified characters, Qian proposed, should not be treated as belonging to the so-called broken style, but rather to an improved style that should be formally used in all writings for educational, literary, academic, and administrative purposes.

Qian's proposal received warm response among fellow language reformers like Hu Shi, Li Jinxi, Zhou Zuoren, and He Zhongying (He 1923; S. Hu 1923; J. Li 1923; Z. R. Zhou 1923). In 1930, Liu Fu and Li Jiarui published *Sòng-Yuán yǐlái súzìpǔ* (*A glossary of popular Chinese characters since Song and Yuan dynasties*), which contained 6,240 simplified characters that were used in twelve publications in the Song, Yuan, Ming, and Qing dynasties. The glossary served as an important database from which simplified characters were selected for official recognition. In 1935, a glossary of simplified characters was compiled under the leadership of Qian Xuantong, which included about 2,400 simplified characters. In the same year, a dozen or so journals decided to adopt more than 300 simplified characters in replacement of their traditional counterparts.

At the urging of language reformers in the educational and cultural fields, the Ministry of Education of the Nationalist Government in August, 1935 promulgated The First List of Simplified Characters containing 324 simplified characters, which were to be promoted in schools and used in all publications. However, it was repealed six months later, reportedly due to the fierce opposition of some high-ranking officials in the government.[1]

9.3.2   **After 1949**

Large-scale script reform was resumed after the founding of the People's Republic of China. Among the first major steps taken by language planning institutions were the reduction of the number of characters in variant forms, and the promulgation of simplified characters for official use. The first list of characters in variant forms was published in December 1955, and included the most commonly used variant forms in contemporary writings. There were 810 groups of characters in variant forms in the list, each of which contained between two and six items. Of the variant forms in each group, only one was chosen as the standard, with all the others discarded as no longer usable. Altogether 1,053 characters were abolished in this exercise, mostly variants with the highest number of strokes and rare or obsolete forms (Y. G. Zhou 1992:168). As a result, the elimination of characters in variant forms achieved a dual goal. It made most of the characters involved easier to write, and also reduced the total number of characters in common use. In contrast to the controversy surrounding other aspects of script simplification, there seems to be general agreement that the reduction of the variant forms of characters represents a very positive achievement in script reform.

In 1956, the Scheme of Simplified Chinese Characters, known later as the First Scheme, was promulgated by the PRC government, and is composed of three lists. List 1 and List 2 contain 230 and 285 simplified characters respectively, representing 544 complicated ones, and List 3 is composed of 54 simplified basic components of characters, namely *piānpáng*. Most of the 230 simplified characters in List 1 had already been extensively used in mass media. It was announced that from the date of publication they were to replace their complicated counterparts as the standard form. The 285 simplified characters in List 2 and the 54 simplified basic components in List 3 were for trial use, and were formally accepted as the standard form in the following years. In 1964, a complete list of 2,236 simplified characters was published which comprised all the simplified characters from List 1 and List 2, as well as characters containing the simplified basic components from List 3.[2] The General List of Simplified Characters published in 1964 was re-published in 1986, involving minor changes to the 1964 version, which saw a few characters resume their complicated forms. Since the 1950s, simplified characters have been used in mainland China as the standard form. Except for special purposes or in such specialized areas as classic studies, all publications are in simplified script.

The adoption of the simplified characters as the standard form in 1955–6 proceeded with considerable care. A list of more than 500 simplified characters was prepared by the Ministry of Education in 1950 for widespread discussion. The Committee on Script Reform was set up in 1952, and approached the simplification of the script in connection with the other aspects of language reform, mainly the promotion of a national spoken standard, the standardization of Modern Written Chinese, and the design of a phonographic writing system. The draft of the First Scheme was completed towards the end of 1954; 300,000 copies were distributed to various sectors of society to solicit comments and suggestions. During this period, 141 simplified characters from the draft scheme were adopted by some print media for trial use. Apart from opposition from some prominent scholars, which included linguists, the responses were generally positive. According to a report (G. Ye 1955), before being submitted to the State Council for final approval, all the characters in the scheme went under close scrutiny by a special team composed of first-rate experts in the field. Having taken feedback from specialists and the general public into consideration, the team voted on the simplified characters and basic components on a case-by-case basis.

At the same time, it was announced that the First Scheme was to be followed by a series of schemes that would continue until all characters that 'needed to be simplified' had undergone the process. In 1964, several years after the promulgation of the First Scheme, the Central Government issued a directive for further simplification of characters. According to the directive, all characters in common use should have the number of strokes reduced to ten or less in order to facilitate the acquisition of literacy by school children and adults.

The Second Scheme of Simplified Chinese Characters was promulgated in December of 1977, and comprised 853 characters. The simplified characters under this scheme fall into two lists. List 1, comprising 248 characters, was put into formal use immediately at the time of publication, and List 2, comprising 605 characters, was for trial use only. Unlike the First Scheme, the Second Scheme was finalized with little input from outside the state language planning institution, and its promulgation was generally considered to be rash and ill-prepared, triggered by political considerations that ignored the need for meticulous planning and extensive consultation. It was reportedly engineered by a few staff members in the state language planning institution who were not qualified to deal with linguistic issues, and little advice was sought from senior experts on script reform or from the general public in the whole process (Y. G. Zhou 1992:172). As expected, the Second Scheme came under criticism immediately after publication, and was repealed in 1986 amid general disapproval. I will discuss this scheme shortly.

9.3.3   Principles underlying simplification

As simplification was never meant to provide a fundamental solution to the reputed problems of the Chinese script, all that was expected of it was that it should alleviate some of the difficulty associated with use of the traditional script, and, what is more important, that it should find ready acceptance by the general public.

The easiest way to achieve this goal was to examine the simplified characters that had already been in popular use for hundreds of years, and grant some of them the status of the standard form. This was essentially what Qian Xuantong did in 1935 when he prepared the list of simplified characters, part of which was accepted by the Nationalist government in the same year. According to official statement, three principles were followed by the Nationalist Government when it promulgated the First List of Simplified Characters in 1935. First, all the simplified characters granted the status of standard had to be already in widespread use among the masses. There would be no recognition of newly simplified characters. Second, only those in most popular use were selected. Third, characters that were already quite simple in graphic shape would not be further simplified.

The 1956 scheme was drafted following basically the same principles, the only difference being that, rather than consisting exclusively of simplified characters in popular use, it also contained a few simplified forms that were newly designed. Generally speaking, characters in the First Scheme fall into several major categories according to which method of simplification is adopted in the process (Y. Fu 1980; Y. G. Zhou 1992:166):

1. complicated characters are replaced by ones with fewer strokes, which may have already been in popular use for informal purposes or may be adapted from the cursive style of the characters;

2. complicated characters are replaced by homophones or near homophones that have fewer strokes;

3. complicated characters are replaced by simplified ones that are newly invented, or that had previously been in limited use.

As will be discussed in detail later, the same set of principles underlay the preparation of the Second Scheme in 1977, only with more weighting given to (2) and (3) than was the case with the First Scheme.

9.4   **Gains and problems**

The main purpose of the First Scheme was to reduce the number of strokes of characters, particularly of those characters in common use. This goal was certainly achieved. Of the 544 characters that underwent simplification, the average number of strokes, 16.08, was reduced almost by half, scoring 8.17 strokes per characters (J. Wang 1995:148). Of the 2,236 simplified characters in the General List, the average number of strokes was reduced from 15.6 to 10.3. As most of the characters involved were commonly used ones, the average number of strokes of the 2,000 most commonly used characters was reduced from 11.2 to 9.8. A survey shows that the average number of strokes of characters used in 100 newspaper editorials was reduced from 9.15 to 7.67 (Y. G. Zhou 1992:168).

Given the fact that 90 per cent of the simplified characters in the First Scheme had already been in popular use for a long time, the promulgation did nothing more than grant official recognition to conventional practices. There is evidence which demonstrates that simplification has gone some way towards comprehensively alleviating the burden of the script's learners and users. It has been established through comparative studies that it is easier for adults to acquire literacy in the simplified script than in the complicated script. It is also much easier for school children to learn to read and write simplified characters. It seems to be a safe assumption that, generally speaking, the simplification of script in the First Scheme has made characters easier to read, write, and recognize on paper and computer screen.

On the other hand, the reform has given rise to some problems. It is the stated aim of script reform to make the script easier to learn, easier to read, easier to write, easier to translate into and from other languages on modern topics and discourse, easier to reproduce by modern printing techniques, and easier to use with computers, etc. As noted in the literature, however, these goals may conflict.

When some simplified characters become easier to learn and write, they may not necessarily be easier to recognize. An ideal writing system has to strike a balance between the legibility and distinctiveness of its basic symbols. It is sometimes maintained that the fewer strokes characters have, the more legible they become. This, obviously, is true only up to a certain point. Characters may become less differentiated from each other as a result of simplification of their graphic structure. Examples are 设 *shè* 'instal' and 没 *méi* 'have not'; 儿 *ér* 'son' and 几 *jǐ* 'several'; and 凤 *fèng* 'phoenix' and 风 *fēng* 'wind'. Readers like myself often pause at these characters to make sure not to take one for the other.

Furthermore, some of the simplified characters offer even fewer cues to their phonetic value than their complicated counterparts. As far as the characters of the *xíngshēng* category that underwent simplification in the First Scheme are concerned, the sound-indicating value of the phonetic determinatives decreased from 0.598 to 0.324 (Shi 1983, 1988:178), which makes these characters more prone to mispronunciation. Related to the decrease in the sound-indicating value due to disruption of the component structure is the increase in the number of symbolic marks. As they are unmotivated, arbitrary symbols that have no recognizable phonetic or semantic value, they are more difficult to memorize than the other types of character components such as phonetic and semantic determinatives. Of the characters involved in the First Scheme, there are 213 which contain symbolic marks before simplification, accounting for 44 per cent of all characters of a composite structure. The number increases to 262 after the simplification, accounting for 60 per cent of the characters at issue. Obviously, the reduction in number of strokes is achieved, in some cases, at the expense of the graphic structure of the characters, making the simplified characters even less predictable in terms of sound and meaning than the complicated ones.

Aside from disagreements stemming from technical considerations involving particular characters, the strongest argument against the simplification of characters is based upon the assertion that it plays a divisive role between past and present, and between mainland China and the other Chinese-speaking communities. It is argued that, since almost all publications before 1956, as well as those from outside mainland Chinese, are in the complicated script, simplification hinders easy access to writings from different times and places.

Arguments along these lines, which virtually repudiate simplification as a viable approach to script reform, hardly stand close scrutiny. As noted earlier, the great majority of the simplified characters in the First Scheme were already quite familiar to general users before they were sanctioned and promoted by language planners in 1956. While it takes some time for people trained in simplified script to learn to write in the complicated one, a reading knowledge of the other type of script is very easy to acquire. Publications printed in simplified script in mainland China sell in Hong Kong, and other Chinese communities. In correspondence between people from mainland China and elsewhere, handwritten characters in different styles are rarely reported to cause any problems in comprehension. As will be discussed below, many of the simplified characters promulgated on the mainland in 1956 were also officially adopted as the standard form in handwriting in Taiwan in 1986 (Luo 1990). When readers who were taught simplified characters in school do not understand classic works in Old Chinese, it is not so much because they do not recognize the characters in their complicated form, but because they are unfamiliar with the lexicon and grammar characteristic of Old Chinese. Difficulties in comprehension due to the differences between the complicated and the simplified characters have been exaggerated.

9.5   **Objections to the Second Scheme**

The failure of the Second Scheme to win widespread support, according to Zhou Youguang (1992), is attributable to two main factors. First, although almost all of the simplified characters in the scheme were gathered from a wide cross-section of users with little innovation on the part of language planners, most of them had been confined to certain geographical areas or to certain sectors of society, or were in use for a limited period of time only. In other words, they were not yet popular enough to be regarded as the conventional simplified forms of the characters involved. The general public found it difficult to accept so many unfamiliar simplified characters. Second, the introduction of such large-scale simplification at the end of the tumultuous decade of the Cultural Revolution was ill-timed. The experience of those years had left the population with a strong aversion to any radical change, including change in linguistic matters.

The failure, I believe, also reflects a fundamental flaw in the guiding principles on script simplification that were formulated in the 1950s and followed in the 1960s and 1970s. According to the original agenda, all characters in common use were gradually to undergo simplification until none of them had more than ten strokes. This goal was set without due consideration of two conflicting features of a writing system, ease of production and ease of recognition. While the former demands minimum differentiation in graphic shape, the latter demands maximum differentiation. When a reduction in the number of strokes makes characters easier to write, it may also make them less differentiated from each other, and thus less easy to recognize. An effective writing system has to strike a balance between the two. Furthermore, as established repeatedly in the literature, the length of a word correlates with the frequency of use, with the most frequently used words tending to be the shortest. In Chinese, the higher the frequency of characters, the lower the average number of strokes tends to be. Wang Fengyang (1992) demonstrates how incidence and the average number of strokes of characters used in *Analects* are correlated, as shown in Table 9.1. Table 9.1 demonstrates that, as is the case with other writing systems, some natural balance is struck in Chinese between frequency and graphic simplicity, with characters in most frequent use simplest in terms of number of strokes.

The plan to reduce the number of strokes of characters in common use to ten or less was ill-founded on two related accounts. First, it fails to recognize that, should most characters in Modern Chinese have fewer than ten strokes, it would be easier for writers, but more difficult for readers. While 65 per cent of the characters that underwent simplification in the First Scheme had fourteen strokes or more, the main target of simplification in the Second Scheme was characters of thirteen strokes or fewer, which accounted for 59 per cent of the characters involved. As a

Table 9.1 Correlation between incidence and average number of strokes of characters used in *Analects*

Incidence	Number of characters	Average number of strokes
500+	4	3.8
100+	24	7.5
50+	27	8.6
40+	18	8.7
30+	16	8.9
20+	39	8.7
10+	129	9.0
5+	202	10.2
4−	923	11.3

result, it effected a substantial increase in the number of characters that were very simple in graphic shape, but were easily confused with each other. Examples are 忑 *gǎn* 'feel' and 忎 *yú* 'stupid', and 亍 *shì* 'thing' and 亐 *gāo* 'tall'.

Second, it fails to pay due recognition to the correlation between frequency of occurrence and average number of strokes. Large-scale simplification of characters with relative low frequency would result in less differentiation within the writing system, without providing any real benefits to writers. As many as 4,500 characters were included in the group of characters in common use which were targeted for simplification in the preparation of the Second Scheme (J. Wang 1995:154). Given the fact that the most common 2,400 characters cover 99 per cent of characters used in modern writings (cf. Table 8.2), there are many items in the Second Scheme that might just as well have been left unsimplified. While 70 per cent of the characters in the First Scheme fell within the range of the 2,000 characters in most frequent use, only 44 per cent in the Second Scheme belonged to this category. There were some simplified characters in the Second Scheme which are very rarely used, with some not even included in dictionaries like *Xīnhuá zìdiǎn*. Although the Second Scheme simplified almost as many characters as the First Scheme, the supposed resultant ease of writing on the part of ordinary users was not as obvious. According to Wang Fengyang (1992:632), the ratio of occurrence in contemporary texts of simplified characters from the First Scheme vs. those from the Second Scheme is 2.8 to 1 in terms of the frequency of character type, and 3.8 to 1 in terms of the frequency of character token. It is also established in Wang Fengyang (1992) that, with regard to the simplified characters in the texts under survey, the average number of strokes per character is reduced by 4.7 for those in the First Scheme, but only by 1 for those in the Second Scheme. This suggests that while the hundreds of simplified characters introduced by the Second Scheme reduced graphic differentiation of the writing system as a whole, benefits for writers were limited because of the relatively low frequency of the characters involved.

9.6   Simplification of script outside mainland China

Simplified characters are not confined to mainland China. After the Nationalist Government moved to Taiwan in 1949, reform of the script through simplification was put back on the agenda of language planning institutions. A resolution was passed by the Legislative Council of the Taiwan Province in 1950 that requested the government to sanction the use of simplified characters on the recommendation of linguistic experts. In 1953 the Ministry of Education also set up a special committee to research the simplification of characters.

Enthusiasm on the island, however, waned drastically as simplification reached full swing on the mainland. In 1956, the same year that simplified characters were formally recognized and promoted in mainland China, the Ministry of Education in Taiwan issued a directive that forbade the use of simplified characters, in order to counteract the 'vandalism of the Communists on the mainland in destroying the traditional script though the promotion of simplified characters' (Fang 1969; B. Zhang 1974). Thus, the simplification of characters became a sensitive political issue in Taiwan (also see L. Chen et al. 1985). The subject was raised again in the late 1960s, with calls for further research into the feasibility of adopting simplified characters. While in actuality a large number of simplified characters have been extensively used in Taiwan, mostly for informal purposes, the language planning institution has maintained its prohibitive stance on the use of simplified characters in publications. *Standard forms of characters in running script* was published in 1980, which was meant to provide the standard graphic form for use in handwriting. Of the 4,010 characters contained in the list, about 1,580 are in simplified form, with about two thirds adopting the same or almost the same graphic shape as the corresponding simplified characters of the mainland. The most obvious difference between Taiwan and mainland China on the issue of simplification of characters is that simplified characters are used in Taiwan mainly in handwriting and seldom in print, whereas on the mainland they are used both in print and in handwriting. Recently, the two sides have made some joint efforts to explore the possibility of unifying the script (Fei 1993). It is anticipated that, if the two sides become closer economically and politically, it will not be long before the same standard in script is adopted in mainland China and Taiwan.

The complex script is the norm in Hong Kong, although simplified characters are popular in handwriting, and tacitly accepted by the Hong Kong Examinations Authority (Ben Kan 1982:2). Singapore, on the other hand, has followed mainland China in script simplification, stipulating in 1976 that a total of 2,238 simplified characters should replace the complicated ones as the standard form.

10.1   Efforts by Western missionaries

Although the 'Phags-pa script, created between 1260 and 1269 at the behest of the founding emperor of the Yuan dynasty, Yuan Shizu, was also used to transcribe Chinese and other languages, it was designed primarily for writing Mongolian. The first schemes specifically designed for the phonetization, or more specifically, romanization of Chinese were all developed by Western missionaries in China. Matteo Ricci, the Jesuit who went to China in 1583 from Italy, is generally believed to be the first person to design a systematic romanized writing for Chinese. His scheme was later modified by another Jesuit missionary in China, Nicolas Trigault. Basically, their schemes served two purposes, to transcribe Chinese proper names, and to help foreigners learn Chinese, in particular the Chinese characters. As recorded in the literature (DeFrancis 1950; J. Li 1935; Ni 1948a; 1948b; Y. G. Zhou 1979:19), quite a few dictionaries were compiled on the basis of these schemes for the convenience of missionaries.

Because of conflict between the Jesuits and the Imperial Court of the Qing Dynasty, the influence of Jesuits in China in the eighteenth century was reduced to a minimum. As a consequence, the romanization of Chinese that they had initiated lay dormant for nearly a century, and was not revived until the early 1800s. The British Protestant missionary Robert Morrison (1782–1834) published a dictionary during 1815–23, in which he introduced a romanization system that he had designed for Mandarin Chinese. After 1840, similar schemes were designed for almost all of the important dialects of Chinese, mainly for the purpose of replacing characters as a bona fide writing system in the translation of the Bible, and for other communicative purposes. Known as *jiàohuì luómǎzì* 'romanized script by the missionary', these schemes were quite influential both in their time and in the years to come. At least seventeen dialects had their own romanized writing systems, and about 137,000 copies of the Bible printed in romanization were sold between 1891 and 1904 (Ni 1948a:18). Although, by the founding of the Republic of China in 1912, the use of these schemes as a regular writing system had declined in all but some isolated parts of China, their contribution to the movement for a phonographic system for Chinese should not be underestimated. They demonstrated, for the first time and on a large scale, that it was possible and feasible to write Chinese for regular purposes with a script other than characters, and to write on the basis of one's own dialect instead of Northern Mandarin. This provided much inspiration for endeavours to reform the Chinese script in the twentieth century, though these later attempts were mainly initiated by native Chinese, and were on a much larger scale, and with further-reaching consequences. As Ni Haishu (1948a:21) put it, 'the achievements of missionary romanization have been cited by almost every worker for the romanization of Chinese as strong evidence in favour of the use of phonetic systems in the promotion of education'.

10.2   Schemes proposed by native Chinese

The year 1892 marks the beginning of the era in which script reform became an integral part of the endeavour to rejuvenate and modernize China. It was then that Lu Zhuangzhang published a phonographic system that he had specifically designed for his native tongue, the dialect of Xiamen, a Southern Min dialect. His goal was clearly stated in the preface to his book:

> Chinese characters are probably the most difficult script in the world . . . I believe that the strength and prosperity of the country depends upon the physical sciences, which can grow and flourish only if all people – men and women, young and old – are eager to learn and sagacious. If they are to be eager to learn and sagacious, then the script needs to be phonetized in such a way that, after they have acquired the alphabet and the spelling, they will know how to read without further instruction. It also depends upon speech and writing being the same so that what is said by the mouth will be understood by the mind. Furthermore it depends upon having a simple script that is easy to learn and write. As a result, this will save more than ten years. If all that time is applied to the study of mathematics, physical sciences, chemistry, and other practical studies, how can there be any fear that our country will not be rich and strong?
>
> (Z. Z. Lu 1892:3)

In terms of the motivation and theoretical assumptions underlying the proposals, what was said in the preface summarizes nicely the features characteristic of Lu's scheme and the dozens of similar schemes proposed by his contemporaries and followers. First, most of the proponents maintained that, from the point of view of learners and users, the Chinese script is inferior to the phonographic writings of Western languages and Japanese, and should be replaced by a phonetic system, or at least supplemented by one. Second, it is obvious that all the proposals were motivated by a strong desire to contribute to the cause of modernizing the country, rather than being a purely intellectual exercise. As noted above, it was widely believed, but never proved, that the difficulty of the writing system was largely responsible for the high rate of illiteracy in China, which in turn accounted for the country's weakness and ineptitude in the face of foreign powers. Since Lu Zhuangzhang, these assumptions have been part of the foundation underlying the whole process of script reform.

This approach to script reform has formed an important part of intellectual life in China ever since, engaging the keenest attention of linguists, educators, and politicians. Roughly speaking, China's one hundred years of script reform via phonetic writing is divisible into four periods. During the first period from 1892, when Lu published his scheme, to 1911, thirty or so schemes of phonetization were proposed. The second period is represented by *zhùyīn zìmǔ*, designed in 1913 and published in 1918, which was the first phonetic writing of Chinese that won official acceptance. Eight years later, *Guóyǔ luómǎzì* was published, which was the most sophisticated though arguably over-complicated scheme of romanization to date. In 1929, *Latinxua sin wenz* was published. These two important schemes of romanization represent the third period of script reform. The fourth period starts with the beginning of the 1950s, when there was a tremendous upsurge of enthusiasm for the romanization of Chinese. In less than a decade, more than 1,000 schemes were submitted to the Committee on Script Reform in Beijing (Y. G. Zhou 1979:50). This enthusiasm showed no sign of abating even after the scheme *Hànyǔ pīnyīn* 'Chinese Phonetic Writing', or *pīnyīn*, was endorsed by the National People's Congress in 1958, and new schemes kept pouring in to the language planning institutions. Largely stimulated by the practical need to design computer input/output systems for the Chinese script, there has been a steady increase in new schemes during the past decade or so (Symposium 1988).

10.3   Groupings of schemes

The more than one thousand schemes of phonetic writing for Chinese that have been proposed during the past century differ mainly along five dimensions: (i) the intended role in relation to the traditional characters; (ii) the graphic form of the script; (iii) the dialect upon which the system is based; (iv) the way in which syllabic structure is represented; (v) the way in which tones are represented.

10.3.1   Intended roles in relation to the traditional characters

All schemes of phonetic writing have been conceived with the aim of tackling the problems that confront the learners and users of characters. The solutions differ with regard to the roles that are stipulated for the schemes in relation to the traditional script. In this regard, four distinct though closely related roles can be identified, namely auxiliary, supplementary, alternative, and superseding.

(1) Auxiliary
A phonetic writing that is intended only to play an auxiliary role is not meant to be a writing system in the strict sense of the word. It does not affect the status of the character script as a writing system. It is merely used to facilitate the learning and use of characters, serving such functions as annotating the pronunciation of characters, transcription, indexing, etc.

The usefulness of an auxiliary phonetic writing, if well designed and promoted, is indisputable. Since such a writing system does not threaten the status quo of the established one, there is usually little resistance to the design and promotion of the system other than on the technical grounds of script form, dialectal base, and the representation of the syllabic structures of characters, etc.

(2) Supplementary
A supplementary phonetic writing is intended to be used together with characters in all situations that characters are used. The phonetic symbols are either used in juxtaposition with characters, creating a new type of symbols that are composed of two parts, i.e., the character and

phonetic symbols that annotate its sound. Or they are used to replace characters in some parts of the text, resulting in a mixed writing system, as we have witnessed for Japanese, where kanji, kana (hiragana and katakana), and romaji can be found together in the same text. The phonetic writing which is assigned a supplementary role is bound to have a considerable effect upon the character script, either substituting a new type of composite symbols for the traditional characters, or reducing the number of characters normally used in writings by customarily encoding some of the words or morphemes with the phonetic symbols. A well-known example of such a supplementary phonetic writing is the Japanese kana.

(3) Alternative

An alternative phonetic writing is one that can properly fulfil the basic functions that are performed by the character script as a writing system. Rather than initiate any change into the logographic writing per se, it takes over some of its functions. More often than not, there is a division of labour between two kinds of autonomous writing systems. One is used for low-level practical purposes in everyday life, while the other for more formal occasions, such as for literary, legal, and academic purposes. If put in place, the two writings would constitute what is known in the linguistic literature as digraphia (Dale 1980; DeFrancis 1984a, and also see Chapter 7). Such a role was intended for most of the schemes of phonetic writing proposed during the past century, although few actually succeeded in attaining that goal, as we will discuss in detail later.

(4) Superseding

A phonetic writing of this type is designed to supersede the logographic system, forcing it into disuse and oblivion, as Quoc Ngu and Hangul did to Chinese characters in Vietnamese and Korean (partially in South Korea and completely in North Korea) respectively. Proponents of a superseding phonetic writing hold the most radical view towards Chinese characters. It is argued that characters are irremediable, and the best way to solve the problems associated with their learning and use is to replace them by a phonographic system that would better meet the needs of a modernizing society. As we will see later, some of the proposed schemes, notably *latinxua sin wenz*, were intended to play exactly such a role.

10.3.2   **Form of script**

The graphic forms of the proposed schemes fall into three major categories: shorthand-style scripts, kana-style scripts, and the roman alphabet.

(1) Shorthand-style scripts

Schemes adopting scripts modelled after shorthand symbols were mainly proposed during the first period from 1892 to 1912. As reported by Zhou Youguang (1979), of the thirty or so popular schemes of this period, five adopted such scripts, although this type fell out of favour with later designers.

(2) Kana-style scripts or characters

The fact that Japanese kana symbols are adapted forms of Chinese characters used purely as phonetic symbols has lent much inspiration to designers of phonetic writing for Chinese, especially during the first and the second period. Most of the schemes proposed during this time were designed after the pattern of kana. Sets of phonetic symbols were proposed which were either based upon existing Chinese characters or their components, or were completely new creations. As reported in Ni (1948a) and Y. G. Zhou (1979), twenty-four of the thirty schemes in the first period adopted this form of script, constituting the mainstream of this period. It culminated in *zhùyīn zìmǔ*, the first phonetic script promulgated by the central government. We will discuss this scheme in more detail later.

In addition, there were some schemes that retained Chinese characters as the basic symbols of the script, but used them largely as phonetic symbols that represent the syllables in the language. Examples are the *yīnbiǎozì* 'phonetic characters' proposed by Zhai Jiaxiong in the mid-1930s, which contained 454 characters that were meant to represent all the Chinese syllables without tonal differentiation, and the scheme proposed by Zhang Gonghui in 1947 which comprised two syllabaries, one with more than 1,000 characters representing all the tonal syllables, and the other with more than 400 characters for non-tonal syllables. The most influential representative of this category is the system of General Chinese Characters (GCC) or, *tōngzì*, proposed by the eminent Chinese linguist Chao Yuen Ren in Chao (1976). *Tōngzì* is based upon a phonological system of Chinese that is a kind of lowest common denominator between the major dialects. Roughly speaking, the phonemic syllables in *tōngzì* comprise the main features of the initial consonants of the Wu dialects, the vowels of Mandarin, and the endings of Cantonese, totalling 2,082 in number. Each syllable is represented by a unique character, which in about 80 per cent of cases may represent a group of regular characters that are etymologically related, hence the name *tōngzì* 'General Chinese character'. Only in about 20 per cent of cases do characters represent homophonous morphemes which are not etymologically related. *Tōngzì* was designed to write Chinese in general, both classical Chinese and modern dialects, and without limitation in style or vocabulary.[1]

(3) The roman alphabet

In comparison, schemes using the roman alphabet were a late development. The first full-scale scheme in this category is represented by Zhu Wenxiong's *Jiāngsū xīn zìmǔ* 'new alphabet of Jiangsu', which appeared in 1906. With the mainstream of schemes during the first and the second period in favour of a kana-style script, romanization did not become a serious contender until near the beginning of the 1920s, but has been the most popular form since then. The most influential ones in this category are *guóyǔ luómǎzì* (proposed in 1926), *latinxua sin wenz* (1929), and *pīnyīn* (1958). These schemes will be discussed in detail later.

There have been two major factors at work in the choice of script form. One is the technical advantages of the script in terms of ease of learning and efficiency of use. The other is how it appeals to the nationalistic sentiment that has traditionally attached itself to the Chinese characters, not necessarily among Western-minded Chinese scholars, but certainly among the general public in China. These two factors may stand in conflict when it comes to the selection of a particular form of script.

Shorthand-style scripts score low on both criteria. The shorthand-style forms are easy to write, but not easy to read, because they are typically comprised of symbols that are not sufficiently differentiated to ensure speedy and unambiguous recognition, and this was soon realized among the designers. For similar views with reference to English, see Sampson (1985). Furthermore, bearing little resemblance to characters, they do not enjoy the reverence that is accorded to the traditional script. Phonetic writings of this category may serve an auxiliary role of subservience to the character script, but they fall well short of the qualifications of a bona fide writing system. Very few of the proposals that were raised after the first period advocated this type of script.

The real competition is between the character-based type, especially those formed after the pattern of kana, and the romanized type.

During the early period, it was the nationalistic affection for the traditional script that prevailed over technical considerations in choice of script form. As characters were regarded by some as an inextricable part of the Chinese language, and Chinese culture for that matter, it was believed, and is still believed by many people that, if the Chinese language is to adopt a phonographic writing system to replace or supplement the logographic one, the basic symbols of the new writing should at least be created from the traditional stock of characters.

As discussed above, some schemes simply adopt regular characters as the basic symbols of the phonetic writing, each representing a single syllable. The major difference between such schemes and the traditional writing is that there are many more phonetic loans in the former than in the latter. To reduce homophony, some schemes introduce distinctions from non-Beijing dialects into the syllabary, resulting in a richer ratio of characters to syllables. *Tōngzì* is such a scheme. As the characters that are retained in such schemes are all traditional ones so far as the graphic shape is concerned, they enjoy whatever reverence has been accorded to the traditional script. Also, because students only have to grapple with around 400–2,000 characters, depending upon which scheme is adopted, instead of the more than 3,000 required for full proficiency in the regular writing system, it alleviates the burden on learners and users.

Schemes of this category, however, have serious shortcomings that prevent them from being accepted beyond a small circle. Obviously, they only alleviate, to some extent, the difficulties encountered by learners and users of characters, rather than provide a thorough solution to the fundamental problems. Furthermore, potential ambiguity poses a serious problem for schemes of this type. While in most cases the characters can be used as pure phonetic symbols without incurring the danger of ambiguity, there are also quite a few cases where the original meanings of the characters used for their phonetic values may persist, engendering meanings that are not intended. Given the logographic nature that has been characteristic of the Chinese script for thousands of years, it is hard for Chinese readers not to 'read into characters'. Also, given the heavy functional load of syllables in Chinese as discussed earlier, it may not always be easy for readers to identify the writer's intended meaning from the whole range of homophonous morphemes that a single character, now employed as a pure phonetic symbol, represents. This probably explains why only a very tiny portion of the proposed schemes advocate this type of all-character script.

To the extent that the kana-type script resembles the graphic shape of the traditional Chinese characters, it is superior to the romanized script in terms of its nationalistic appeal. As the kana-type symbols are not conventional characters either, they serve better as phonetic symbols, being free from the semantic meaning that has been associated with logographic characters.

In comparison with kana-type symbols, on the other hand, the roman alphabet scores higher in terms of technical convenience and efficiency. It is economical in terms of the number of basic symbols, and it is easy to memorize as the letters have already been in common use in the everyday life. As the most widely used script at the international level, it serves Chinese better in relating to the world. The romanized script normally represents the language in a phonemic manner, which is more precise and flexible than the semi-phonemic and semi-syllabic representation that is typically adopted by a kana-type script. Furthermore, the roman letters are easier to write, as the ending strokes easily lead to the beginning strokes of the following letters, and easy to recognize. In comparison, kana-type letters, like those in *zhùyīn zìmǔ*, are less differentiated than roman letters in terms of graphic shape, and are more prone to confusion in handwriting. Also, based upon characters, typical kana-type symbols still preserve the visually solitary shape, making it less easy to mark word boundaries in text. What is more, only a language with a very simple syllable structure, such as Japanese, is suitable for such a script.

It took several decades for technical efficiency to become the more important factor in the choice of script form. Since the 1930s, the roman alphabet has become the mainstream type of script, having been adopted in all the important schemes like *guóyǔ luómǎzì, latinxua sin wenz*, and *pīnyīn*. However, this does not mean that there is no resistance to this script. The roman alphabet is a foreign script both in origin and graphic form. It does not appeal to those who insist that a phonetic Chinese script should draw upon indigenous resources rather than borrow from the outside. Views like this have often struck a sympathetic chord with nationalistic-minded Chinese of the twentieth century. A good example is Mao Zedong, who, while endorsing the phonetization of the Chinese writing system with enthusiasm, insisted in the early 1950s that it should be national in form, and should be elaborated on the basis of the existing Chinese characters. In the explanatory note that accompanied the introduction of the romanized *pīnyīn* in 1956, there was a whole section devoted to the justification of adopting this non-Chinese script for the new phonetic writing. While there is no denying that technical efficiency has prevailed over nationalistic sentiment in the mainstream of script reform, the view in favour of a native script for the phonetic writing of Chinese is far from being abandoned in Chinese communities. The kana-type *zhùyīn zìmǔ* is still the normal phonetic script used in Taiwan, rather than the roman-based *guóyǔ luómǎzì* that was promulgated by the same government. It appears that the tension between technical efficiency and nationalistic sentiment will remain an issue in the field for many years to come.

10.3.3 Dialectal basis

As discussed earlier, in relation to dialects, Chinese characters function somewhat like algebraic symbols, which can be realized by different though systematically related phonetic values by speakers of different dialects. In designing a phonetic writing for Chinese, the issue naturally arises as to what particular phonological system of Chinese is to be represented.

As regards the dialectal basis, schemes of phonetic writing of Chinese that have been proposed so far fall into two major groups, those that are non-dialect specific, or inter-dialectal, and those that are dialect-specific.

(1) Non-dialect specific

Some romanized schemes are designed to serve as the writing system of all Chinese dialects, playing basically the same role as the traditional Chinese script, but, in theory at least, without the problems associated with characters. Such a writing system is possible in principle, by virtue of the fact that almost all the modern dialects of Chinese can be traced to the phonological system of Medieval Chinese as represented in *Qièyùn* (see Chapter 2). It can be demonstrated that the modern dialects were derived from the *Qièyùn* system by means of systematic phonological rules that relate particular phonemes and tonemes in the former to the corresponding segments in the latter. The differences between dialects are manifested in terms of the different phonological rules that were operative in the course of derivation. Instead of being based on any particular modern dialect, an inter-dialectal phonetic writing typically represents an approximation of the phonological system of *Qièyùn*. Speakers of modern dialects arrive at the specific pronunciation in the particular dialect by applying to the word a set of phonological rules equivalent to those operative in the historical derivation of the word from the *Qièyùn* system. In other words, the same set of phonological rules that operated diachronically is meant to work synchronically to derive the specific pronunciation of the word forms in the modern dialect.

The first scheme in this category is called *La romanisation inter-dialectique* 'The interdialectic romanization', proposed by the Catholic priests Henri Lamasse and Ernest Jasmin in 1931–2 (L. Wang 1940:363; Y. G. Zhou 1979:24). Based upon the pronunciation of Chinese as represented in *Qièyùn*, it is meant to be realized differently in different dialects. Chinese linguists Wang Li (1940) and Chao Yuen Ren (1976) each designed systems based on roughly the same principle. Wang's was called *wényán luómǎzì* 'Classical literary Chinese romanization', and was intended mainly to encode Old Chinese rather than Modern Chinese. Chao's system was called General Chinese Romanization, and, as a romanized form of *tōngzì*, was intended be to a full-scale writing system suitable for all dialects and for all literary styles (see Chao 1976).

(2) Dialect-specific

The great majority of the proposed schemes are dialect-specific, either representing the phonology of a single dialect, or based mainly upon one dialect while incorporating a few features from other dialects.

Along the same line as pursued by the missionaries in the nineteenth century, most of the schemes proposed by native Chinese over the two decades after Lu Zhuangzhang (1892) were based upon non-Mandarin dialects. Among the dialects represented in this way are Southern Min, Cantonese, and Wu (Ni 1948a; 1948b; Y. G. Zhou 1979). Concomitant with the advocacy of *guóyǔ*, the trend moved towards taking Northern Mandarin, especially the Beijing dialect, as the basis of romanization. As discussed in detail in Chapter 2, starting from 1913, serious attempts were made to decide upon a standard pronunciation of *guóyǔ* on a character-by-character basis. Several prominent romanization schemes proposed since then, including *zhùyīn zìmǔ*, *guóyǔ luómǎzì*, and *pīnyīn*, were designed to represent the newly established Modern Standard Chinese.

On the other hand, the idea of basing the phonetic writing of Chinese on a single dialect, or on Modern Standard Chinese, was explicitly rejected by proponents of *latinxua sin wenz* in favour of separate romanizations for each of the major dialects in China. Full-scale *latinxua sin wenz* schemes were proposed for the major dialects.

In spite of their theoretical soundness, all schemes of interdialectical romanization have had very little impact beyond a small group of linguistic experts. They are hardly learned by anyone and little known outside a narrow academic circle. Most academics consider the creation of such schemes to be more of an intellectual exercise in historical phonology, than an activity that has any practical applications. The reason for the lack of success, as I see it, lies in the fact that while such systems have lost most of the disambiguating power of the logographic script, the way in which they encode phonological information does not represent any significant compensatory gain. As the basic symbols in such a system are supposed to represent pure phonetic value, the ease of recognition afforded by the logographic system with its distinct graphic forms for homophonous morphemes is lost. On the other hand, as the 'phonographic' symbols are quite removed from the actual pronunciations in any of the Chinese dialects, it demands a lot of effort on the part of users before they can establish the correspondences between the graphemes and their speech.

In more serious contention are the two mutually opposing approaches: those advocating a single phonographic system for the standard Modern Spoken Chinese and those arguing for separate systems for different dialects. The former are represented by proponents of *zhùyīn zìmǔ*, *guóyǔ luómǎzì*, and *pīnyīn*, and the latter by the missionaries, by proponents of a large portion of the phonetic scripts before *zhùyīn zìmǔ*, and by proponents of *latinxua sin wenz*. The controversy between the two groups is essentially a matter of whether to assign primacy to the standardization of the Chinese language for the whole Chinese community, as emphasized by the former group, or to assign primacy to easy access to literacy, especially on the part of native speakers of dialects other than Northern Mandarin, as maintained by the latter group. For a detailed analysis, see Chapter 7.

It seems then that whatever approach is adopted with regard to the dialectal base of romanization, it will be weighted against the speakers of Southern dialects. Either they have to work harder to learn a phonographic writing system that is removed from their own speech, or they will achieve literacy in a writing that is little used beyond their own dialectal areas. The difficult in learning the standard phonographic writing based upon Northern Mandarin is relieved only if the speakers of Southern dialects become truly bilingual, speaking Northern Mandarin in addition to their own dialect.

10.3.4   **Representation of syllabic structure**

Phonographic schemes differ with regard to the manner in which the segmental structure of syllables is represented. They fall into three major groups, namely, syllabic, syllabo-phonemic, and phonemic.

(1) Syllabic

One symbol is used to represent a whole syllable as do characters in the traditional script. All schemes comprising characters used as purely phonetic symbols belong to this category, such as those proposed by Zhai Jiaxiong, Zhang Gonghui, and Chao Yuen Ren (1976) that were discussed earlier.

(2) Syllabo-phonemic

Two or three phonetic symbols are used to represent the syllabic structure of the character, some encoding phonemes and some encoding syllables. Schemes using two symbols are known as *shuāngpīn* 'double spelling', and those using three as *sānpīn* 'triple spelling'. Schemes of double spelling may use one symbol for the initial, representing a phoneme, and the other for the final, representing a syllable. Alternatively, they may use one symbol for the initial and the medial, when there is one, and the other for the remaining part of the final. With schemes of triple spelling, the medial is always represented by a separate symbol, with the initial and the remaining part of the final represented by the other two respectively. Almost all the schemes adopting a kana-type script represent the syllabic structure in this syllabo-phonemic fashion.

(3) Phonemic
Each segment is represented by one symbol. The majority of the romanized schemes adopt this method of representation.

The syllabic representation found little favour in script reform, mainly for the reason that more than 400 distinct phonetic symbols are needed in such a writing system, making it clumsy in comparison to the other types. The main choice has been between syllabo-phonemic and phonemic representation.

The syllabo-phonemic method of representation relates closely to an age-long linguistic tradition in which the phonetic value of a character is indicated by two other characters according to the so-called *fǎnqiè* method: one character having the same initial as the character in question, and the second having the same final and tone. It is as if one were to indicate the pronunciation of the word 'pie' by (*p*)ea and m(*y*). However, in the case of this type of phonetic writing, pure phonetic symbols are used instead of characters. A feature of the syllabo-phonemic method of representation is that, although it needs more distinct letters than the phonemic system, the average length of the written word is shorter in the former than in the latter.

The phonemic representation reflects a more sophisticated analysis of the syllabic structure. In comparison with the syllabo-phonemic system, it is characterized by two features that make it decidedly preferable over most phonetic writings. First, it employs a smaller inventory of phonetic letters. Second, it is capable of representing a greater variety of syllabic types, and thus is better suited to many functions that the phonographic system is expected to serve, such as transcribing from other dialects or languages.

10.3.5   **Representation of tones**
Schemes also differ with regard to whether tones of syllable are marked or not, and how they are marked. Differentiation of homophones is the major consideration in favour of indicating tones, since without tone marks, homophonous words will make up one third of the vocabulary in Modern Chinese. Those who have dispensed with tone marks in their

schemes argue that it would be very uneconomical to indicate tones when the great majority of the potential ambiguities are actually resolved by context.

Latinxua sin wenz is the most important scheme which does not indicate tones except in the case of ambiguity, like *maai* 'buy' and *mai* 'sell'. *Guóyǔ luómǎzì*, on the other hand, has developed a complicated way of indicating different tones in spelling. Other schemes choose to indicate tones in terms of numbers, or diacritical marks which are placed in one of the four corners of the word, or superimposed on the main vowels of the word. The advantage of indicating tones with numbers or diacritical marks rather than spelling is that it gives users more flexibility. They may decide to use the tone marks only when there is a need to do so. On the other hand, these tone-indicating symbols which are independent of the spelling of words may turn out to be very inconvenient in handwriting, and more importantly, in input and output on computer.

10.4 Five representative schemes

To illustrate the above discussion on the major aspects of the schemes of phonetic writing of Chinese, let us briefly examine five schemes that have played important roles in the script reform movement during the past 100 years, with special attention to the functions they are intended to serve within the broad context of language reform.

(1) Wang Zhao's *guānhuà zìmǔ* 'Mandarin phonetic alphabet'
Proposed in 1900, Wang Zhao's *guānhuà zìmǔ* was the most influential of the thirty schemes proposed during the first period of script reform (Z. Wang 1900). The alphabet contains forty-nine symbols for initials and twelve symbols for finals, representing the syllabic structure of characters by the method of double spelling. It differs from most of its contemporary and ensuing schemes in that the medial sound is integrated with the initial rather than the final, as shown in Table 10.1. Tones are marked with a dot in one of the four corners of the word. The symbols are all adapted from component parts of characters, assuming a graphic form that is very similar to that of kana. As discussed earlier, given that the

Table 10.1 Scheme of *guānhuà zìmǔ*

INITIALS			
七 [pi]	夂 [pʰi]	十 [mi]	
⼘ [pu]	扌 [pʰu]	才 [mu]	⺪ [fu]
忄 [t]	牛 [tʰ]	亻 [n]	⼘ [l]
乛 [ti]	匚 [tʰi]	ㅌ [ni]	厶 [li]
𠂆 [tu]	土 [tʰu]	乂 [nu]	乇 [lu]	口 [ly]
七 [k]	屮 [kʰ]	扌 [h]	
𠃌 [ku]	⼁ [kʰu]	ㄅ [hu]	
⼚ [tɕ]	廾 [tɕʰ]	乂 [ç]	
₽ [tɕy]	屮 [tɕʰy]	丿 [çy]	
ᒪ [tʂ]	八 [tʂʰ]	寸 [ʂ]	日 [ɹ]
丁 [tʂu]	刀 [tʂʰu]	乜 [ʂu]	入 [ɹu]
乛 [ts]	干 [tsʰ]	乄 [s]	
二 [tsu]	⼚ [tsʰu]	ㄎ [su]	
〈 [i]	丑 [u]	于 [y]	

FINALS			
㇌ [a]	Ｖ [ɛ]	㇈ [o]	
一 [ai]	ㄱ [ei]	㇈ [au]	㇑ [ou]
㇇ [an]	L [ən]	㇈ [aŋ]	ㄱ [əŋ]
⼉ [ɚ]			

traditional reverence towards Chinese characters was still prevalent among the masses of Chinese at that time, *guānhuà zìmǔ*'s close resemblance to the character script contributed to its popularity during the first period of the movement.

Guānhuà zìmǔ was later expanded, by Lao Naixuan, to write other dialects, mainly Wu, Cantonese, and Min. New symbols were designed and added to Wang's scheme to accommodate sounds not found in the Beijing dialect. The scheme, including its variants for other dialects, found favour among literati and bureaucrats in China, and was promoted on a scale unmatched by any other contemporary schemes. A large number of books were compiled and published, on a wide range of subjects like ethics, history, geography, geology, botany, zoology, etc. It was reported that more than 60,000 copies of books in this script were sold in a decade after its publication, and there were many newspapers and magazines printed in this script. It was also used for posters and personal communications (Ni 1948a; 1948b; Y. G. Zhou 1979).

As was typical of the schemes proposed during the first period, *guānhuà zìmǔ* was intended to serve a dual function in much the same way as kana in Japanese. First, it played an auxiliary role in relation to characters, providing an aid to their pronunciation. Second, it aimed to serve as a fully independent writing system that was an alternative to the character script, mainly for those who could not afford the time and energy needed for the mastery of characters. On one hand, Wang Zhao maintained that it was impractical to abolish characters, because of the existence of the myriad of Chinese classics; on the other hand, he argued that there should be an alternative script like *guānhuà zìmǔ* that is much easier to learn, but fully capable of serving the needs of everyday, non-literary functions. What Wang Zhao had in mind is a typical case of digraphia: the character script was to become a High writing system, learned by people of sufficient leisure, and *guānhuà zìmǔ* a Low writing system used only for the mundane, practical purposes of everyday life.

(2) *Zhùyīn zìmǔ*

Promulgated in 1918 by the Ministry of Education of the Republic of China, *zhùyīn zìmǔ* was the first phonographic writing of Chinese that was sanctioned and promoted by the language planning institution of the government. In much the same way as Wang Zhao's *guānhuà zìmǔ*, the symbols of *zhùyīn zìmǔ* were adapted from simple characters in Old Chinese, characterized by few strokes and simple forms. It adopted the method of triple spelling in the representation of the syllabic structure. In the beginning, the *yángpíng, shǎng, qù* and *rù* tones were marked by a dot positioned in one of the four corners of the word, with *yīnpíng* unmarked. Later, the dot in different positions was replaced by four distinct diacritic marks which were superimposed on the word. Concerning the dialectal base, it was intended at the beginning to represent a phonological system that was based upon the Beijing dialect, but also included features from other dialects, notably the Nanjing dialect. Later on, it was decided that it was to be based exclusively on the Beijing dialect. As a result, some symbols were abolished that represented sounds not found in the Beijing

Table 10.2 Scheme of *zhùyīn zìmǔ*

INITIALS				
ㄅ [p]	ㄆ [p]	ㄇ [m]	ㄈ [f]	ㄪ [v]
ㄉ [t]	ㄊ [t]	ㄋ [n]		ㄌ [l]
ㄍ [k]	ㄎ [k]	ㄫ [ŋ]	ㄏ [x]	
ㄐ [tɕ]	ㄑ [tɕ]	ㄬ [n̠]	ㄒ [ɕ]	
ㄓ [tʂ]	ㄔ [tʂ]		ㄕ [ʂ]	ㄖ [ɹ]
ㄗ [ts]	ㄘ [ts]		ㄙ [s]	

MEDIALS		
ㄧ [i]	ㄨ [u]	ㄩ [y]

FINALS					
ㄚ [a]	ㄛ [o]	ㄜ [ɣ]	ㄝ [ɛ]	ㄞ [ai]	ㄟ [ei]	ㄠ [ao]
ㄡ [ou]	ㄢ [an]	ㄣ [ən]	ㄤ [aŋ]	ㄥ [əŋ]	ㄦ [ɚ]	

dialect. *Zhùyīn zìmǔ* is generally taken to be the culmination of the first stage of script reform that was initiated by Lu Zhuangzhang in 1892. With respect to the script form, dialectal base, and representation of the syllabic structure and tones, it embodies the major features characteristic of the mainstream of schemes proposed during the first period. However, *zhùyīn zìmǔ* stands in remarkable contrast to the previous schemes with regard to the stated purpose of the phonetic writing. Most of the earlier schemes, as mentioned above, were intended to serve at least one of the three major functions in relation to the character script, namely supplementary, alternative, or superseding, in addition to the auxiliary role. At the time of promulgation, it was stated explicitly in the official document that *zhùyīn zìmǔ* was only to serve an auxiliary role, i.e., that of annotating the pronunciation of characters. In comparison with the aspirations of the proponents of the earlier schemes, this represents a more conservative stance towards the traditional character script. Some of its chief designers did conceive of a more active role for *zhùyīn zìmǔ*, intending it to serve a supplementary or alternative function. For instance, Li Jinxi (1923) advocated that characters in all publications should be accompanied by *zhùyīn zìmǔ*, which essentially means that the traditional characters should be replaced in publication by a new type of script comprising characters in juxtaposition with *zhùyīn zìmǔ*. It was hoped that, with the widespread use of *zhùyīn zìmǔ* under the auspices of the government, the phonetic script could in practice play a role beyond the auxiliary or the supplementary one, and either serve as a bona fide alternative to the character script, or supersede the latter in due course. Such expectations were to be disappointed.

So far as the auxiliary function is concerned, *zhùyīn zìmǔ*, or *zhùyīn fúhǎo*, as it was called later, has been very successful in facilitating the learning of character pronunciation in Northern Mandarin, especially in the Beijing dialect. It was a valuable tool in the promotion of *guóyǔ* during the several decades after its promulgation. It was replaced by *pīnyīn* in mainland China after 1958, but has been in continuous use in Taiwan.

(3) Guóyǔ luómǎzì

Designed by a group of eminent linguists and scholars of the time, *guóyǔ luómǎzì*, or *gwoyeu romatzyh* as originally spelled, was published in 1926, and promulgated by the government in 1928, representing the first romanized system that was officially recognized by the language planning institution in China. Adopting a phonemic representation, *guóyǔ luómǎzì* was in the main based upon the Beijing dialect, with some features from other Northern Mandarin dialects added in. It was intended to serve as the standard romanization of Chinese characters for all relevant purposes at that time, such as the transcription of proper nouns, in a context where the widespread use of several other schemes of romanization such as the Wade–Giles system, and the Postal system, had created considerable chaos.

Guóyǔ luómǎzì is characterized by the different function it was meant to play in relation to the character script. Not satisfied with the conservative stance the government assumed on the role of *zhùyīn zìmǔ*, a group of liberal intellectuals launched a heated debate on the fate of the character script in the late 1910s. In the then influential journals such as *Xīn Qīngnián* (*La Jeunesse*), *Guóyǔ Yuèkān* (*National Language Monthly*), and *Guóyǔ Zhōukān* (*National Language Weekly*) the majority of articles

Table 10.3 Scheme of *guóyǔ luómǎzì*

		INITIALS		
b [p]	p [pʰ]	m [m]	f [f]	v [v]
d [t]	t [tʰ]	n [n]	l [l]	
g [k]	k [kʰ]	ng [ŋ]	x [x]	
j [tɕ]	ch [tɕʰ]	gn [ɳ]	sh [ɕ]ᵃ	
j [tʂ]	ch [tʂʰ]		sh [ʂ]	r [ɹ]ᵇ
tz [ts]	ts [tsʰ]		s [s]	z [z]
		FINALS		
y [ɿ] or [ʅ]	i [i]	u [u]	iu [y]	
a [a]	ia [ia]	ua [ua]		
o [o]	io [iɔ]	uo [uo]		
e [ɣ]				
e [ɛ]	ie [iɛ]		iue [yɛ]	
ai [ai]	iai [iai]	uai [uai]		
ei [ei]		uei [uei]		
au [au]	iau [iau]			
ou [ou]	iou [iou]			
an [an]	ian [iɛn]	uan [uan]	iuan [yɛn]	
en [ən]	in [in]	uen [un]	iun [yn]	
ang [aŋ]	iang [iaŋ]	uang [uaŋ]		
eng [əŋ]	ing [iŋ]	ueng [uəŋ]		
ong [uŋ]	iong [yŋ]			
el [ɚ]				

a before [i] or [y]
b before other sounds

entertained a fairly radical view, advocating the replacement of the character script by one that is easier to learn and use (X. Qian 1918b; S. Fu 1919; Chao 1923; J. Li 1923). As remarked in Zhou Youguang (1979:42), the call to abolish characters in favour of a romanized alphabet reached a peak around 1923. As almost all of the designers of *guóyǔ luómǎzì* were ardent supporters of this radical view, it is only natural that, aside from serving the immediate auxiliary role of sound annotation, etc., their scheme was designed in such a way that it would be capable of serving all the functions expected of a bona fide writing system, and supersede characters in due course.

In *guóyǔ luómǎzì*, tones are represented in terms of spellings, instead of by diacritical marks. This, it has been argued, makes the system unnecessarily complicated. Due to that and some other factors, it turned out that the system itself was not as popular as *zhùyīn zìmǔ*. However, it was influential in that it ushered in a new period in the design of phonetic writings for Chinese: one that is characterized by a switch from character-based symbols to the roman alphabet as the preferred script, and by the renewed interest, after the conservative stance of *zhùyīn zìmǔ*, in the more fundamental roles to be assigned to schemes over and above the function of annotating character pronunciations.

It is worth noting that indicating tones in spelling in *guóyǔ luómǎzì*, rather than in terms of superimposed diacritics as in other schemes, may have given it an important 'second life' as a useful tool for teaching Chinese to foreigners in Western universities. Students may find the complicated spelling rules irritating at first, but it is more likely than with other schemes that they will be rewarded with speaking correct tones. The reason *guóyǔ luómǎzì* is useful in instilling correct tones is that Western students are accustomed to thinking that a word is 'a different word' if it is spelled differently. Using *guóyǔ luómǎzì*, they have to think of the correct tone every time they use a syllable for any purpose.[2]

(4) *Latinxua sin wenz*

Designed by several prominent Chinese communist scholars in exile in the Soviet Union, in collaboration with Soviet linguists, *latinxua sin wenz* was first published in 1929 in the Soviet Union. First employed among the 100,000 Chinese living in the Soviet Union, and later introduced into China, it was the first romanized scheme that was put to large-scale use as a fully independent writing system, intended to supersede the character script.

Latinxua sin wenz differs from the preceding schemes in three remarkable aspects. First, all of the three schemes discussed above were designed and promoted as part of the effort to promote a national language based on the Beijing dialect, making it easier to learn by providing a set of symbols that could be used to annotate the pronunciation of characters in that dialect. Both in theory and in practice, the proponents of *latinxua sin wenz* were opposed to making the Beijing dialect the base of a standard national language for speakers of all the Chinese dialects, labelling the National Language Movement as an elitist endeavour that

Table 10.4 Scheme of *latinxua sin wenz*

		INITIALS		
b [p]	p [pʰ]	m [m]	f [f]	
d [t]	t [tʰ]	n [n]		l [l]
g [k]	k [kʰ]	ng [ŋ]	x [x]ᵃ	
g [tɕ]	k [tɕʰ]		x [ɕ]ᵇ	
zh [tʂ]	ch [tʂʰ]		sh [ʂ]	rh [ɻ]
z [ts]	c [tsʰ]		s [s]	r [ɚ]

		FINALS		
	i [i]	u [u]	y [y]	
a [a]	ia [ia]	ua [ua]		
o [o]		uo [uo]	yo [yo]	
e [ɣ]				
	ie [iɛ]		ye [yɛ]	
ai [ai]		uai [uai]		
ei [ei]		ui [uei]		
ao [au]	iao [iau]			
ou [ou]	iu [iou]			
an [an]	ian [iɛn]	uan [uan]	yan [yɛn]	
en [ən]	in [in]	un [un]	yn [yn]	
ang [aŋ]	iang [iaŋ]	uang [uaŋ]		
eng [əŋ]	ing [iŋ]	ung [uŋ]	yng [yŋ]	

a except before [i] or [y]
b before [i] or [y]

placed the speakers of non-Mandarin dialects at a linguistic disadvantage (see Chapter 7). Furthermore, it was asserted that, if the romanized writing was to be based upon the Beijing dialect, it would be as difficult to learn as a foreign language for native speakers of Southern dialects like Wu, Min, or Cantonese. Instead of basing the romanized writing on the pronunciation of one particular dialect, they maintained, a separate scheme should be designed for each of the important dialects, thus ensuring easy access to literacy by its native speakers. As a result, there were at least thirteen schemes of *latinxua sin wenz* published for the major Chinese dialects. The most influential was the one based upon Northern Mandarin, which was due solely to the larger population of the native speakers of the dialect. The phonology is very similar to that of old *guóyīn*, incorporating a number of features outside the contemporary Beijing dialect. *Latinxua sin wenz* also differs from the other schemes in that tones are not marked unless absolutely necessary, which constitutes one of the most important features that make it 'reasonably simple' (Ni 1948a:213).

Another feature that sets *latinxua sin wenz* apart from other schemes is the radical attitude its proponents held in relation to characters. While the auxiliary role of annotating the sound of characters was intended to be an important function of the above three schemes, *latinxua sin wenz* was designed, first and foremost, to supersede the character script. It was asserted that the Chinese characters were a product of the old feudal society, and had become a tool with which the ruling class oppressed the labouring masses. They were an insurmountable impediment to higher literacy, and so unsuitable for a modern society. Because of that, they reasoned, they should be abolished in favour of a purely phonetic writing.

Latinxua sin wenz is notable as the scheme that was designed with the most radical intentions in relation to the traditional characters. In spite of indifference and hostility on the part of the Nationalist government towards the scheme, *latinxua sin wenz* was very popular as an autonomous writing system in some parts of the country, particularly in those regions in the Northwestern part of China that were under the control of the Communist Party. The government in those regions even granted it status as an official writing system, announcing that documents written in *latinxua sin wenz* should enjoy the same legal force as those in the character script. This was largely due to the support of a large number of prominent left-wing and liberal scholars. According to Ni Haishu (1948b:209), more than 300 publications totalling half a million copies appeared in *latinxua sin wenz*. What is more important, by its considerable success, it demonstrated to later proponents of script reform just what a phonetic writing of Chinese could achieve, thus paving the way for an even more influential scheme, *Hànyǔ pīnyīn*, that was to be published in the 1950s.

(5) *Hànyǔ pīnyīn*

Designed during the mid-1950s and promulgated in 1958 by the government of the People's Republic of China, *Hànyǔ pīnyīn*, or, in short form, *pīnyīn*, adopts the roman alphabet and assumes a phonemic representation, basically along the same lines as *guóyǔ luómǎzì* and *latinxua sin wenz*, as shown in Tables 3.1 and 3.2.[3] The superimposed diacritical marks have been borrowed from *zhùyīn zìmǔ* to indicate four tones of *yīnpíng, yángpíng, shǎng* and *qù*.

Unlike the other schemes, however, *pīnyīn* has received the full support of the state government, in a way not testified in any earlier period of language reform in China. It is the official phonographic scheme of Chinese in China, being extensively employed in all relevant areas such as textbooks, reference works, communications, sign languages, etc. It is the most popular phonographic system of Chinese outside China, widely taught in schools and used in publications. It was adopted by the International Standardization Organization in 1982 as the standard form for the transcription of Chinese words. It is also the system that has enabled characters to be arranged in an orderly way. Most notably, it is commonly used in the input/output system in Chinese word processing. Most popular Chinese word processors, like NJ Star, Xia Li Ba Ren, or New Tianma, have *pīnyīn*-character conversion as its main input/output method.

There are two aspects of *pīnyīn* which are worth discussing here, one with respect to the dialect base of the system, the other concerning the functions it is intended to serve.

Pīnyīn is based exclusively upon the pronunciation of the Beijing dialect. In contrast to the *latinxua sin wenz* approach of separate schemes for the major dialects, no attempt has been made on the part of the language planning institution to design similar *pīnyīn* schemes for other dialects. As discussed above, the *latinxua sin wenz* approach of designing separate schemes for each of the major dialects is based on a rejection of the concept of a Modern Standard Chinese based on a particular dialect. This concept of a standard national language, in the form of *pǔtōnghuà*, was wholeheartedly embraced by the newly established government. In fact, one of the major stated functions of *pīnyīn* is to facilitate the acquisition of *pǔtōnghuà* by speakers of other dialects. Thus, rather than assign primacy to creating easy access to literacy, as the *latinxua sin wenz* camp had done, the government of the People's Republic of China has opted for establishing uniformity of language (Y. Z. Wu 1958; Y. Z. Wu and J. Li 1958).

With regard to the intended function of the phonetic writing, *pīnyīn* also retreated from the more radical position of *latinxua sin wenz*. While *latinxua sin wenz* was to function as an alternative and superseding writing system in relation to the character script, *pīnyīn* is intended to serve a mere auxiliary role.

It must be pointed out, however, that a close examination of the relevant literature reveals that there has been considerable vacillation on the part of the language planning institution concerning the function of *pīnyīn*. There is ample evidence that when the Committee on Script Reform first set to the task of designing a phonetic scheme in the 1950s, there was no doubt in the mind of the designers that they were to come up with a scheme that could function as a bona fide writing system, one which would eventually supersede the character script. Zhou Youguang, one of the chief designers of *pīnyīn*, remarked four decades later that the design of a new phonetic scheme in the early 1950s was prompted by the dissatisfaction on the part of the state language planning institution and senior state leaders with the previous schemes like *zhùyīn zìmǔ*, *guóyǔ luómǎzì* and *latinxua sin wenz*. They held that while these schemes were suitable for auxiliary purposes, they fell short of serving as all-purpose writing systems, and hence a new scheme was needed (Y. G. Zhou 1992:217). Mao Zedong was quoted as saying in the early 1950s: 'The writing system must be reformed, and it should take the phonetic direction common to the languages of the world' (DeFrancis 1979; Y. Z. Wu 1978:101). The question at the time was not whether there was need for a phonographic writing system, but how long it would take for the phonographic system to completely supersede the characters.

When *pīnyīn* was promulgated in 1958, however, there was an obvious retreat from the previous stance on its role. *Pīnyīn* is intended to serve an auxiliary role, mainly as a sound-annotating tool to facilitate the learning and use of characters, in much the same way as *zhùyīn zìmǔ* and *guóyǔ luómǎzì*. Furthermore, as *pīnyīn* is based on the Beijing dialect, which provides the standard pronunciation of *pǔtōnghuà*, it also functions as an aid in promoting Modern Standard Chinese among the native speakers of other dialects. When the first draft of the *pīnyīn* scheme was distributed to the participants of the National Conference on Script Reform convened in October 1955, it was called *Hànyǔ pīnyīn wénzì (lādīng zìmǔ shì) cǎo'àn chūgǎo* 'First draft of phonetic writing system of

Chinese (in Latin alphabet)'. When promulgated in 1958, it was changed to *Hànyǔ pīnyīn fāng'àn* 'phonetic scheme of Chinese' with the crucial term *wénzì* 'writing system' deleted. Also, it was stated in explicit terms that *pīnyīn*'s role in relation to Chinese characters was not intended to be a supplementary, alternative, or superseding one.

10.5   Phonetization in Taiwan and elsewhere

As noted in Chapter 7, *zhùyīn zìmǔ* and *guóyǔ luōmǎzì* were respectively renamed *zhùyīn fúhào* 'sound-annotating symbols' in 1930 and *yìyīn fúhào* 'transliteration symbols' in 1940 to dispel any faint hope that they were to be used as bona fide writing systems. The new names precisely indicate the functions *zhùyīn zìmǔ* and *guóyǔ luōmǎzì* have been serving in Taiwan since then. *Zhuyin zìmǔ* has served an auxiliary or supplementary role in language instruction, while *guóyǔ luōmǎzì* is mainly used to transliterate Chinese names into other languages. In May 1984, the Ministry of Education published a revised version of *guóyǔ luōmǎzì* for trial use (Ben Kan Zhiliaoshi 1986). At the same time, it announced that the name *yìyīn fúhào* was changed to *Guóyǔ zhùyīn fúhào dì èr shì* 'Sound-annotating symbols of *guóyǔ* (scheme 2)'. The scheme was formally promulgated in January 1986, as presented in Table 10.5.

With tones marked by diacritics and other minor modifications, the revised version is much closer to *pīnyīn* than *guóyǔ luómǎzì* is. At the time of writing, there are growing calls in Taiwan for it to take over the functions of *zhùyīn zìmǔ* in language instruction.[4]

Phonetization of Chinese in other Chinese communities including Hong Kong and Singapore is largely confined to the transliteration of Chinese proper names into languages using phonographic writing systems. While it is almost always in Latin script, it displays much more variation than in mainland China or Taiwan in terms of the phonographic schemes adopted and the dialects upon which they are based. The Wade–Giles scheme is still used by some people and transliteration is much more likely to be based upon the predominant local non-Northern Mandarin dialect rather than Modern Standard Chinese.

Table 10.5 Scheme of *guóyǔ zhùyīn fúhào dì èr shì*

INITIALS

b [p]	p [pʰ]	m [m]	f [f]	
d [t]	t [tʰ]	n [n]		l [l]
g [k]	k [kʰ]		h [x]	
j [tɕ]	ch [tɕʰ]		sh [ɕ]*a*	
j [tʂ]	ch [tʂʰ]		sh [ʂ]	r [ɻ]*b*
tz [ts]	ts [tsʰ]		s [s]	

FINALS

r [ɻ]	i or yi [i]	u or wu [u]	iu or yu [y]
z [ɿ]			
a [a]	ia [ia]	ua [ua]	
o [o]	io [iɔ]	uo [uo]	
e [ɣ]			
ê [ɛ]	ie [iɛ]	iue [yɛ]	
ai [ai]	iai [iai]	uai [uai]	
ei [ei]		uei [uei]	
au [au]	iau [iau]		
ou [ou]	iou [iou]		
an [an]	ian [iɛn]	uan [uan]	iuan [yɛn]
en [ən]	in [in]	uen [un]	iun [yn]
ang [aŋ]	iang [iaŋ]	uang [uaŋ]	iung [yŋ]
eng [ən]	ing [iŋ]	ung [uəŋ]	
er [ɚ]			

---

a before [i] or [y]
b before other sounds

11 Use and reform of the Chinese writing system: present and future

11.1 Recent developments

11.1.1 Deviations from official policy

Since the late 1970s, much activity in the educational, cultural, and scientific fields that were almost dormant during the Cultural Revolution has been enthusiastically resumed. On the front of script reform, however, in spite of renewed efforts on the part of the language planning institutions to continue with the agenda drawn up in the 1950s and 1960s, there has been an obvious trend among the general public to break away from the tight controls that have been in place since the 1950s. In comparison with the twenty-year period following 1956, the 1980s and 1990s have witnessed more deviation from the standard in the use of characters.

First, the original complex forms of simplified characters are staging a comeback. In spite of language planning institutions issuing a succession of regulations and directives prohibiting their use, they are everywhere to be seen – on the signboards of streets, stores, schools, companies, and even government institutions, as well as in advertisements, slogans, television subtitles, etc. According to a recent survey of forty-eight universities in Beijing, twenty-five use complex characters in their signs, and of fifty-one restaurants chosen at random in Beijing, forty-three use complex characters in their signs (Zhong 1990). The percentage is even higher in Southern Chinese cities like Xiamen and Guangzhou (Fei and Qi 1986; Dai 1991). The calligraphic works of senior politicians published in prominent places in newspapers contain a large number of complex characters, much to the dismay of language planners who expect these writers to pay more attention to official policy on the use of script.

This phenomenon is attributable to several factors. First, the renewed interest in the complex script is closely related to the widespread assumption that users of the complex script are more learned, cultivated, or simply more affluent than users of the simplified script. This assumption is presumably derived from the fact that it is the complex script, rather than the simplified one, that was used in the myriad of Chinese classics. Association with a time-honoured literary heritage lends the complex script an aura of prestige that was all the more attractive at a time when society was recovering from the devastating consequences of the Cultural Revolution, which had among its stated goals the destruction of China's cultural heritage. The association of the complex script with the prestige of tradition is further reinforced by the fact that most highly esteemed scholars and eminent calligraphers are more accustomed to writing in the complex script, as most of them finished school well before the promulgation of the simplification scheme in 1956. When their calligraphic works appear in prominent places, they contribute to the supposed refinement of the complex script.

On some occasions, the use of the complex script is justified on the grounds that it would better accommodate readers in overseas Chinese communities like Taiwan, Hong Kong, etc., where only the complex script is customarily used. When the overseas edition of *Rénmín Rìbào* was started in July 1985, it was published in the complex script instead of the simplified one.[1] As overseas Chinese communities are economically better developed than mainland China, the complex script is associated with affluence in the minds of some people.

At the same time, a large number of unauthorized simplified characters have appeared in public places. Some of them are from the now abolished Second Scheme of Simplified Chinese Characters, but most are recent inventions. Although they are mostly used by people with little education, or confined to highly specialized contexts, they are widespread enough to catch the attention of the general public, who may in turn adopt them in their own writing.

The extensive use of complex characters and unauthorized simplified characters in China since the early 1980s contrasts sharply with the considerable uniformity in the use of script before that time. Deviation from the promulgated standard in script use has occurred in the context of fundamental changes that took place in post-Mao China. Following the adoption of a more liberal, laissez-faire policy by the central government, there has been more diversity in all aspects of Chinese society, including the political, economic, cultural, and literary arenas. Regulations on language issues are beginning to lose the authority or binding force they used to enjoy in the 1960s and 1970s.

From 1986 onwards, the State Language Commission, formerly the Committee on Script Reform, has reacted to the increasing deviations from the standard by issuing a series of directives which have aimed to redress what they see as a chaotic situation in the use of script. It has been reiterated that the complex characters can be used only in publication of classics in *wényán*, and that the standard form of characters as promulgated by language planning institutions should be closely observed in publications and other writings for public display. These directives have been accompanied by administrative measures that attempt to bring the community back in line with the official policy on the use of script. Amid the fanfare surrounding the publication of some of the directives, according to newspaper reports, stores in Beijing were forced to replace signboards containing 'unauthorized' characters at great cost. It is highly doubtful, however, that the widespread use of these so-called unauthorized characters will be checked by such official exercises. Anyone on a casual tour in the major Chinese cities, especially in Southern China, will conclude from what Chinese writings are on display in public places that the prescriptive stance of the language planning institutions has had little effect in preventing further deviation from the standard script. All evidence suggests that, although publications in print are still overwhelmingly in simplified characters in mainland China, and in the traditional complex script in Taiwan, a situation is emerging in all the Chinese communities in which the complex and the simplified script are used in a mixed way on all other occasions.

11.1.2 Official policy on script reform under challenge

For more than two decades following 1956, there were very few who dared to challenge the official policy on script reform, and even fewer who could have their opposing opinions openly published. While comments or suggestions on individual simplified characters did appear in journals and newspapers, any dissident voice against simplification as an approach to script reform, or against phonetization as a long term goal was effectively muted.

The situation has changed considerably since the late 1970s. People feel freer to express their views on all aspects of language planning. While the promotion of Modern Standard Chinese and the standardization of Modern Written Chinese have been readily accepted by the general public and experts alike, there is much less consensus on script reform. The official policy since the 1950s has come under closer scrutiny, and become a topic for heated debate.

As discussed in Chapter 10, it was explicitly stated in the 1950s that the fundamental goal of language reform in China was to eventually switch from the logographic writing system to a phonographic one, and most of the measures adopted in language reform were meant to contribute to this objective. In spite of the fact that this agenda allegedly represented the consensus of expert opinion on the issue and had the personal endorsement of Mao Zedong and other senior state politicians, its feasibility and desirability are now called into serious question. Arguments against replacement of the traditional Chinese script by a romanized one are much more publicized than before.

It is argued that the shortcomings of the character script as elaborated in Chapter 9 have been exaggerated by proponents of the phonetization of the writing system. In comparison with users of phonographic writing systems, Chinese may not necessarily be at such a linguistic disadvantage. It is claimed that while Chinese readers have to learn about 3,000 characters in order to be able to read *Renmín Rìbào*, English readers have to learn in the order of 50,000 words to attain the same level of comprehension with *The New York Times*. The reason for this lies in the fact that the 3,000 Chinese characters can be used to combine into hundreds and thousands of words, whereas most of the English words have to be learned one by one. The burden on learners of the Chinese script, it is argued, is not that much heavier than that on learners of the English script after all. As they see it, the proposal to abolish the logographic characters in favour of a phonographic system is nothing more than another manifestation of a radical revolutionary attitude towards traditional Chinese values and heritage, which, although well intended, does not offer any real solution to the problems confronting the nation. The backwardness of the country as a whole, they believe, cannot be attributed to the difficulty of its writing system. The rapid economic development of Taiwan over the past decades has been cited as evidence against the allegation that the traditional Chinese script is poorly suited to modern times. Japan has often been cited as another example. In spite of its proverbially complex writing system, Japan has achieved a literacy rate comparable to that of any other industralized nation.

At the same time, we are reminded that characters were not indigenous to the languages in which they have been superseded, but rather had been borrowed because those languages had no writing system of their own. As Coulmas (1989, 1992) reports, there are no recorded instances of a logographic system that is native to a language being superseded by a phonographic system for that language, and Chinese seems unlikely to

prove an exception. With these and similar arguments against the abolition of the logographic script receiving much more publicity than before,
phonetization is now perceived by a growing number of people as far too
radical an approach to script reform to be acceptable in the foreseeable
future.

The simplification approach pursued so far has also met with chal-
lenges. As discussed in Chapter 9, it has been suggested that simplified
characters should be abolished in favour of the original complex ones, on
the grounds that simplification has restricted easy access to the Chinese
classics, and to Chinese communities outside mainland China. While
this view has not won general support, it does indicate a level of concern about the negative effects of simplification as an approach to script
reform.

At the same time, there are increasing calls for a more tolerant attitude
to be taken towards the use of complex characters that were supposedly
made obsolete by the promulgation of their simplified counterparts.
The official stance forbidding the use of complex characters in public
places is criticized as being too rigid, and sometimes unreasonable. It is
maintained that, while it may be desirable to impose a standard script
in printed materials, people should have more freedom in the choice of
script for handwritten works, including those for public display. It is also
proposed that the complex script should be restored in print in mainland
China, both for the sake of easier differentiation of characters, and to
ensure wider access to readers outside the mainland. On the other hand,
the simplified script should only be used in handwriting to provide economy of effort. As people read much more than they write, such measures
would maximize the benefits for both readers and writers (Shi 1988).

Those in favour of further simplification argue that there are still
a considerable number of characters which, owing to the complexity of
their graphic structure, should be simplified in the interests of ease of
recognition and ease of writing. It is pointed out that, of the 2,236
simplified characters in the General List published in 1964, there are
1,752 which are only partially simplified, containing components that
can and should be further simplified, as they have already been elsewhere as independent characters or component parts. Furthermore, in
the National Standard set of 6,763 characters for computer use (GB
Code), there are 138 characters which cannot be written properly within

the matrix composed of 15×16 dots, and have to be represented expediently in an ad hoc manner. It is desirable that these characters undergo simplification.

The majority of participants in the debate seem to hold the opinion that the best strategy in script reform at present is to maintain the status quo. On the one hand, they do not like the idea of restoring the complex script used before the 1950s. Given that hundreds of millions of people in mainland China have already been trained in the simplified script, it would be highly uneconomical to change its writing system merely to accommodate other Chinese communities. The proposed practice to read in the complex script but write in the simplified one, in their view, would only lead to a heavier burden on the part of learners, who would have to know both simplified and complex scripts in order to be literate. On the other hand, they are opposed to any further simplification on a scale similar to that of the First and the Second Scheme, mainly for the reasons elaborated in Chapter 9. There is a growing voice which argues that the approach of simplification has reached the end of its usefulness, and that, to further alleviate the burden of the learners and users of the Chinese script, an approach of optimization, instead of simplification, should be adopted. I will return to this later.

11.2   Change in policy on script reform

The arguments against phonetization and further large-scale simplification that appeared in the late 1970s eventually had an impact on the decision making of language planning institutions. In January 1986, thirty years after the First National Conference on Script Reform, the Second National Conference on Language and Script was convened in Beijing. This conference marks some obvious changes in official policy on script reform.

As expected, the aims of the 1986 Conference were to review what had been achieved so far in language reform, and to draw up goals and strategies for the future. For the first time since the 1950s, phonetization of the writing system was dropped from the agenda of language reform, although the conference fell short of admitting that it was unrealistic to expect the logographic script ever to be superseded by a phonographic writing system.

At the same time, the Second Scheme of Simplified Chinese Characters promulgated in 1977 was formally repealed on the grounds that it would too greatly inconvenience the compilation of dictionaries and character fonts for computer use. It was revealed at the meeting that, when it was realized that opposition to the Second Scheme was so strong that its abolition appeared inevitable, the language planning institution prepared another list of characters to be simplified, altogether containing 111 characters, which it hoped would receive a more favourable reception.[2] It turned out that even the much more conservative scheme failed to win the approval of participant experts and the legislature (D. Liu 1986:27; Y. G. Zhou 1992; J. Wang 1995). It was resolved at the conference that a more cautious attitude would be adopted towards any further simplification of the script. What this actually means is that while some characters may still undergo simplification in the future, any exercise in simplification of the scale of the First and the Second Scheme would be avoided. The resolution in effect indicates that the goal set in the 1950s, and reiterated in 1964, to reduce the number of strokes of common characters to 10 or less has been abandoned.

11.3   Prospects of script reform

11.3.1   Roles of phonographic schemes

As an auxiliary writing system, *pīnyīn* is well established, having been put to a wide range of uses both inside and outside mainland China. While the ambitious goal of replacing the logographic script with a phonographic one has been all but abandoned, attempts are still being made to further the uses of *pīnyīn* beyond that of an auxiliary system. Basic Rules of the Orthography of Chinese in *Pīnyīn* was promulgated in 1988, which aims to provide the prerequisite conditions for the use of *pīnyīn* as a writing system that may serve a supplementary or alternative role (Y. G. Zhou 1992:286–98).

It is believed that if *pīnyīn* is ever to play a broader role, it should start with beginning school children. All Year 1 school children in China learn *pīnyīn* as an auxiliary system before they start learning characters, and normally become quite proficient in it. As they advance to the higher grades and learn more characters, however, they mostly lose the skills in *pīnyīn*. This loss of proficiency in *pīnyīn* has encountered little surprise or regret on the part of educators or linguists. In a sense, *pīnyīn* is meant to serve approximately the same role in schools as the ITA system that was experimented with in the USA and England. Rather than being treated as full-fledged writing systems, they are intended to function as auxiliary systems that facilitate acquisition of the traditional writing system (Venezky 1970). One of the major reasons that such an auxiliary system fails to become a bona fide writing system is that very few publications are printed in it. Although there are some publications in China, including a monthly newspaper, that are printed exclusively in *pīnyīn*, they have hardly any impact upon the general public. Without enough opportunities to practise *pīnyīn*, and without enough motivation, *pīnyīn* drops out of use before students graduate from primary school. An experiment has been in progress in Heilongjiang province in northeastern China that attempts to develop *pīnyīn* into a regular writing system in order that school children might gain literacy in this phonographic writing several years earlier than is usual with the character script. Students are encouraged to write in *pīnyīn* from Year 1, and devote much less time than usual to learning characters. At the same time, they are provided with a large amount of reading materials printed in *pīnyīn*. It is hoped that such measures will serve to develop their writing skills from an early age without being hindered by the difficulties involved in learning characters, and, at the same time, help to retain their proficiency in *pīnyīn* as an alternative writing system after they later acquire literacy in the character script (Ding et al. 1985). The experiments, according to reports, have been a great success so far as the development of the writing skills of students at an early age is concerned.[3] As students use *pīnyīn* for words they have not yet learned how to write in characters, they are able to express themselves in writing much more freely than is usually the case before.

Although the standardization of orthography in *pīnyīn* will be conducive to improvement in the quality and quantity of writings and publications in *pīnyīn*, it is unlikely that *pīnyīn* will play a role beyond the transitional one even in this case, unless and until society at large becomes more receptive to writings in a script other than the logographic characters. In the foreseeable future, it seems that the major role of *pīnyīn* will be confined to an auxiliary one. The same holds for *zhùyīn zìmǔ* and *guóyǔ luómǎzì* in Taiwan.

11.3.2   **Optimization of the traditional writing system**
There is growing consensus that, instead of simplification or phonetization, the best approach to adapt the traditional writing system to modern society should be what is called optimization (X. Qiu 1988; N. Wang 1991; Z. T. Chen 1992; Y. G. Zhou 1992). Aiming to make the best use of the logographic script, optimization includes the following major tasks.

(1) To delimit the number of characters in common use
It is suggested that it is the very large number of Chinese characters which have to be learned in the acquisition of literacy that accounts for much of the difficulty with the writing system. As noted in Chapter 9, there are in the order of 60,000 characters recorded in dictionaries, which include distinctive types of characters, and variant tokens of the same character type. These characters differ greatly with regard to frequency of usage. Although the most common 3,000 cover more than 99 per cent of all characters used in modern writings, the other characters may also show up occasionally, most often in proper names or in writings of a highly literary style containing a large number of expressions in Old Chinese. This adds to the burden of readers, writers, printers, designers of Chinese word processing software, etc.

As has often been the case with language planning issues in China, inspiration has been drawn from Japanese efforts to delimit the legitimate number of characters used in contemporary writings to less than 2,000. It is suggested that it would be a great relief to Chinese if the same course were followed for the Chinese script.

Following the determination of the frequency of all Chinese characters in modern writings as discussed in Chapter 8, it has been proposed that the number of characters used should be limited to 3,000 in Chinese newspapers, as recommended by the Chinese Press Association (Y. Lin 1971:xxx), or to 7,000 in all modern publications, as suggested by Zhou Youguang (1992:158). Those not included in lists of most frequently used characters should be replaced by those in the lists with the same phonetic or semantic value. With the publication of the character set for computer use (GB code) in 1981, the number of characters for general use in computer processing of the Chinese script in mainland China has been effectively delimited. However, there are so far no restrictions upon newspapers or publishing houses with regard to the number of characters used. It is proposed that language planning institutions should extend such restrictions beyond computer use, and there are signs that such action is being contemplated (Y. Fu 1989a; Y. G. Zhou 1992).

(2) To improve on the sound and meaning indicating capability of characters

Given that characters of the *xíngshēng* category comprise about 90 per cent of characters in common use in Modern Chinese, the script would be easier to learn and use if the phonetic and semantic components of the compounds were better indicators of the phonetic and semantic values. It is even suggested that the writing system should undergo a radical change in the structuring of characters so that each syllable is indicated by one and only one phonetic indicative, and characters belonging to the same thesaurus-type category should share the same semantic component. This proposal is of course unlikely to win widespread approval for reasons similar to those underlying the lack of general support for the use of phonographic scripts as bona fide writing systems, as detailed in Chapter 10.

Nevertheless, there is growing recognition of the need to pay more attention to the function of character components within the whole writing system when they are subjected to simplification. Characters involved in the process should not be treated in isolation, but in relation to other characters that contain the same or similar phonetic or semantic components. It is preferable for characters to indicate their phonetic and semantic value in a clearer and more predictable way after simplification. At the same time, the number of symbolic marks should be reduced to a minimum. An increase in the number and incidence of such marks in the Second Scheme, as observed in Chapter 9, was an important reason for its rejection. The First Scheme is also inadequate in this respect. The symbolic mark 一, for instance, has been chosen to replace ten distinct components which are used as phonetic or semantic determinatives in dozens of characters, greatly reducing the sound- and meaning-indicating capability of the characters involved. The ten components in question, furthermore, are replaced by the simplified mark only in some characters, but not in other characters, where they are still used as phonetic or semantic components. This no doubt adds to the burden of learners. Such oversights, it is suggested, would be the target of rectification in the optimization of the script.

(3) To standardize the ordering of characters

Differences between dictionaries, catalogues, etc. in the ordering of characters in terms of graphic structure, as noted in Chapter 9, have created a great deal of inconvenience to users. Standardization of the ordering of characters for such purposes is also one of the important tasks in the optimization of the Chinese writing system. This would require standardization of the type, designation, and ordering of radicals, as well as standardization in terms of the number and ordering of the strokes of characters. Prepared by the language planning institution in 1983, a draft of scheme for character indexing by radicals has been distributed for discussion. It is hoped that, when finalized, the system will serve as the standard for all purposes that require the ordering of characters.

In a country with an entrenched tradition for government to regulate the use of writing system, script reform will continue to be a subject of attention from educators, scholars, and language planning institutions in China. With phonetization or further large-scale simplification of the Chinese writing system appearing to be all but ruled out, most of the discussion on script reform since the early 1990s is directed towards aspects of optimization as discussed above. It is likely that proposals on the delimitation of the number of characters for everyday use, and on modification of the graphic structure of some individual characters in conformity with the principles of optimization, will be adopted by language planning institutions in due course.

I have described and analysed the development of Modern Chinese since the late nineteenth century from historical and sociolinguistic perspectives, concentrating on three major aspects, namely, Modern Spoken Chinese, Modern Written Chinese, and the Modern Chinese writing system.

As the fundamental institution of society, language both influences and reflects the development of the community in which it is used. The development of Modern Chinese since the late nineteenth century constitutes an integral part of the history of Chinese society and Chinese people over the period, and is best understood in that context. All the major changes to the language during the period followed events of historical significance, which include military defeats of China by Western powers in the nineteenth century, the overthrow of the imperial Qing dynasty and the founding the Republic of China in the early 1910s, the New Culture Movement in the late 1910s, and the founding of the People's Republic of China in 1949. Linguistic standards, particularly in relation to the written style, and the writing system, had been firmly in place in the country before modern times. They were for the most part enforced by official institutions, and held in reverence by the general public. The historical events in modern times prompted reform-minded scholars, educators, and politicians to take a critical examination of the Chinese language in close connection with the social, political, economic, educational, and cultural aspects of the country, and at the same time created a society that was more receptive to changes and innovations initiated into the language.

It is no coincidence that this period also marks the general modernization of China as a nation state. Almost all of the efforts on language reform were driven by the desire to make the language more suitable for a modernizing China. Consensus built up early on in the period that the wide diversity in spoken dialects, a standard written style completely divorced from contemporary vernacular, and a logographic writing system stood as serious impediments to the progress of the country. Drawing on the experience of a similar undertaking in Japan, the Chinese decided that the language must undergo dramatic reform to fit in with a modernizing society. Over the past century or so, a spoken standard based upon Northern Mandarin has been established and popularized, a written style that is basically based upon Northern Mandarin has been established as the written norm, the writing system has undergone considerable simplification, and several phonetic schemes have been designed and used extensively to alleviate the difficulties in the acquisition and use of the traditional script. Norms and standards developed in mainland China have generally been followed in other major Chinese communities like Taiwan, Hong Kong, and Singapore, although each of the latter places has also developed its own localized norms at the same time. The changes to Modern Chinese over the period are unparalleled in Chinese history in terms of depth, range, and implications.

The development of the three major aspects of Modern Chinese has been closely interrelated, and ensued on the interaction of linguistic, and social, historical factors. The National Language Movement, which aimed to establish and promote a spoken standard across the land, preceded the efforts to replace *wényán* with *báihuà* as the basis of a modern written standard. Since the switch from *wényán* to *báihuà* was first and foremost motivated by the fact that the latter is much closer than the former to the contemporary vernacular of Northern Mandarin, the movement in no small measure facilitated the acceptance by the community of a new written standard that was essentially based upon the spoken standard that was being popularized. In the undertaking to make the Chinese script easier to acquire and use, moreover, phonetization emerged as a serious option only after the written language moved away from Old Chinese towards the contemporary vernacular as its base. The logophoricity of the traditional Chinese script has operated as the single most important linguistic factor throughout the development of Modern Chinese, accounting for the lion's share of the strengths and weaknesses ascribed to the writing system, and underlying most features relating to spoken and written Chinese.

Notes

1 Introduction

1. It is almost certain that those innovations occurred in everyday vernacular earlier than in writing. The problem is that, without written records, it is impossible to ascertain when they first emerged in the language.

2. Mainly on the basis of the divergence of *wényán* 'literary written style' and *báihuà* 'vernacular written style', Lü Shuxiang (1985a, 1985b) proposes that the history of Chinese is divided into two major periods, Old Chinese and Modern Chinese, with the appearance of substantial texts in mainly vernacular style serving as the line of demarcation. The former covers the period from the earliest records down to the late Tang dynasty, and the latter starts from the late Tang dynasty and extends into the twentieth century. From this perspective, what is presented as Modern Chinese in Table 1.1 is actually an extension of Pre-modern Chinese. Other ways of periodization have been proposed in China and in the West. Many linguists maintain that it is preferable to set Pre-modern Chinese apart from Modern Chinese, on the grounds that the language in the Pre-modern period displays many features that are absent in Modern Chinese, and also on the grounds that it would be inconvenient to use the same term to refer to the language in transition and the resulting language (Peyraube 1988, 1996; J. Liu et al. 1992; S. Jiang 1994).

   The English word 'modern' covers the meanings of *jìndài* 'recent times' and *xiàndài* 'present times' in Chinese. To avoid ambiguity, I use 'pre-modern' for *jìndài*, and 'modern' for *xiàndài*.

3. Given such difference among the Chinese dialects, it is no wonder that they are more often than not referred to as separate languages by linguists and the general public alike (Li and Thompson 1981; DeFrancis 1984b, 1989). In other words, the terms language and dialect are sometimes used interchangeably with respect to the regional varieties of Chinese, as readers will find in this book, in a way similar to what is reported for Western societies (Fasold 1984, 1990; Wardhaugh 1986:25). In spite of the ambiguities and obscurities often attaching to the terms 'language' and 'dialect', linguists have been trying to establish the distinctive definitive features that are associated with language and dialect respectively, and establish criteria that may be applied to specific codes in determining their appropriate classification. Generally speaking, there are two distinct dimensions involved in the various usages of language and dialect in Western scholarship. One is structural, and the other is functional. In the structural usage, the overriding consideration is genetic relationship. Speech forms must be developed from one earlier speech form before they can be called dialects. If not, they are called different languages. Thus, language can be used to refer to either a single linguistic norm or to a group of genetically related norms, while a dialect refers to one of the norms in the group. It is often assumed that dialects must also be mutually intelligible. In the functional usage, on the other hand, the overriding consideration is the use that speakers make of the codes they master. From this perspective, a language is defined as a superposed norm used by speakers whose first and ordinary language may be different. In other words, a language is the medium of communication between speakers of different dialects. As proposed by Haugen (1966), functionally a dialect may be defined as an undeveloped (or underdeveloped) language, in the sense that it has not been employed in all the functions that a language can perform in a society larger than that of the local tribe or peasant village. For a functionally defined dialect to develop into a language, it must undergo the process of standardization or codification, and elaboration, ensuring its competence to serve diverse functions. Furthermore, both standardization and elaboration are possible only if a written language is developed on the basis of the vernacular (Haugen 1983; Cooper 1989; Coulmas 1989). Thus, a dialect in functional terms does not count as a language unless it has

developed a standard written code of its own. As generally accepted in the literature (Ferguson 1968; Kloss 1968; Fasold 1984; Cooper 1989), the most important criterion that differentiates a standard language from an unstandardized vernacular is that the former has a written code, with dictionaries, grammar books, and similar codifying materials developed for it, so that it can be learned as a subject, and can be the medium in which all modern knowledge can be taught at an advanced level, while the latter does not.

When these criteria are applied to Chinese, we find that this conclusion is not far from what has been generally assumed with regard to the Chinese dialects. By the structural criterion, all the seven major Chinese dialects are entitled to the name 'language', because, as discussed earlier, they are mutually unintelligible and each in turn comprises a group of genetically related varieties. In so far as they are learned and used by speakers of other codes as lingua franca, all the major dialects can again be called languages. As each of the dialect groups contains dialects which may be mutually unintelligible, there are usually one or two dialects, normally those highest in prestige, that serve as the lingua franca among the unintelligible dialects in the same group: for instance, the dialect of Guangzhou (Canton) for the Cantonese group; the dialect of Mei County for Kejia; the dialect of Xiamen (Amoy) or Fuzhou for the Southern Min dialect; and the dialect of Suzhou or Shanghai for the Wu dialect. These dialects are learned by speakers of the other dialects in the group, and used as the lingua franca within the group. From this functional perspective, it is again justified to treat what have been known as dialects as languages.

There is one important aspect in which the various geographical varieties of Chinese other than Mandarin are justifiably called dialects, or underdeveloped languages: except for Mandarin, none of these dialect groups have an established writing tradition, in spite of the fact that they represent very large populations and are distributed over very large geographical areas – often much larger than was the case with most of the Modern European languages. I will elaborate on this in later chapters.

In the following chapters of the book, I will use terms like 'language', 'dialect', 'variety', and 'speech form' in accordance with established usage without further elaboration. In cases where they seem to be used rather loosely, I trust they will not cause any ambiguity in the context.

4. The term 'mandarin' is used to translate *guānhuà* in Chinese, which is used in at least two related senses. As the designation of a group of regional dialects, it is used as the name of a family of Northern Chinese speech forms, viz. Beifanghua 'northern speech' as in this chapter. It is also used as the designation of a social speech form, referring to the standard language or koine spoken by officials and educated people from the Yuan dynasty up to the early twentieth century, when it was replaced by *guóyǔ* 'national language'. *Guānhuà* as a social speech form was based upon *guānhuà* as a family of geographical dialects.

5. There are also many Chinese linguists who maintain that Min should be divided into two major groups, Southern Min and Northern Min, resulting in a framework of eight, instead of seven, major dialect groups. Atlas (1987/1991), on the other hand, has adopted a framework under which the Chinese dialects fall into ten major groups. It has also adopted a somewhat different scheme of grouping for Mandarin, according to which there are eight subgroups: Northeastern, Beijing, Beifang (jilu), Jiaoliao, Zhongyuan, Lanyin, Southwestern, and Jianghuai. For a more detailed discussion, see R. Li (1988) and Ting (1996).

2 Establishment and promotion of Modern Spoken Chinese

1. The dialect of Beijing in the twentieth century is considerably different from that in the Yuan dynasty. The majority of the residents in Beijing from around 1400 onwards were migrants,

mostly from Anhui and Shanxi provinces in the Ming dynasty, and from the northeastern provinces and Hebei province in the Qing dynasty.

2. This is quoted from Coblin (1997:51).

3. I suppose it was much the same situation with the standard spoken Chinese before *guānhuà*.

4. The term *guóyǔ* before modern times was usually used to refer to the native language of the ruling non-Han dynasty. For example, the word in writings of the Qing dynasty before the twentieth century normally refers to Manchu.

5. The chaos that occurred during the promotion of the national language in the old national pronunciation contributed to the switch to a new standard of pronunciation. It was reported that, on cases where the stipulated old national pronunciation differed from the Beijing pronunciation, instructors in a primary school fought against each other over which should be taken as the correct one, and the principal had to admit that both pronunciations were correct (J. Li 1935:97).

6. Fu Sinian noted in his memoir that, in the 1920s, when he spoke in the Beijing dialect, he was ridiculed by his family in the Shandong province as 'talking like an old maid'.

7. The term *pǔtōnghuà* first appeared in Zhu Wenxiong's *Jiāngsū xīn zìmǔ*, which was published in 1906. It was defined as 'the speech form that can be used in all provinces'.

8. According to Wang Li (1980a:191–2), the definition that *pǔtōnghuà* is based on Northern Mandarin as its base dialect means that its lexical norms should be based on those of Northern Mandarin.

9. The statistics here are far from being generally accepted. Zhou Youguang (1992:39) reported that some people estimated in 1988 that only about 10 per cent of the population in mainland China speak *pǔtōnghuà*.

3 Norms and variations of Modern Standard Chinese

1. When applying the Western phonemics to the analysis of Chinese, linguists differ greatly with regard to the number and nature of phonemes in Modern Standard Chinese (see Hockett 1947; Z. W. Lu 1956; J. Zhang 1957; S. Xu 1957; Norman 1988). Chao (1934), which has become a classic treatise on the issue, argues that as palatals are in complementary distribution with the dental sibilants, the retroflexes, and the velars, they can be treated as allophonic with either the dental sibilants or the velars. A similar situation obtains with vowels. Scholars like Xu Shirong (1957) and Norman (1988) maintain that from a phonemic point of view, Modern Standard Chinese exhibits five vocalic contrasts, with a great variety of allophonic variations. Hockett (1947), on the other hand, worked with two vowels [a] and [e] and three semi-vowels [i], [u], and [r], while Zhang Jing (1957) identified thirty-five vowel phonemes.

2. It is stated in Ji (1988:65) that although rhotacization may stand to enrich the vocabulary and enhance the expressive power of the language, rhotacized words should not be admitted into *pǔtōnghuà* in large quantities because they are only used in limited geographical areas. In other words, they are labelled as dialectalisms.

4 The standard and dialects

1. 'Diglossia' was first only used with reference to varieties of the same language in Ferguson (1959). It was later extended by Fishman (1967) and others to situations where different languages are involved.

2. The practice was later discouraged in a directive jointly issued by the State Language Commission and the Ministry for Broadcasting, Film, and Television in 1987.

5 Development and promotion of Modern Written Chinese

1. For instance, it is observed that traditional Northern Mandarin differs from the Southern dialects with respect to yes/no questions. Of the following patterns, (1) and (2) are used in the former, and (3) in the latter:

   (1) VP *bù* 'not' VP
   (2) VP *méiyǒu* 'have-not'
   (3) adverb VP

   In the traditional *báihuà* literature, as expected, (1) and (2) are normally found; but (3) is also occasionally used, presumably by writers from the Southern dialect areas. The choice between (1) and (2) on the one hand, and (3) on the other, has been cited as evidence in ascertaining the identity of the author of *Jīn píng méi* (see Zhu 1985; Hashimoto 1988).

2. There were some novelists in the late Qing who experimented with writing in Southern dialects like Cantonese and Wu, and produced novels such as *Jiǔ wěi guī* and *Hǎi shàng huā liè zhuàn*. All such works had only very limited circulation, far less popular than contemporary writings in *báihuà* based on Northern Mandarin. That their experimental attempts proved to be abortive, according to Doleželová-Velingerová (1977:23), was both because of the difficulties of transcribing the pronunciation of these Southern dialects in Chinese characters and because of the limited numbers of readers who were able to understand the texts. For more details, see Chapter 7.

3. As quoted in Davies (1992:203), the regional dialect background of 213 writers who were active from the early twentieth century onwards is as follows: Beijing 2 per cent, other North Mandarin 14 per cent, South-West Mandarin 22 per cent, South (Jiang-Huai) Mandarin 11 per cent, Wu 40 per cent, Cantonese 6 per cent, Min 5 per cent.

4. There is ample evidence that the inventory of the basic syllables in Chinese as spoken in the eighth century was reduced by half as compared with what was represented in *Qièyùn* compiled in 601. It was further reduced by at least another half in the fourteenth century, as shown in *Zhōngyuán yīnyùn* compiled in 1324 (for a detailed account, see L. Wang 1980b).

5. According to the latest statistics in Beijing Yuyan Xueyuan (1986), the average length of words in Modern Written Chinese is 1.48 syllables. In the fields of social and natural sciences, di- and multi-syllabic words make up 51 per cent of the vocabulary in texts. For more details, see Part III.

6. Chao Yuen Ren (1980) illustrated this point in an insightful manner when he composed two short stories using *wényán* words which are pronounced exactly the same except for the tone in some cases, but are represented by different characters. The texts do not make any sense if transcribed into a romanized system.

7. These people succeeded to some extent. In addition to the examples to be discussed later, a well-known example of their achievements is the introduction into Modern Written Chinese of the distinct third person pronouns for masculine, feminine, and neuter gender. Three different characters are now used for this purpose, although there is no difference in actual pronunciation. Furthermore, Western punctuation marks have been systematically introduced into Chinese, and firmly established. The overwhelming majority of publications in mainland China have adopted the left to right horizontal arrangement of characters in the same style as in Western languages instead of the traditional up to down vertical format.

8. Journalism is the field where *wényán* holds on most tenaciously. Until the end of the 1940s, almost twenty years after the movement of promoting *báihuà*, a large portion of editorials and news reports were still written in *wényán* instead of *báihuà*. The situation has changed

somewhat since then. But still, expressions characteristic of Old Chinese are ubiquitous in Chinese newspapers and journals published in every Chinese community, especially for titles. I examined at random the front page of the 25 February 1992 issue of *Rénmín Rìbào*. Of the eleven titles on the page, five contain words and expressions that are distinctively *wényán*.

6 Norms and variations of Modern Written Chinese

1. Gunn (1991:196) observes that the construction appears rarely in the late 1920s, and it gains in frequency during the 1930s.
2. *Bèi* was occasionally found to be used for situations other than undesirable ones in traditional *báihuà*, as reported in Gunn 1991. Such examples were few and far between before the twentieth century, and should be considered to be exceptional.
3. This example is borrowed from Kubler (1985:140).
4. There were two important reasons for the switch to Japanese as the main source of books on western learning to be translated into Chinese. First, by the end of the twentieth century, almost all of the important works in the West, particularly in political sciences, economy, and sociology had been translated into Japanese. Second, after the Sino-Japanese War in 1894, thousands of Chinese students went to Japan to study there, and were exposed to western learning via Japanese. Since the written Japanese at that time contained a large number of Chinese characters it was much easier for Chinese to translate from Japanese than from European languages.
5. It is reported that a working group has been set up in Taiwan under government auspices to reduce terminological discrepancies between Taiwan and mainland China (see *Zhōngyāng Rìbào* (*Central Daily News*), International Edition, 30 May 1992, p. 7).

7 Dialect writing

1. No writing before the Qing dynasty has been found that was composed exclusively in one of the Southern dialects. *Shāngē* 'Folk songs' compiled by Feng Menglong in the late Ming dynasty is the first important literary work that contains a substantial amount of elements from the Wu dialect.
2. Among the writing systems designed by the missionaries, that for writing in Southern Min has been the most influential one. According to Zhou Youguang (1992:209), there are at least 50,000 women who are still using the writing system which was designed specifically to write in the Xiamen dialect.
3. All the devices listed here have actually been used in the development of writing in Mandarin-based *báihuà*. On the other hand, there are still words in Northern Mandarin that do not have conventional representation in characters (see Chapter 3 with reference to the Beijing dialect). It seems that if there is a will, a fully-fledged writing system in Chinese characters can be developed for any of the Chinese dialects. The fact that the present-day Chinese script is much better adapted for writing in Northern Mandarin than Southern dialects is nothing more than the result of the historical, demographic, and political factors under discussion here.
4. At a time when the promotion of Northern Mandarin as a lingua franca across Chinese dialects had achieved far from satisfactory success even among officials and educated people, separate phonetic writing systems for different dialects seemed to be the only means of attaining the goal of *wǒ shǒu xiě wǒ kǒu* 'my hand writes as my mouth speaks'. See Chapter 5 for further discussion.
5. For a more elaborated account of this point, see P. Chen (1996b).

8 **Basic features of the Chinese writing system**

1. There are two exceptions to the statement that one character represents one syllable: (1) The character *ér* represents a rhotacized sound that is generally considered not to be a full syllable; (2) There are a few characters, mostly coined during the past century, that represent more than one syllable, like 瓩 *qiānwǎ* 'kilowatt' and 浬 *hǎilǐ* 'nautical mile'. These characters have been withdrawn from regular use by the language planning institution in mainland Chinese, and replaced with two-character words.

2. *Xíngshēng* characters which are homophonous may contain different phonetic determinatives which are not related. Furthermore, the phonetic determinatives are all independent characters with their own meaning. Sometimes, a grapheme can serve either as a phonetic or a semantic determinative.

3. Sometimes, a grapheme has more than one meaning. Given that the relationships among the meanings represented by a single grapheme may range from closely derivative to unrelated, it is not always easy to draw a sharp distinction between a polysemous morpheme and homographic morphemes, It is safe, however, to assume that distinct characters which have the same phonetic value as in Table 8.3 represent at least as many distinct morphemes.

9 **Simplification of the traditional writing system**

1. After they were officially withdrawn, the simplified characters were still used in some publications, particularly in the Communist controlled areas.

2. The basic components comprising List 3 actually appear in simplified form only in about one third of all containing characters in the 1964 General List of Simplified Characters.

10 **Phonetization of Chinese**

1. A peculiar script, called *nǚshū* 'woman script', has recently been found in the Hunan province, China, which is used to write a local dialect the genetic affiliation of which has not been finally clarified yet. It is composed of about 1,000 basic phonographic symbols, which are similar in function to the *yīnbiāozì* and *tōngzì* under discussion here. About 80 per cent of the symbols were adapted from regular Chinese characters, assuming graphic shapes which are usually longer than the latter, and tilt towards the right. It has been used exclusively among women mainly for writing lyrics and stories.

2. I am grateful to Perry Link for this observation (personal communication).

3. It was revealed by Liu Yongquan that expert linguists from the Soviet Union who participated in the design of a phonetic writing system for Chinese in the early 1950s tried in vain to persuade the Chinese to adopt a Cyrillic script.

4. The great majority of publications in Taiwan are printed in vertical lines from right to left. While roman letters are rarely arranged in the vertical order, *zhùyīn zìmǔ* fits in well with both horizontal and vertical writings. This is an important reason why *zhùyīn zìmǔ* still prevails over romanization in Taiwan.

11 **Use and reform of the Chinese writing system: present and future**

1. The newspaper switched to the simplified script years later.

2. The revised Second Scheme is composed of two lists. List 1 is made up of ninety-one simplified characters which are not to appear in simplified forms elsewhere as component parts of other characters, and List 2 has twenty which assume the simplified form both as autonomous characters and as component parts of other characters (J. Wang 1995).

3. It was reported that the experiment was later extended to other parts of the country, involving hundreds of thousands of school children.

References

Atlas 1987/1991. *Language atlas of China* (Part I and Part II), Steven A. Wurm et al. (eds.). Hong Kong: Longman Group (Far East) Ltd.

Bao, Mingwei 1955. Lüèlùn Hànzú gòngtóngyǔ de xíngchéng hé fāzhǎn. In: Yushu Hu (ed.), 1980, 41–9.

Barnes, Dayle 1977. To ER or not to ER. *Journal of Chinese linguistics* 5(2), 211–36.

Bauer, Robert S. 1988. Written Cantonese of Hong Kong. *Cahiers de Linguistique Asie Orientale* 17, 245–93.

Beijing Yuyan Xueyuan 1986. *Xiàndài Hànyǔ pínlǜ cídiǎn*. Beijing: Beijing Yǔyán Xuéyuàn Chūbǎnshè.

Ben Kan Bianjizu 1982. Xiānggǎng Kǎoshìjú duì jiǎntǐzì de tàidù. *Yǔwén Jiànshè Tōngxùn* 7, 2–3.

Ben Kan Zhiliaoshi 1986. Taiwan zhèngshì gōngbù shǐyòng "guóyǔ zhùyīn fúhào dì èr shì". *Yǔwén Jiànshè* 7, 57–9.

Bolinger, Dwight 1946. Visual morphemes. *Language* 22, 333–40.

Bolton, Kingsley and Kwok, Helen (eds.) 1992. *Sociolinguistics today: international perspectives*. London: Routledge.

Bradley, David 1992. Chinese as a pluricentric language. In Michael G. Clyne (ed.), *Pluricentric languages: contributions to the sociology of language*, 305–24. Berlin: Mouton de Gruyter.

Chan, Marjorie K. M. and Tai, James H.-Y. 1995. Some reflections on the periodization of the Chinese language. MS. The Ohio State University.

Chang, Baoru 1989. Xiàndài Hànyǔ pínlǜ cídiǎn de yánzhì. In Yuan Chen (ed.), 30–59.

Chao, Yuen Ren 1923. Guóyǔ luómǎzì de yánjiū. In Guoyu (ed.), 87–117.

1930. A system of tone letters. *Le Maître Phonétique* troisième série 30, 24–7.

1934. The non-uniqueness of phonemic solutions of phonetic systems. *Bulletin of the Institute of History and Philology* 4, 363–97; also reprinted in Martin Joos (ed.), *Readings in linguistics*, 38–54. Washington, DC: ACLS.

1976. A preliminary sketch of General Chinese. In Anwar S. Dil (ed.), *Aspects of Chinese sociolinguistics: essays by Yuan Ren Chao*, 106–43. Stanford: Stanford University Press.

1980. *Yǔyán wèntì*. Beijing: Shāngwù Yìnshūguǎn.

Chen, Chungyu 1983. A fifth tone in the Mandarin spoken in Singapore. *Journal of Chinese Linguistics* 11(1), 93–119.

1986. Xīnjiāpō Huáyǔ yǔfǎ tèzhēng. *Yǔyán Yánjiū* 1, 138–52.

Chen, Duxiu 1917. Wénxué gémìng lùn. In Jiabi Zhao (ed.), 1935, 44–7.

Chen, Engquan (ed.) 1989. *Shuāngyǔ shuāngfāngyán*. Guangzhou: Zhōngshān Dàxué Chūbǎnshè.

Chen, Jianmin 1989. *Yǔyán wénhuà shèhuì xīntàn*. Shanghai: Shanghai Jiàoyù Chūbǎnshè.

Chen, Jianmin and Zhu, Wanjin 1992. Yǔyán de shìchǎng jiàzhí. *Yǔyán Wénzì Yìngyòng* 2, 59–66.

Chen, Lifu et al. 1985. *Zhōngguó wénzì yǔ Zhōngguó wénhuà lùnwénjí*. Taipei: Zhōnghuá Mínguó Kǒng Mèng Xuéhuì.

Chen, Mingyuan 1981. Shùlǐ tǒngjì zài Hànyǔ yánjiū zhōng de yìngyòng. *Zhōngguó Yǔwén* 6, 466–74.

Chen, Ping 1993. Modern Written Chinese in development. *Language in Society* 22(4), 505–37.

1994. Four projected functions of new writing systems of Chinese. *Anthropological Linguistics* 36(3), 366–81.

1996a. Toward a phonographic writing system of Chinese: a case study in writing reform. *International Journal of Sociology of Language* 122, 1–46.

1996b. Modern Written Chinese, dialects, and regional identity. *Language Problems and Language Planning* 20(3), 223–43.

Chen, Songcen 1990. Shàoxīngshì chéngqū pǔtōnghuà de shèhuì fēnbù jí qí fāzhǎn qūshì. *Yǔwén Jiànshè* 1, 41–7.

Chen, Wangdao 1934. Guānyú dàzhòngyǔ wénxué de jiànshè. In Zhong Ren (ed.), Part 3, 4–7.

Chen, Weizhan 1988. Wǒ duì Hànzì qiántú de yìxiē kànfǎ. In Seminar, 39–49.

Chen, Yuan (ed.) 1989. *Xiàndài Hànyǔ dìngliàng fēnxī*. Shanghai: Shanghai Jiàoyù Chūbǎnshè.

Chen, Zhangtai 1990. Guānyú pǔtōnghuà yǔ fāngyán de jǐ ge wèntí. *Yǔwén Jiànshè* 4, 27–9.

1992. Lùn Hànzì jiǎnhuà. *Yǔyán Wénzì Yìngyòng* 2, 1–6.

Chen, Zizhan 1934. Wényán, báihuà, dàzhòngyǔ. In Zhong Ren (ed.), Part 3, 1–3.

Cheng, Robert L. 1978. Taiwanese morphemes in search of Chinese characters. *Journal of Chinese linguistics* 6, 306–14.

1979. Language unification movement in Taiwan: present and future. In McCormack and Wurm (eds.), *Language and society: anthropological issues*, 541–79. The Hague: Mouton.

1985. A comparison of Taiwanese, Taiwan Mandarin and Peking Mandarin. *Language* 61(1), 352–77.

1986. Contradictions in Chinese language reform. *International Journal of the Sociology of Language* 59, 87–96.

1989. Essays on written Taiwanese. Taipei: Zìlì Wǎnbào Wénhuà Chūbǎnbù.

Cheng, Robert L. and Huang, Shuanfan (eds.) 1988. *The Structure of Taiwanese: a modern synthesis*. Taipei: Wenhe Chuban Youxian Gongsi.

Christian, Donna 1988. Language planning: the view from linguistics. In Frederick Newmeyer (ed.), *Linguistics: the Cambridge survey* volume IV: *The socio-cultural context*, 193–209. Cambridge University Press.

Clyne, Michael 1992. Language planning. In William Bright (ed.), *International Encyclopedia of Linguistics*, 84–7. New York and Oxford: Oxford University Press.

Coblin, W. South 1997. Notes on the sound system of Late Ming Guanhua. MS. University of Iowa.

1998. A brief history of Mandarin. MS. University of Iowa.

Cooper, Robert L. 1989. *Language planning and social change*. Cambridge: Cambridge University Press.

Coulmas, Florian 1989. The writing system of the world. London: Basil Blackwell.

1992. Writing systems. In William Bright (ed.), *International Encyclopedia of Linguistics* volume IV, 253–57. New York and Oxford: Oxford University Press.

Dai, Zhaoming 1991. Fántǐ fēng, "shì fán xiě jiǎn" hé yǔwén lìfǎ wèntí. *Yǔyán Wénzì Yìngyòng* 1, 49–55.

Dale, Ian R. H. 1980. Digraphia. *International Journal of the Sociology of Language* 26, 5–13.

Davies, Peter 1992. The non-Beijing dialect component in Modern Standard Chinese. In Bolton and Kwok (eds.), 192–206.

DeFrancis, John 1950. *Nationalism and language reform in China*. Princeton: Princeton University Press.

1979. Mao Tse-tung and writing reform. In Joshua A. Fogel and William T. Rowe (eds.), *Perspectives on a changing China*, 137–54. Boulder, Colorado: Westview Press.

1984a. Digraphia. *Word* 35(1), 59–66.

1984b. *The Chinese language: fact and fantasy*. Honolulu: University of Hawaii Press.

1989. *Visible speech: the diverse oneness of writing systems*. Honolulu: University of Hawaii Press.

Ding, Yicheng, Li, Nan and Bao, Quan'en 1985. "Zhùyīn shízì, tíqián dúxiě" shìyàn bàogào. *Yǔwén Xiàndàihuà* 8, 134–48.

Doleželová-Valingerová, Melina 1977. The origin of Modern Chinese literature. In Merle Goldman (ed.), *Modern Chinese literature in the May Fourth era*, Harvard East Asian Series, no. 89, 17–35. Cambridge, Massachusetts: Harvard University Press.

Erbaugh, Mary S. 1995. Southern Chinese dialects: a medium for reconciliation within Greater China. *Language in Society* 24, 79–94.

Fan, Guo and Wu, Xinjie 1992. Xiānggǎng diànhuàbù Guǎngzhōuhuà páijiǎn xìtǒng píngshù. MS. Hong Kong: Hong Kong Baptist College.

Fan, Keyu 1993. Cóng "shéngcí shóu zì shuō" kàn cíyì hé gòucí yǔsùyì de guānxì. *Yǔyán Wénzì Yìngyòng* 1, 49–55.

Fang, Shidu 1969. *Wǔshí nián lái Zhōngguó Guóyǔ yùndòng shǐ*. Taipei: Guóyǔ Rìbào Shè.

Fasold, Ralph 1984. *The sociolinguistics of society*. London: Basil Blackwell.

1990. *The sociolinguistics of language*. London: Basil Blackwell.

Fei, Jinchang 1993. Hǎixiá liǎng àn xiànxíng hànzì zìxíng de bǐjiǎo fēnxī. *Yǔyán Wénzì Yìngyòng* 1, 37–48.

Fei, Jinchang and Qi, Wen 1986. Shāngdiàn yòngzì diàochá bàogào. *Yǔwén Jiànshè* 1, 30–52.

Ferguson, Charles A. 1959. Diglossia. *Word* 15, 325–40.

1968. Language development. In Fishman et al. (eds.), 27–35.

Fishman, Joshua A. 1967. Bilingualism with and without diglossia; diglossia with and without bilingualism. *Journal of Social Issues* 13(2), 29–38.

Fishman, Joshua A., Ferguson, Charles and Das Gupta, Jyotirindra (eds.) 1968. *Language problems of developing nations*. New York: John Wiley & Sons.

Fu, Sinian. 1917. Wén yán héyī cǎoyì. In Jiabi Zhao (ed.), 1935, 121–6.

1918. Zěnyàng zuò báihuàwén. In Jiabi Zhao (ed.), 1935, 217–27.

1919. Hànyǔ gǎi yòng pīnyīn wénzì de chūbù tán. In Jiabi Zhao (ed.), 1935, 147–64.

Fu, Yonghe 1980. Cóng Hànzì jiǎnhuà fāng'àn dào jiǎnhuàzì zǒngbiǎo. *Yǔwén Xiàndàihuà* 3, 188–9.

1989. Xiàndài Hànyǔ chángyòngzìbiǎo de yánzhì. In Yuan Chen (ed.), 107–15.

Gao, Tianru 1993. *Zhōngguó xiàndài yǔyán jìhuà de lǐlùn hé shíjiàn*. Shanghai: Fùdàn Dàxué Chūbǎnshè.

Gelb, I. J. 1963. *A study of writing*. 2nd edition. Chicago: The University of Chicago Press.

Guan, Xiechu 1988. *Hànzì jiǎnhuà wèntí*. In Symposium, 108–9.

Gunn, Edward 1991. *Rewriting Chinese: Style and innovation in twentieth-century Chinese prose*. Stanford University Press.

Guo, Youpeng 1990. Húběi Shíyàn Shì pǔtōnghuà yǔ fāngyán de shǐyòng qíngkuàng. *Zhōngguó Yǔwèn* 6, 427–32.

Guoyu Yanjiuhui (ed.) 1923. *Guóyǔ Yuèkàn: Hànzì gǎigé hào*. Reprinted by Beijing: Wénzì Gǎigé Chūbǎnshè.

Haas, William 1983. Determining the level of a script. In Florian Coulmas and Konrad Ehlich (eds.), *Writing in Focus* 1983, 15–29, Berlin: Mouton.

Haas, William (ed.) 1976. *Writing without letters*. Manchester University Press.

Hashimoto, Anne Yue 1988. Hànyǔ fāngyán yǔfǎ de bǐjiào yánjiū. *Bulletin of the Institute of History and Philology* 59(1), 23–41. Academia Sinica.

Haugen, Einar 1966. Dialect, language, nation. *American Anthropologist* 68, 922–35.

1983. The implementation of corpus planning: theory and practice. In Juan Cobarrubias and Joshua A. Fishman (eds.), 1983, *Progress of language planning: international perspectives*, 269–89. Berlin: Mouton.

He, Zhongying 1923. Hànzì gǎigé de lìshǐguān. In Guoyu Yanjiuhui (ed.), 1923, 125–31.

Hill, Archibald A. 1967. The typology of writing systems. In William M. Austin (ed.), *Papers in linguistics: in honor of Leon Dostert*, 92–9. The Hague: Mouton.

Ho, Wai Kit 1989. *Yìxué xīnlùn*. Taipei: Shulin.

Hockett, Charles 1947. Peiping phonology. *Journal of the American Oriental Society* 67, 253–67.

Hong, Weiren 1992a. *Táiwān yǔyán wēijī*. Taiwan: Qiánwèi Chūbǎnshè.

1992b. *Táiyǔ wénxué yǔ Táiyǔ wénzì*. Taiwan: Qiánwèi Chūbǎnshè.

Hoosain, Rumjahn 1991. *Psycholinguistic implications for linguistic relativity: a case study of Chinese*. New Jersey: Lawrence Erlbaum.

Hsu, Raymond S. W. 1979. What is standard Chinese? In Lord (ed.), 1979, 115–41.

Hu, Mingyang 1991. *Yǔyánxué lùnwén xuǎn*. Beijing: Zhōngguó Rénmín Dàxué Chūbǎnshè.

Hu, Qiguang 1990. Wǒguó jìndài de liǎng cì shūmiànyǔ gǎigé yùndòng. *Yǔwén Xiàndàihuà* 9, 226–39.

Hu, Shi 1917. Wénxué gǎiliáng chúyì. In Jiabi Zhao (ed.), 1935, 34–43.

1918. Jiànshè de wénxué gémìng lùn. In Jiabi Zhao (ed.), 1935, 127–40.

1923. Juǎntóu yǔ. In Guoyu Yanjiuhui (ed.), 1923, 1–4.

1935. Dǎoyán. In Jiabi Zhao (ed.), 1935, 1–32.

Hu, Yushu (ed.) 1980. *Xiàndài Hànyú cānkǎo zīliào*. Shanghai: Shanghai Jiàoyù Chūbǎnshè.

Huang, Guoying 1988. Táiwān dāngdài xiǎoshuō de cíhuì yǔfǎ tèdiǎn. *Zhōngguó Yǔwén* 3, 194–201.

Huang, Shuanfan 1988. A sociolinguistic profile of Taipei (1). In Cheng and Huang (eds.), 1988, 301–33.

1993. *Yǔyán, shèhuì yǔ zúqún yìshì*. Taipei: Wénhè Chūbǎnshè.

Ji, Xianlin (ed.) 1988. *Zhōngguó dà bǎikē quánshū: yǔyán wénzì*. Beijing: Zhōngguó Dà Bǎikē Quánshū Chūbǎnshè.

Jiang, Shanguo 1987. *Hànzìxué*. Shanghai: Shanghai Jiàoyù Chūbǎnshè.

Jiang, Shaoyu. 1994. *Jìndài Hànyǔ yánjiū gàikuàng*. Beijing: Beijing Dàxué Chūbǎnshè.

Kalmar, Ivan, et al. 1987. Language attitudes in Guangzhou, China. *Language in Society* 16, 499–508.

Kloss, Heinz 1968. Notes concerning a language-nation typology. In Fishman et al. (eds.), 69–86.

Kubler, Cornelius C. 1985. *The development of Mandarin in Taiwan: a case study of language contact*. Taipei: Student Book Co., Ltd.

Kublen, Cornelius C. and Ho, George T. C. 1984. *Varieties of spoken Standard Chinese*, volume II: *A speaker from Taipei*, 1–13. Dordrecht: Foris Publications.

Kuo, Eddie C. Y. 1985. *Xīnjiāpō de yǔyán yu shèhuì*. Taipei: Cheng Chung Book Co. Ltd.

Lee, Kuan Yew 1990. Opening address. In Xinjiapo Huawen Yanjiuhui (ed.), 1990, 7–9.

Leung, Yin-bing 1994. A survey on the uses of dialects in the Pearl River Delta Region. MS. The University of Queensland.

Li, Charles N. and Thompson, Sandra A. 1981. *Mandarin Chinese: a functional reference grammar*. Berkeley and Los Angeles: University of California Press.

Li, Chen-ching 1982. The sociolinguistic context of Mandarin in Taiwan: trends and development. In C. Chu, W. S. Coblin and F. F. Tsao (eds.), *Papers from the 14th International Conference on Sino-Tibetan Languages & Linguistics*, 259–275. Taipei: Student Book Company.

Li, Jinxi 1923. Hànzì gémìngjūn qiánjìn de yì tiáo dàdào. In Guoyu Yanjiuhui (ed.), 1923, 27–65.

————— 1935. *Guóyǔ yùndòng shǐgāng* Shanghai: Shāngwù Yìnshūguǎn.

Li, Qingmei 1992. Hǎixiá liǎng'àn zìyīn bǐjiào. *Yǔyán Yánjiū yǔ Yìngyòng* 3, 42–8.

Li, Rong 1988. Guānhuà fāngyán de fēnqū. *Fāngyán* 1, 2–5.

————— 1990. Pǔtōnghuà yǔ fāngyán. *Zhōngguó Yǔwén* 5, 321–4.

Li, Rulong 1988. Lùn pǔtōnghuà de pǔjí hé guīfàn. *Yǔwén Jiànshè* 2, 43–6.

————— 1995. Mǐnnán fāngyán dìqū de yǔyán shēnghuó. *Yǔwén Yánjiū* 2, 34–7.

Li, Xindi 1995. Jìndài Hànyǔ gòngtóngyǔ yǔyīn de gòuchéng, yǎnjìn yǔ liànghuà fēnxī. *Yǔyán Yánjiū* 2, 1–23.

Li, Xinkui 1980. Lùn jìndài Hànyǔ gòngtóngyǔ de biāozhǔnyīn. In Xinkui Li (ed.), 1993, 150–67.

————— 1987. Hànyǔ gòngtóngyǔ de xíngchéng hé fāzhǎn. In Xinkui Li (ed.), 1993, 265–95.

Li, Xinkui (ed.) 1993. *Lǐ Xīnkuí zìxuǎnjí*. Henan Jiàoyù Chūbǎnshè.

Li, Xueqin 1985. Kǎogǔ fāxiàn yǔ Zhōngguó de wénzì qǐyuán. In Shouhe Ding et al. (eds.), *Zhōngguó wénhuà yánjiū jíkān* volume II, 146–57. Shanghai: Fùdàn Dàxué Chūbǎnshè.

Liang, James C. P., DeFrancis, John, and Han, Y. H. 1982. *Varieties of Spoken Standard Chinese* volume I: *A speaker from Tianjin*. Dordrecht: Foris Publications.

Liang, Yuzhang 1990. Fúzhōu fāngyán cíhuì lǐ pǔtōnghuà cír tìhuàn xiànxiàng. *Yǔwén Jiànshè* 6, 14–18.

Lin, Lianhe 1980. Guānyú hànzì tǒngjì tèzhēng de jǐ ge wèntí. *Yǔwén Xiàndàihuà* 1, 135–50.

Lin, Yutang 1971. *Chinese–English dictionary of modern usage*. Hong Kong: Chinese University Press.

Liu, Bannong 1917. Wǒ zhī wénxué gǎiliáng guān. In Jiabi Zhao (ed.), 1935, 63–73.

Liu, Daosheng 1986. Xīnshíqī de yǔyán wénzì gōngzuò. In Proceedings 1987, 16–34.

Liu, Hong 1993. Yǔyán tàidù duì yǔyán shǐyòng hé yǔyán biànhuà de yǐngxiǎng. *Yǔyán Wénzì Yìngyòng* 3, 93–102.

Liu, Jian et al. 1992. *Jìndài Hànyǔ xūcí yánjiū*. Beijing: Yǔwén Chūbǎnshè.

Liu, Yongquan 1986. Terminological development and organization in China. *International Journal of the Sociology of Language* 59, 33–46.

Liu, Zhaoxiong 1993. Lùn pǔtōnghuà de quèlì hé tuīguǎng. *Yǔyán Wénzì Yìngyòng* 2, 57–65.

Lock, Graham 1989. Aspects of variation and change in the Mandarin Chinese spoken in Singapore. *Australian Journal of Linguistics* 9, 277–94.

Lord, Robert (ed.) 1979. *Hong Kong language papers*. Hong Kong: Hong Kong University Press.

Lu, Guoyao 1994. Míng dài guānhuà jíqí jīchǔ fāngyán wèntí. In *Lǔ Guóyáo Zìxuǎnjí*, 292–304. Henan Jiàoyù Chūbǎnshè.

Lu, Shaochang 1985. Tán Xīnjiāpō tuīguǎng huáyǔ de jīngyàn. *Yǔwén Jiànshè Tōngxùn* 17, 21–4.

1990. Xīnjiāpō Huáyǔ cíhuì de kǎochá. In Xinjiapo Huawen Yanjiuhui (ed.), 1990, 336–41.

Lu, Zhiwei 1956. Guānyú Běijīnghuà yǔyīn xìtǒng de jǐ gè wèntí. In Xiandai Hanyu guifan wenti xueshu huiyi mishuchu (ed.), *Xiàndài hànyǔ guīfàn wèntí xuéshù huìyì wénjiàn huìbiān*, 48–68. Beijing: Wénzì Gǎigé Chūbǎnshè.

Lu, Zhuangzhang 1892. *Yímùliǎorán chūjiè: Zhōngguó qièyīn xīn zì Xiàqiāng*. Reprinted in 1956. Beijing: Wénzì Gǎigé Chūbǎnshè.

Luo, Changpei and Lü, Shuxiang 1955. Xiàndài Hànyǔ guīfàn wèntí. In Yushu Hu (ed.), 1980, 81–106.

Luo, Yi 1990. Táiwān "Biāozhǔn Xíngshū Fànběn" chūbǎn shí zhōunián. *Yǔwén Jiànshè* 6, 53–60.

Lü, Shuxiang 1985a. *Jìndài Hànyǔ zǐdàicí*. Shanghai: Xuélín Chūbǎnshè.

1985b. *Jìndài Hànyǔ dúběn* xù. In Jian Liu, *Jìndài Hànyǔ dúběn*, 1–4, Shanghai: Shanghai Jiàoyù Chūbǎnshè.

Lü, Shuxiang and Zhu, Dexi 1952. *Yǔfǎ xiūcí jiǎnghuà*. Beijing: Kāimíng Shūdiàn.

Ma, Zuyi 1984. *Zhōngguó fānyì jiǎnshǐ: Wǔsì yùndòng yǐqián bùfèn*. Beijing: Zhōngguó Duìwài Fānyì Chūbǎn Gōngsī.

Mair, Victor H. 1991. Preface: Building the future of information processing in East Asia; demands facing linguistic and technological reality. In: Victor H. Mair and Yongquan Liu (eds.) *Characters and Computers*, 1–8. IOS Press.

1994. Buddhism and the rise of the written vernacular in East Asia: The making of national languages. *The Journal of Asian Studies* 53(3), 707–51.

Masini, Federico 1993. *The formation of Modern Chinese lexicon and its evolution toward a national language: the period from 1840–1898*. Monograph Series Number 6 of *Journal of Chinese Linguistics*.

Mao, Zedong 1969. *Selected works of Mao Zedong*. Beijing: Rénmín Chūbǎnshè.

Mei, Tsulin 1994. Tángdài, Sòngdài gōnggòngyǔ de yǔfǎ hé xiàndài fāngyán de yǔfǎ. In Paul Jen-Kuei Li, Chu-Ren Huang, and Chih-Chen Jane Tang (eds.), *Zhōngguó jìnnèi yǔyán jí yǔyánxué* 2, 61–97. Taipei, Taiwan.

Miao, Jin'an 1989. Xiānggǎng de yǔwén zhèngcè hé yǔwén guīhuà. In Engquang Chen (ed.), 1989, 106–11.

Newman, John 1988. Singapore's speak Mandarin campaign. *Journal of Multilingual and Multicultural Development* 9(5), 437–48.

Ng, Bee Chin 1985. A study of the variable /sh/ in Singapore Mandarin. *Papers in South-East Asian Linguistics* No. 9: *Language policy, language planning and sociolinguistics in South-East Asia*, 31–7. *Pacific Linguistics*, A-67, 1985.

Ni, Haishu 1948a. *Zhōngguó pīnyīn wénzì gàilùn*. Shanghai: Shídài Shūbào
    Chūbǎnshè.
    1948b. *Zhōngguó pīnyīn wénzì yùndòng shǐ*. Shanghai: Shídài Shūbào
    Chūbǎnshè.
    1959. *Qīngmò Hànyǔ pīnyīn yùndòng biānniánshǐ*. Shanghai: Shanghai
    Rénmín Chūbǎnshè.
Ni, Haishu (ed.) 1949. *Zhōngguó yǔwén de xīnshēng*. Shanghai: Shídài Shūbào
    Chūbǎnshè.
    1958. *Qīngmò wénzì gǎigé wénjí*. Beijing: Wénzì Gǎigé Chūbǎnshè.
Norman, Jerry 1988. *Chinese*. Cambridge: Cambridge University Press.
Ohta, Tatsuo 1991. *Hànyǔ shǐ tōngkǎo*, Chinese translation of *Chugokugo-shi
    tsuko* by Jiang Lansheng and Bai Weiguo. Chongqing: Chongqing
    Chūbǎnshè.
Peyraube, Alain. 1988. *Syntaxe diachronique du Chinois*. Paris: Collège de
    France, Institut des Hautes Etudes Chinoises.
    1995. Westernization of the Chinese grammar in the 20th century:
    myth or reality? Paper delivered at the Symposium 'Prisma Sprache'.
    Bad-Homburg, 1–25.
    1996. Recent issues in Chinese historical syntax. In James C.-T. Huang and
    Y.–H. Audrey Li (eds.), *New horizons in Chinese linguistics*, 161–213.
    Dordrecht: Kluwer Academic Publishers.
Pierson, Herbert D. 1988. Xiānggǎng dìqū de yǔyán tàidù hé yǔyán yìngyòng: diù
    pǔtōnghuà de kǎochá. *Zhōngguó Yǔwén* 6, 423–30.
Platt, John T. 1985. Bilingual policies in a multilingual society: reflections of the
    Singapore Mandarin Campaign in the English language press. In David
    Bradley (ed.), *Papers in South-East Asian linguistics* No. 9. *Language policy,
    language planning and sociolinguistics in South-East Asia*, 15–30. *Pacific
    Linguistics* A-67.
Proceedings 1957. *Dì yí cì quánguó wénzì gǎigé huìyì wénjiàn huìbiān*. Beijing:
    Wénzì Gǎigé Chūbǎnshè.
Proceedings 1987. *Xīnshíqī de yǔyán wénzì gōngzuò: quánguó yǔyán wénzì
    gōngzuò huìyì wénjiàn huìbiān*. Beijing: Yǔwén Chūbǎnshè.
Pulgram, Ernst 1976. The typologies of writing-systems. In Haas (ed.), 1976, 1–28.
Qian, Nairong (ed.) 1990. *Xiàndài Hànyǔ*. Beijing: Gāoděng Jiàoyù Chūbǎnshè.
Qian, Xuantong 1918a. *Chángshì jí* xù. In Jiabi Zhao (ed.), 1935, 105–10.
    1918b. Zhōngguó jīnhòu zhī wénzì wèntí. In Jiabi Zhao (ed.), 1935, 141–5.
    1922. Jiǎnshěng xiànxíng hànzì de bǐhuà àn. In Guoyu Yanjiuhui (ed.), 1923,
    160–163.
    1923. Hànzì gémìng. In Guoyu Yanjiuhui (ed.), 1923, 5–25.
Qiu, Xigui 1987. Tántan hànzì zhěnglǐ gōngzuò zhōng kěyǐ cānkǎo de mǒuxiē lìshǐ
    jīngyàn. *Yǔwén Jiànshè* 2, 3–12.
    1988. *Wénzìxué gàiyào*. Beijing: Shāngwù Yìnshūguǎn.

Qiu, Zhiqun and van den Berg, Marinus 1994. Táiwān yǔyán xiànzhuàng de chūbù yánjiū. *Zhōngguó Yǔwén* 4, 254–61.

Qu, Qiubai 1931a. Guǐménguān yǐwài de zhànzhēng. In Ni (ed.), 1949, 10–29.

1931b. Luómǎzì de xīn Zhōngguówén háishì ròumázì de xīn Zhōngguówén. In Ni (ed.), 1949, 29–47.

Ramsey, Robert S. 1987. *The languages of China*. Princeton University Press.

Reform 1958. *Reform of the Chinese written language*. Beijing: Foreign Languages Press.

Ren, Zhong (ed.) 1934. *Wényán, báihuà, dàzhòngyǔ lùnzhàn jí*. Shanghai: Mínzhòng Dúwù Chūbǎnshè.

Renmin Ribao 1955. Zhèngquède shǐyòng zǔguó de yǔyán, wèi yǔyán de cúnjié he jiànkàng ér dòuzhēng, Editorial on 26 October, In Yushu Hu (ed.), 1980, 50–60.

Romaine, Suzanne 1995. *Bilingualism*. Second edition. London: Blackwell.

Rubin, Joan 1977. Language standardisation in Indonesia. In Joan Rubin, Björn H. Jernudd, Jyotirindra Das Gupta, Joshua A. Fishman, and Charles A. Ferguson (eds.), *Language planning processes*, 157–79, The Hague: Mouton.

Sampson, Geoffrey 1985. *Writing systems: a linguistic introduction*. London: Hutchinson.

1994. Chinese script and the diversity of writing systems. *Linguistics* 32, 117–32.

Shao, Rongfen 1982. *Quèyùn yīnxì*. Beijing: Zhōngguó Shèhuì Kēxué Chūbǎnshè.

Shen, Jiong 1987. Běijīng huà hékǒuhū língshēngmǔ de yǔyīn fēnxī. *Zhōngguó Yǔwén* 5, 352–62.

Shi, Youwei 1983. Jiǎntǐzì yǔ fántǐzì biāoyīndù bǐjiào. *Yǔwén Tōngxùn* 11, 3–13.

1988. Hànzì de chóngxīn fāxiàn. In Seminar, 1988, 172–87.

Su, Jinzhi 1991. Mǐn fāngyánqū de yǔmǎ xuǎnzé. *Yǔwén Jiànshè* 12, 15–18.

Su, Peicheng 1992. Xiàndài hànzì yánjiū jiǎnshù. *Yǔwén Jiànshè* 7, 6–14.

Symposium 1988. *Hànzì wèntí xuéshù tǎolùnhuì lùnwénjí*. Zhongguo Shehui Kexueyuan Yuyan Wenzi Yingyong Yanjiusuo (ed.). Beijing: Yǔwén Chūbǎnshè.

Tan, Bi'an 1956. *Wǎn Qīng de báihuàwén yùndòng*. Wuhan: Húběi Rénmín Chūbǎnshè.

Ting, Pang-hsin 1996. Review of *Language Atlas of China (Parts I and II)*, *International Review of Chinese Linguistics* 1(1), 89–92.

Trager, George L. 1974. Writing and writing systems. In Thomas Sebeok (ed.), *Current trends in linguistics*, volume XII: *Linguistics and adjacent arts and sciences*, 373–496. The Hague: Mouton Publishers.

Tse, Kwock-Ping J. 1986. Standardization of Chinese in Taiwan. *International Journal of the Sociology of Language* 59, 25–32.

T'sou, Benjamin K. 1986. Language planning in Hong Kong: quo vadis? Paper
    presented at Conference on language policy and language planning in
    Hong Kong.
van den Berg, M. E. 1988. Taiwan's sociolinguistic setting. In Cheng and Huang
    (eds.), 1988, 243–59.
Venezky, Richard L. 1970. Principles for the design of practical writing systems.
    Anthropological Linguistics 12(7): 256–70.
Wang, Biao 1985. Pǔtōnghuà gāo shuǐpíng de zài Xīnjiāng tōngxíng. *Yǔwén
    Jiànshè Tōngxùn* 16, 2–4.
Wang, Fengyang 1992. *Wénzìxué*. Changchun: Jílín Wénshǐ Chūbǎnshè.
Wang, Huidi 1990. Xīnjiāpō Huáyǔ cíhuì de tèdiǎn. In Xinjiapo Huayu Yanjiuhui
    (ed.), 1990, 346–56.
Wang, Jun 1995. *Dāngdài Zhōngguó de wénzì gǎigé*. Dāngdài Zhōngguó
    Chūbǎnshè.
Wang, Kaiyang 1992. Hànzì yōuyuè zhū shuō xiàn yí. *Yǔwén Jiànshè* 4, 8–13.
Wang, Li. 1940. Hànzì gǎigé. Reprinted in *Wáng Lì wénjí* volume VII, 1990. Jinan:
    Shāndōng Jiàoyù Chūbǎnshè.
    1954. Lùn Hànzú biāozhǔnyǔ. In Yushu Hu (ed.), 1980, 23–40.
    1979. Báihuàwén yùndòng de yìyì. *Zhōngguó Yǔwén* 3, 161–2.
    1980a. Tuīguǎng pǔtōnghuà de sàn gè wèntí. *Yǔwén Xiàndàihuà* 2, 187–98.
    1980b. *Hànyǔ shǐgǎo*. Beijing: Zhōnghuá Shūjú.
Wang, Li et al. 1956. *Hànyǔ de gòngtóngyǔ hé biāozhǔnyīn*. Beijing: Zhōnghuá
    Shūjú.
Wang, Maozu 1934. Jìn xí wényán yǔ qiáng lìng dújīng. In Zhong Ren (ed.), Part 1,
    1–9.
Wang, Ning 1991. Hànzì de yōuhuà yǔ jiǎnhuà. *Zhōngguó Shèhuì Kēxié* 1, 69–80.
Wang, Shuqin 1992. Nóngcūn zhōngxiǎoxué fāngyán jiāoxué lìng rén dānyōu.
    Guāngmíng Rìbào, 21 June 1992.
Wang, Yiding 1991. Zǒuguò guānjiàn niándài. *Zhōngyāng Rìbào* International
    Edition, 17 October 1991.
Wang, Zhao 1900. Guānhuà héshēng zìmǔ xù. In Ni (ed.), 1958, 19–23.
Wardhaugh, Ronald 1986. *An introduction to sociolinguistics*. London: Basil
    Blackwell.
Williams, S. Wells 1883. *The Middle Kingdom*. London: W. H. Allen & Co.
Wu, Renyi and Yin, Binyong 1984. Pǔtōnghuà shèhuì diàochá. *Wénzì Gǎigé* 11,
    37–8.
Wu, Wenchao 1980. The adoption of the Chinese Phonetic Alphabet as the
    international standard for romanization of Chinese names of persons and
    places. *Journal of Chinese Linguistics* 8(2), 320–1.
Wu, Yingcheng 1990. Cóng Xīnjiāpō Huáyǔ jùfǎ shíkuàng diàochá tǎolùn Huáyǔ
    jùfǎ guīfànhuà wèntí. In Xinjiapo Huawen Yanjiuhui (ed.), 1990, 118–23.

Wu, Yuzhang [Yuchang] 1958. Report on the current tasks of reforming the written language and the draft scheme for a Chinese Phonetic Alphabet. In Reform, 1958, 30–54.

    1978. *Wénzì gǎigé wénjí*. Beijing: Zhōngguó Rénmín Dàxué Chūbǎnshè.

Wu, Yuzhang [Yuchang] and Li, Jinxi [Li, Chin-hsi] 1958. A summary of the efforts of the Chinese people over the past sixty years for a phonetic alphabet. In Reform, 1958, 63–70.

Wu, Zhankun and Ma, Guofan 1988. *Hànzì hé hànzì gǎigé shǐ*. Changsha: Húnán Rénmín Chūbǎnshè.

Xia, Mianzun 1934. Xiān shǐ báihuàwén chéng huà. In Zhong Ren (ed.), 1934, Part 2, 1–4.

Xinjiapo Huawen Yanjiuhui (ed.) 1990. *Shìjiè Huáwén jiàoxué yántǎohuì lùnwénjí*. Singapore.

Xiong, Yuezhi. 1994. *Xīxué dōng jiàn yǔ wǎn Qīng shèhuì*. Shanghai: Shànghǎi Rénmín Chūbǎnshè.

Xu, Baohua and Zhan, Bohui 1988. Hànyǔ fāngyán. In Xianlin Ji (ed.), 1988, 137–49.

Xu, Jidun 1992. *Táiyǔ wénzìhuà de fāngxiàng*. Taipei: Zìlì Wǎnbào Shè Wénhuà Chūbǎnbù.

Xu, Maoyong 1934. Guānyú wényánwén. In Zhong Ren (ed.), 1934, Part 1, 68–72.

Xu, Shirong 1957. Běijīng yǔyīn yīnwèi jiǎnshù. In Yushu Hu (ed.), 1980, 351–8.

    1979. Pǔtōnghuà yǔyīn he Běijīng tǔyīn de jièxiàn. *Yǔyán Jiàoxué Yǔ Yánjiū* 1, 7–22.

    1995. Sìshí niáng lai de pǔtōnghuà yǔyīn gūifàn. *Yǔwén Jiànshè* 6, 1–6.

Yang, Paul Fumian 1995. Luo Minjian, Li Maduo *Pú Hàn Cídiǎn* suǒ jìlù de Míng dài guānhuà. *Zhōngguó Yǔyánxuébào* No. 5, 35–81.

Yao, Youchun 1989. Yīng kāizhǎn duì dìfāng pǔtōnghuà de yánjiū *Yǔwén Jiànshè* 3, 18–21.

Ye, Chuqiang 1965. Xiàndài tōngyòng hànzì dúyīn de fēnxī tǒngjì. *Zhōngguó Yǔwén* 3, 201–5.

Ye, Gongchuo 1955. Guānyú hànzì jiǎnhuà gōngzuò de bàogào. In Proceedings, 1957, 20–36.

Yi, Feng 1992. Hànyǔ fāngyán shìlì tànwēi. *Yǔwén Jiànshè Tōngxùn* 37, 60–2.

Yin, Binyong 1988. Guānyú Hànzì píngjià de jǐ gè jīběn wèntì. In Seminar, 1988, 251–62.

    1991. Xiàndài Hànzì de dìngliàng yánjiū. *Yǔwén Jiànshè* 11, 19–21.

You, Rujie 1992. *Hànyǔ fāngyánxué dǎolùn*. Shanghai: Shànghǎi Jiàoyù Chūbǎnshè.

Young, Russell L., Huang, Shuanfan, Ochoa, Alberto, and Kuhlman, Natalie 1992. Language attitudes in Taiwan. *International Journal of the Sociology of Language* 98, 5–14.

Yu, Jingtao 1934. Xiǎoxué dújīng yǔ xuéxí wényánwén. In Zhong Ren (ed.) 1934, Part 1, 17–23.

Yuwen Jianshe 1992. Zhōnggòng Guǎngdōng shěngwěi, Guǎngdōng shěng rénmín zhèngfǔ guānyú dàlì tuīguǎng pǔtōnghuà de juédìng. *Yǔwén Jiànshè* 4, 2–3.

Zhang, Boyu 1974. *Táiwān dìqū guóyǔ yùndòng shǐliǎo.* Taipei: Shāngwù Yìnshūguǎn.

Zhang, Guangyu 1991. Hànyǔ fāngyán fāzhǎn de bùpínghéngxìng. *Zhōngguó Yǔwén* 6, 431–8.

Zhang, Jing 1957. Tán Běijīng huà de yīnwèi, In Yushu Hu (ed.), 1980, 338–46.

Zhang, Qingchang 1990. Bǐbǐ kàn: 'Hànyǔ Pīnyīn Fāng'àn' gēn Luómǎ zìmǔ Sīláfū zìmǔ jǐ zhǒng zhǔyào Hànyǔ pīnyīn fāng'àn de bǐjiào. *Shìjiè Hànyǔ Jiàoxiè* 1, 1–14.

Zhang, Shuzheng 1994. Xiàndài Hànyǔ fāngyán yīnxì jiǎnhuà de qūshì yǔ tūiguǎng pǔtōnghuà. *Yǔyán Wénzì Yìngyòng* 1, 48–53.

Zhang, Weidong 1992. Lùn *Xí Rú Ěr Mù Zī* de jìyīn xìngzhì. In *Jìniàn Wáng Lì Xiānshēng 90 dànchén wénjí*, 224–42. Jinan: Shāngdōng Jiàoyù Chūbǎnshè.

Zhang, Xunru 1956. Běijīnghuà li qīngshēng de gōngyòng. In Yushu Hu (ed.), 1980, 468–70.

Zhao, Jiabi (ed.) 1935 *Zhōngguó xīnwénxué dàxì*, volume I: *jiànshè lǐlùn jí*. Shanghai: Liángyǒu Túshū Yìnshuā Gōngsī.

Zhong, Zhemin 1990. Jiāqiáng shèhuì yòngzì guǎnlǐ, cùjìn yǔyán wénzì guīfànhuà. *Yǔwén Jiànshè* 5, 6–12.

Zhongguo Shehui Kexueyuan Yuyan Yanjiusuo 1979. *Xiàndài Hànyǔ cídiǎn.* Beijing: Shāngwù Yìnshūguǎn.

Zhou, Qinghai 1990. Xīnjiāpō Huárén yǔyán móshì de zhuǎnyí. In Xinjiapo Huawen Yanjiuhui (ed.), 1990, 483–90.

Zhou, Xiaobing 1989. Xīnjiāpō Huáyǔ xiǎoshuō de yǔfǎ tèdiǎn. In Enquan Chen (ed.), 1989, 212–22.

Zhou, Yang (ed.) 1986. *Zhōngguó dà bǎikē quánshū: Zhōngguó wénxué.* Beijing: Zhōngguó Dà Bǎiké Quánshū Chūbǎnshè.

Zhou, Youguang 1979. *Hànzì gǎigé gàilùn.* Third Edition. Beijing: Wénzì Gǎigé Chūbǎnshè.

1992. *Zhōngguó yǔwén zònghéngtán.* Beijing: Rénmín Jiàoyù Chūbǎnshè.

Zhou, Zumou 1988. Hànzì. In Xianlin Ji (ed.), 1988, 195–9.

Zhou, Zuoren 1923. Hànzì gǎigé de wǒ jiàn. In Guoyu Yanjiuhui (ed.), 1923, 71–3.

Zhu, Dexi 1985. Hànyǔ fāngyán lǐ de liǎng zhǒng fǎnfù wènjù. *Zhōngguó Yǔwén* 1, 10–20.

Index

affix-like morphemes in Chinese, 96–7, 110
Analects, 7, 79, 160–1
annotated national character, *see zhùyīn guózì*
Archaic Chinese, 1
Atlas, 204 n. 5

bāgǔwén, 73, 75
báihuà, 22, 68–75
  new-style, 76
  traditional, 69, 76, 93
Basic Rules of the Orthography of
  Chinese in *Pīnyīn*, 197
Bauer, Robert, 116
bèi, 93–4, 208 (ch. 6 n. 2)
Beifanghua, 2; *see also* Mandarin
Beijing, dialect of, 10–12, 14, 16, 19, 21,
  37–41, 205 n. 1
Beijing Television (BTV), 38, 40
běiyīn, 10; *see also* Beijing, dialect of
běnzì, 116
bidialectalism, 30, 204–5 n. 3
biétǐ, 150
bilingualism, 50, 52–3, 204–5 n. 3
Bolinger, Dwight, 132
Book of history, see Shū jīng
Book of odes, see Shī jīng
Bradley, David, 49
broken style, *see pòtǐ*
bronze script, *see jīnwén*
bùshǒu, 144

Cantonese, 2, 28–29, 45, 51–2, 54–5,
  57–9, 62–3, 99
  phonetic schemes for, 120, 174–5,
  179
  written, 52, 114–15, 117, 207 n. 2
cǎoshū, 149
Central People's Radio Station (CPBS),
  38, 42
Chan, Marjorie K. M., 1
Chang Baoru, 136
Chao Yuen Ren, 19, 21, 169, 174, 183,
  206 (ch. 3 n. 1)
Chaucer, 73, 115
Chen Chungyu, 49
Chen Duxiu, 72, 74–5

Chen Enquan, 55, 57
Chen Guofu, 120
Chen Jianmin, 51, 94
Chen Lifu, 162
Chen Mingyuan, 139
Chen Ping, 127, 208 (ch. 7 n. 5)
Chen Songcen, 30, 42–4, 54
Chen Wangdao, 80–1
Chen Zhangtai, 45, 199
Cheng, Robert L., 47, 98, 116, 127
China Central Television (CCTV), 38,
  40, 42, 53, 58
Chinese characters
  composite, *see hétǐzì*
  homophony of, 137–8, 140
  number of, 135–6, 157
  ordering of, 143–5, 200–1
  simple, *see dútǐzì*
Chinese Language Ordinance, 32, 62
Chinese Press Association, 199
Chinese word processors, 187
Christian, Donna, 89
Cíhǎi, 144
Classical literary Chinese
  romanization, *see wényán luómǎzì*
clerical script, *see lìshū*
Clyne, Michael, 124
Coblin, South, 11, 206 (ch. 2 n. 2)
Commission for Unifying Reading
  Pronunciation, *see Dúyīn Tǒngyī Huì*
Committee for *Guóyǔ* Promotion of
  the Ministry of Education, *see Jiàoyùbù Guóyǔ Tuīxíng Wěiyuánhuì*
Committee on Script Reform, 155, 166,
  188, 192; *see also* State Language
  Commission
Communist Party of China, language
  policy before 1949, 121, 186
compound indicative, *see huìyì*
Confucius, 8
Cooper, Robert L., 89, 109, 124
corpus planning, 88–9, 109–13
Coulmas, Florian, 102, 124, 131, 134,
  194
Cultural Revolution, 26, 160, 191